The Pronunciation of English

For *Carol*

The Pronunciation of English

A Course Book

Charles W. Kreidler

Second Edition

Blackwell
Publishing

350 Main Street, Malden, MA 02148-5020, USA
108 Cowley Road, Oxford OX4 1JF, UK
550 Swanston Street, Carlton, Victoria 3053, Australia

First edition published 1989
Second edition published 2004 by Blackwell Publishing Ltd

Library of Congress Cataloging-in-Publication Data

Kreidler, Charles W., 1924–
   The pronunciation of English : a course book / Charles W. Kreidler.—
2nd ed.
      p. cm.
Includes bibliographical references (p.   ) and index.
   ISBN 1–4051–1335–9 (alk. paper) — ISBN 1–4051–1336–7 (pbk. : alk.
paper)
      1. English language—Pronunciation.   2. English
language—Pronunciation—Problems, exercises, etc.   3. English
language—Pronunciation by foreign speakers.   4. English
language—Pronunciation by foreign speakers—Problems, exercises, etc.
   I. Title.
   PE1137.K84 2004
   421'.52—dc22
                                                           2003015474

A catalogue record for this title is available from the British Library.

Set in 10/12.5pt Palatino
by Graphicraft Limited, Hong Kong
Printed and bound in the United Kingdom
by MPG Books Ltd, Bodmin, Cornwall

For further information on
Blackwell Publishing, visit our website:
http://www.blackwellpublishing.com

Contents

Preface to the Second Edition

When I wrote *The Pronunciation of English* fifteen years ago, I expected that it would serve as a textbook for advanced students of English and linguistics, many of whom were preparing for a career as teachers of English as a second or foreign language. My aim was to present the facts of pronunciation in the principal native-speaker varieties of the language and to use generative phonology as the theoretical basis for the presentation. I hoped for a double accomplishment: to give students who are not native speakers of English a better 'feel' for the spoken language, and to lead native speakers to a more specific awareness of the knowledge they acquired early in life. The present edition has the same general purpose.

The method of presenting the material also remains the same. In the original preface I wrote:

> I believe that learning linguistics requires a heavy involvement with data. The student needs to *do* analysis, going from observed facts to general statements and then testing these with more observations.

More than 80 exercises scattered throughout the book are meant to lead the student to participate continually in the development of the topics treated.

Innovations in the present edition are due mostly to the feedback I have received from those who used the earlier work in teaching and/or studying. I have tried to incorporate the perspectives achieved in the 'new phonologies' of the past decade and a half, but most of what is new in this second edition has a pedagogic purpose: deletion of some material that turned out to be unnecessary, more attention to the definition of technical terms, more charts and figures to illustrate, and a glossary.

I am grateful to all who have commented on the earlier edition and to the Blackwell staff for their smooth efficiency in producing this book. Responsibility for the contents rests with me, of course.

C. W. K.

About this Book

Each of the 14 chapters begins with one or more paragraphs which are intended to tell briefly the content of the chapter. Each ends with a summary, which briefly reviews the content of the chapter and also tries to show the importance of what has been treated, or to describe some problems in analyzing not taken up within the chapter. The last section, called Notes, suggests readings in other books for those who want to extend their exploration of these topics.

Linguistics, like every academic discipline, has its own technical terms, and some of them are used in this book. These terms are in **bold print** when they are first introduced. Some of the terms, such as **suffix**, may already be familiar to you; some, like **allophone**, are likely to be new; and some will probably be familiar to you but you will find that they are used here in a more specialized way; **accent**, **assimilation**, and **stop** are examples. The Glossary provides definitions or explanations, with examples.

Description of pronunciations also requires the use of special symbols, which are introduced from chapter 2 on. As with technical terms, several of these symbols will be unfamiliar to you and some – ordinary letters of the Roman alphabet – you will already know. But every symbol will consistently have a specific value, always representing the same speech sound or phoneme. Keep in mind that we are dealing with speech, not spelling, and that English spelling does not consistently represent what people pronounce. When a symbol – one or two letters – appears between slant lines, it represents an English phoneme; for example, /k/ represents the phoneme that occurs at the beginning of the words *cat* and *kitten* and in the middle of *second*, *chicken*, *token*, and *liquor*. Symbols in square brackets represent speech sounds or phones; *cold* and *scold* both have the phoneme /k/ but the phoneme is pronounced with aspiration, [kʰ], in *cold* but without aspiration, [k], in *scold*. A tick (') is used to mark the stressed syllable of a word (the syllable following the tick); for example, 'origin, o'riginal, origi'nality. Other special signs are explained as they are introduced.

Each chapter contains some exercises. These have different names but the names always appear in SMALL CAPITALS, like this. Most exercises have just one answer for each question or task; in some cases there is more than one correct answer; and in other cases the questions asked are mainly intended to introduce a discussion. Each exercise is followed by a FEEDBACK, sometimes right after the exercise, sometimes at the end of the chapter. Try to do each exercise by yourself before looking at the feedback.

If you are a native speaker of English, you may find that some of the descriptive statements and some of the illustrative utterances do not agree with what you say. This is inevitable. There is a limit to the variation that can be dealt with in a single book. While we cannot deal in detail with every variety of the language, we hope to provide a basis for understanding what kinds of variation exist.

1

Language and Speech

This book is an attempt to answer a question: How is English pronounced? The question is deceptively simple, and it cannot have a simple answer. English today is the native language of nearly 400 million people and the second language of many others scattered all over the world. A language so widespread is bound to be different in different places. We are all aware that the Scots and the Australians, Londoners and New Yorkers, Irish, New Zealanders, South Africans, Jamaicans, Welsh, and Canadians do not sound the same when they speak. How can anyone describe the pronunciation of so many different people?

The diversity is real and must be treated in an account of how English is pronounced, but the commonality is greater. There is much more to be said about what is common to all speakers of English than there is regarding what is different. Furthermore, although to describe pronunciation obviously requires us to tell what people do with their voices, we will be, in a sense, more concerned with the language they possess in common.

1.1 Language variation

In every language there is variety. A language varies from one place to another, from one era to another, from one occasion to another. The differences may be in choice of words to express a meaning, as with *petrol* versus *gas(oline)* or *dual carriageway* versus *divided highway*. Differences exist in word formation: for the past tense of the verb *dive* does one say *dived* or *dove*? There are possible differences in the ways that words are put together to form phrases and sentences: would you say, for instance, *They gave it me*, or *They gave me it*, or *They gave it to me*? In this book we are concerned with differences in pronunciation. Some words are spoken differently by different speakers of English, for instance *either*, *garage*, and *tomato*. We are more concerned, however, with systematic differences; for example, some speakers of English pronounce an R in such words as *car* and *horn* and other speakers do not; for the former *spa* and *spar* sound different, for the latter group the two words are homophones. There are interesting differences in the vowel systems of different dialects: how different are *stock* and *stalk* (and *stork*), for instance?

We can discuss language variation under two headings: differences among people, the users of language, and differences in the uses of language, the ways in which people employ language on different occasions.

First, we are all aware of the differences of the sort mentioned in the first paragraph, above. People who live in different areas speak different **regional**, or **geographic**, **dialects**. The geographic differences in English reflect the different times in which speakers of English settled in an area, how diverse they were in their origins, how much contact they have had with other speakers of the language and what influence there has been from speakers of other languages.

Geographic dialects are not the only kind of difference among speakers of a language. In any locality different people grow up with different advantages and opportunities for education; the forms of language used by the more educated are generally considered more prestigious than the forms used by the less educated (but that doesn't mean that the less educated want to talk differently). Such differences are social dialects. We may also speak of age dialects – nobody expects teenagers to talk like their grandparents, or vice versa – and sex dialects – men and women use language differently. The differences of these sorts are mostly in vocabulary, however, and are not of great concern in a book on pronunciation. The geographic differences are important for this book. The next section briefly traces the expansion of the English language to account for the major varieties of the language in our times. Chapter 4 contains a more technical account of what these differences are.

1.2   A very brief history of the English language

When Angles, Saxons, and Jutes migrated from the continent of Europe to the island of Britain in the fifth century AD, they spoke a language which was to become English. Within two centuries they had subjugated, intermarried with, or pushed back the people who were there before them, until varieties of English were being spoken in most of what is now England and in the lowlands of Scotland (though some have maintained that Scots is a language related to English rather than a dialect of it). The Celtic languages of the original inhabitants were confined to Cornwall, Wales, and the highlands and islands of Scotland. In the centuries that followed regional varieties of English developed in a feudal society that had no ruling class nor dominant center.

With the Norman Conquest in 1066 French became the language of the ruling class, the language of government, just as Latin was the language of religion. Varieties of English developed a grammar quite different from pre-Norman English and a double-barreled vocabulary with numerous synonyms of the type *deep/profound, ring/circle, last/endure*. When London grew in importance as the political capital and later as the commercial capital, English displaced French in official functions and the variety spoken in London began to be a standard form, helped by printers like William Caxton in the late fifteenth century who made the London dialect the norm for written English. With the establishment of a strong, centralized kingdom under the Tudors in the sixteenth century the importance of London continued to grow, but until the Industrial Revolution, at the beginning of the nineteenth century, most Englishmen spoke some regional variety of English.

The Industrial Revolution brought rural populations into the cities. During the nineteenth century a larger middle class came into existence, and the idea of belonging to the middle class became associated with speaking a particular form of English. This particular way of speaking came to be called Received Pronunciation (RP). In the twentieth century the British Broadcasting Corporation selected and trained announcers to speak with an RP 'accent,' and RP has been the variety that most foreigners have chosen to learn. But to this day only a small portion of the English population speak RP. Regional and urban dialects remain.

In the sixteenth and seventeenth centuries English monarchs began to annex their Celtic-speaking neighbors to the English crown. In Wales English was established by law as the official language of trade, law, and education in the middle of the sixteenth century, but it did not spread widely as the language of daily life until the nineteenth century.

When James VI of Scotland became James I of England he united the crowns and sought to promote throughout Scotland the reading of the English Bible and the establishment of English schools to make this possible.

Though there were settlements of English-speakers in Ireland from the Norman era on, the Anglicization of Ireland is something that began in the sixteenth and seventeenth centuries, with usurpation of Irish estates and settlement of English and Scottish loyalists there.

The Englishes of Wales, Scotland, and Ireland are essentially the forms of English adopted centuries ago by peoples speaking Welsh, Scots Gaelic, and Irish Gaelic, with the inevitable changes that have occurred in the succeeding period of time, and with the constant influence of RP as a prestige model.

If Welsh, Scottish, and Irish English had their origins in the sixteenth and seventeenth centuries, the establishment of English in North America came very shortly after. Newfoundland, Britain's first overseas colony, was claimed for the English Crown in 1588; Jamestown was founded in Virginia in 1607 and Plymouth in Massachusetts in 1620. In the early eighteenth century England gained control of the Maritime provinces of Canada and near the end of that century laid claim to the whole country. Unlike Ireland, Wales, and Scotland, where English was imposed largely on people of Celtic language background, in North America English was the language of people who came from the British Isles or the language learned by people who came later from other parts of Europe. The same is largely true of South Africa, Australia, and New Zealand.

Settlement of the major English-speaking countries of the southern hemisphere dates from the late eighteenth and early nineteenth centuries. The first colony was planted in Australia in 1788, the first settlement of New Zealand in 1792, though in both countries large-scale immigration did not occur until the middle of the nineteenth century. Britain took possession of the Cape Colony in South Africa in 1806, and migration from England and Scotland grew rapidly after 1820.

It is well to remember that most people who went out to settle Britain's overseas colonies originated from the northern and western parts of England or from the lower class of London and did not speak the variety which was to become Standard British English. RP has been, however, a prestige norm in most parts of the Commonwealth – less perhaps in Canada than in the southern hemisphere. Contrariwise, those who take pride in being Australian or South African are likely to hold fast to the pronunciations which are endemic. In those two countries one finds a range of dialect differences from Broad Australian or Broad South African to RP or near-RP.

1.3   Speech and language

In discussing the pronunciation of English we can focus on one or both of two aspects. On one hand, we may want to describe what people do when they are speaking English. This is the aspect of speech, an activity carried on by people who use English for communicating. On the other hand, we may address the question 'What are the characteristics of English words and sentences that are realized in speech?' This is the aspect of language, a code which exists, handed down from the past with slight changes made by each generation, something that is known by those who speak and understand English.

Speech is not the same as language. For one thing, the voice has characteristics which may carry extra messages: we can often identify someone we know by his or her voice (over the telephone, for instance), and we can sometimes determine something of the speaker's mood – anger, elation, nervousness, impatience, fatigue – from the way of speaking, as distinct from what is said. More important, speech is an activity which is carried on in numerous events; language is knowledge, a code which is known and shared by people who use their knowledge for transmitting and interpreting messages in these events. When someone is speaking, anyone who is close enough can hear – the sound waves set up in the air by the speaker reach the eardrums of the hearer. But only a person who knows the language can understand what is said.

Because we are interested in pronunciation from both these aspects, we will make use of information and concepts drawn from two disciplines, **phonetics** and **phonology**. Phonetics deals with speech in its purely physical aspects –

the way sounds are articulated by the speaker, the acoustic properties of sound waves, and the effects that these have on the ear of the hearer (and on the ear of the speaker, for that matter). Phonology is concerned with the way speech sounds are organized into a system, the sound system of a specific language. Phonology relates the physical facts of speech to other linguistic knowledge which speakers possess, knowledge of vocabulary and grammar.

Phonology is concerned with describing pronunciations but, more than that, with accounting for what is relevant in pronunciations, what makes it possible to communicate, what makes one utterance different from another.

Because we are interested in both speech and language, we need certain terms to use in describing both. We start with terms that have to do with speech:

We use the term **discourse** to refer to any act of speech which occurs in a given place and during a given period of time. The word *text* is used by some authors with this meaning, described as 'anything from a single proverb to a whole play, from a momentary cry for help to an all-day discussion of a committee' (Halliday and Hasan 1976: 3). In this book we are concerned mostly with spoken discourse. A written discourse may be the record of something that has been spoken, or it may originate for the purpose of being performed aloud, like a speech or play, or it may exist without ever having been spoken or intended to be spoken, like most articles and books.

A discourse consists of at least one **utterance**, which is defined as a stretch of speech produced by a single speaker, with silence before and after on the part of that speaker. Two utterances in a discourse may be (partly) simultaneous, but only when two people speak at the same time. By definition one person cannot produce two utterances at the same time, though of course speakers may make several false starts and may not complete what they intended to say.

An utterance consists of at least one **tone unit**, a stretch of speech which has a melody or intonation, one of a fairly small inventory of intonation contours that exist in the language. The melody results from the physical fact that the speaker's vocal cords vibrate at different frequencies in the articulation of the tone unit, producing parts of it at different pitches. The action of the vocal cords is described further in chapter 2, and the intonations are outlined in chapter 10.

A tone unit consists of at least one **syllable** and usually a number of syllables. The syllable is an element which is recognized in all descriptions of speech, and yet one that is hard to define. A syllable consists of a vowel sound, usually with consonants before and after it. When a tone unit consists of several syllables, which is usually the case, they differ in prominence. Relative prominence is due to some combination of factors: greater force with which air is expelled from the lungs, higher pitch or changing pitch, the duration, or timing, of the syllable. These matters are discussed in greater detail in chapter 5.

A syllable consists of at least one **segment** and usually more than one. In the production of speech the speaker's vocal organs are constantly moving from one position to another; speech is a dynamic process. Nevertheless, we perceive a succession of different sounds, a chain of speech made up of different segments linked to one another. (In the word *meat*, to take a very short example, we think that we articulate three distinct sounds in sequence. This is not quite true. The vocal organs do not assume one position, then another, and then another; they are in motion as long as we are talking. Nevertheless, our perceptions have a reality of their own, and we adopt the convenient fiction that any syllable can be described as a sequence of segments.)

The elements listed so far occur more or less sequentially: the utterances of a discourse occur one after another, tone units follow one another, syllables occur in succession, and within syllables the segments come one after another (though there is more overlap than we might think). The last elements of speech to be mentioned occur simultaneously. In the production, or articulation, of a segment the vocal organs have some particular configuration – the lips are rounded or stretched, the tongue is low in the mouth or not, it has a flat surface or not, air is escaping through the mouth or through the nose or not escaping at all, the vocal cords are vibrating or not, etc. Each such position or movement is an **articulatory feature**. These features always occur in simultaneous bundles; no segment can consist of a single feature. The segment [m], which occurs at the beginning of the word *meat*, is produced with the vocal cords vibrating, the lips closed together, and air coming out through the nose. These are three articulatory features combined. Other segments may be voiced (made with vocal cords vibrating), labial (articulated with one or both lips), or nasal (produced with air flowing through the nasal cavity), but only [m] is all three – a voiced labial nasal.

We will also need to refer to units of language from time to time in this book. Some terms for units of language are familiar to you. In our use of language we express ourselves much of the time in **sentences**. Sentences consist of **phrases**, and phrases consist of **words**. Words belong to different classes; major classes are called nouns, verbs, adjectives, adverbs; minor classes are determiners, prepositions, conjunctions, and others. But we need to introduce a few terms which are not necessarily part of the layperson's usage.

Every word consists of at least one **morpheme**, a minimal unit that contributes in some way to the meaning of the whole word. If we compare the words *honest, dishonest, honestly,* and *honesty,* we will surely decide that they all share some meaning and that the first word, *honest,* has only this meaning and cannot be divided into smaller meaningful units. On the other hand, *dishonest* is obviously *dis-* + *honest; honestly* is *honest* + *-ly;* and *honesty* is the same *honest* + *-y,* or perhaps *honest* + *-ty,* analogous to *certainty* and *loyalty.* Each of these meaningful units is a morpheme: *honest, dis-, -ly, -ty.* The first of these is a **base** morpheme, the last three are **affixes**, which only exist in combination with a base. The first of these, *dis-,* is a **prefix**, and *-ly* and *-ty* are **suffixes**.

Usually a morpheme is expressed in just one way, in some sequence of the **phonemes** of the language. The phoneme is the unit which makes the connection between sound and meaning. A phoneme is a unit of sound in a particular language which is capable of differentiating morphemes, the units of meaning of that language. The morpheme *meat* is a sequence of three phonemes, which we represent as /m/ for the first, /ii/ for the second, and /t/ for the third, thus /miit/. The morpheme *beet* has a different initial phoneme, which we represent as /b/, thus /biit/, and the morphemes *moot* and *boot* have a different medial phoneme, written /uu/ – /muut/ and /buut/. The morpheme *team* has the same phonemes as *meat*, but in a different order, /tiim/, and *tomb* has the same phonemes as *moot*, in a different arrangement – /tuum/. *Eat, tea, too, bee, beam, boom* are six other morphemes which contain some selection of these five phonemes: /b/, /m/, /t/, /ii/, /uu/. In our transcription these six morphemes are written /iit, tii, tuu, bii, biim, buum/.

Different morphemes have different meanings, but they may sound the same. English *meat* and *meet* are **homonyms**; they are expressed by the same sequence of the same phonemes, /miit/. Similarly, *beet* and *beat* are homonyms, /biit/, and so are *tee* and *tea*, /tii/; *team* and *teem*, /tiim/; *be* and *bee*, /bii/; *too* and *two*, /tuu/.

As these examples show, we use a letter or a combination of two letters to represent each English phoneme and always between slant lines. A phoneme is not a letter. A language has phonemes whether it is written in an alphabetic system or not – indeed, whether it has ever been written or not. Besides, a phoneme may be represented by different letters or sequences of letters, like the *ee* and *ea* of the examples above; two letters may represent the same phoneme, as in *kit* and *cat*; or two different phonemes may be represented in spelling by the same letter or letters, like the *th* in *thy* and *thigh*.

One might also be inclined to equate the term 'phoneme' with 'sound' or 'speech sound' or 'segment'. That is not accurate, as the next paragraphs will show.

If you get ready to pronounce – but don't pronounce – *meet, moot, beet, boot*, you will find that all four words begin with lips closed. You should also find that with *meet* and *beet* the lips are stretched but with *moot* and *boot* they are slightly pursed or rounded. We think of *meet* and *moot* as beginning the same way, and likewise *beet* and *boot*. That is true, but not true. *Meet* and *moot* begin with the same phoneme, /m/, but they begin with different segments; the two segments have some articulatory features in common and they differ in another feature, the shape of the lips. Analogous statements can be made about *beet* and *boot*, of course; they begin with the same phoneme, /b/, but the phoneme is realized as different segments.

Let's try another experiment. Get ready to pronounce the words *geese* and *goose* but don't say anything. Instead, note the position and shape of your tongue and lips. You have the back of your tongue raised, touching the roof of the mouth toward the back – you may be able to recognize that the tongue's contact is in different places on the roof of the mouth. At the same time the lips are stretched for *geese* and rounded for *goose* – at the very beginning. Next, get ready to say *glee* and *glue* and compare. Some features, in the sounds that you are ready to make, are the same and some are different. The tongue-back, or **dorsum**, is in contact with the roof of the mouth for all of these. At the same time there is lip-stretching for *geese* and *glee*, lip-rounding for *goose* and *glue*. In addition, you note that the sides of the tongue are curled inward for *glee* and *glue*. Now get ready to say *greet* and *grew* and observe. The back of your tongue is again touching the roof of the mouth, and the lips are stretched for *greet*, rounded for *grew*, and the tip of the tongue is drawn back and bunched up.

The point we want to make is an important one: any speaker of English feels that the six words, *geese, goose, glee, glue, greet, grew*, all begin with the same sound. They don't; they begin with the same phoneme, which we represent this way, /g/. A phoneme is an abstract unit which is realized in speech as different segments in different positions. These different segments are the **allophones** of the phoneme. All six allophones are alike in being dorsal stops – the breath stream is built up behind the closure made with the tongue-back, or dorsum, against the soft palate, ready to be released when pronunciation occurs. There is another common feature, not so easy to observe: the vocal cords are in a position to begin vibrating. In addition to these shared features, there are other features which are only partly shared, present in some of the six but not all: lip-rounding or stretching, lateral tongue curl, retracted tongue tip. The features which are present in all the allophones are **distinctive features**; those which are present in one or several but not all the allophones are **redundant features**. It is fairly easy to see that the redundant features, in these cases, are 'borrowed' from other phonemes: lip-rounding is a feature of /uu/ in *goose, glue, grew* while lip-stretching is characteristic of the vowel /ii/ in the other words; lateral tongue curl, occurring with the /g/ of *glee* and *glue* is properly the feature of /l/; in *greet* and *grew* there is the tongue-retraction which is associated with /r/. But redundant features are not necessarily borrowed from neighboring phonemes. Notice carefully the difference between the beginning sound of *team* and the second sound of *steam*. Both words contain an instance of the phoneme /t/. The initial /t/ is aspirated; it is followed by a puff of air that comes from the throat. When /t/ follows /s/, it has no such aspiration. The aspiration is a redundant feature, but it has nothing to do with neighboring phonemes.

Phonemes, then, vary in pronunciation. They combine with other phonemes in sequence to express morphemes, and because they enter into such sequences they contrast with other phonemes, thus serving to differentiate morphemes. *Glue* is different from *clue* and *grew* from *crew*; *glue* contrasts with *blue*, and *blue* with *brew*; *boot* is distinct from *beet*, and *beet* from *meet*. **Minimal pairs** like these establish what every speaker of English knows: that /g/, /k/, /b/, /m/, /l/, /r/, /ii/ and /uu/ are separate phonemes: they are capable of signaling differences of meaning. To describe the sound system of English means to establish the phonemes of the language, to tell in what possible sequences they can occur, and what varying pronunciations each phoneme has in its various positions of occurrence.

1.4 Phonological analysis

A language is a number of things together. It is a collection of meaningful elements called morphemes; the technical name for this collection is the **lexicon**. And a language is a collection of rules for putting morphemes together to form words and for putting words together to form sentences. The rules for forming words are the **morphology** of the language, and the rules for forming sentences make up the **syntax**. Lexicon, morphology, and syntax are not abstractions; they are knowledge which speakers of the language possess, a knowledge which is largely unconscious for native speakers who acquired the language in the earliest years of life.

Phonology may also be thought of a collection of phonemes and a collection of rules for putting these units together to express the meanings of morphemes, words, and sentences. Phonology is no more an abstraction than lexicon, morphology, and syntax; it is knowledge, largely unconscious, which speakers have and which enables them to communicate, to express meanings which other speakers of the language will understand.

The native speaker of the language is aware of phonemes; the trained phonetician recognizes the variation of these – that each phoneme is pronounced differently in different contexts – as allophones. Phonological analysis is the grouping of segments into phonemes. The linguist observes that in English an aspirated [tʰ] occurs in certain positions, word-initially for one, and an unaspirated [t] occurs in other positions, as for example after /s/. The two are not in contrast; they are similar, sharing most of their articulatory features. The linguist decides that they are allophones of a single phoneme. On the other hand, the linguist establishes that /k/ and /g/, /b/ and /m/, /ii/ and /uu/ are separate phonemes in English.

The development of phonological analysis – and the creation of such terms as **phoneme**, **allophone**, **minimal pair** – was the work of linguists who belong to the discipline of structural linguistics. Structural phonology – sometimes called autonomous phonology or classical phonology – followed procedures which regarded language as an object for empirical investigation, with scrupulous avoidance of mentalistic terms and careful separation of phonological investigation from considerations of a grammatical or lexical nature.

Since the late 1950s many linguists have become adherents to the theory of generative grammar, which regards language as an inseparable whole. A generative grammar of a language is, supposedly, a description of the competence of a speaker of that language, the knowledge which makes him or her capable of producing and interpreting sentences in the language. Phonology, in a generative framework, cannot be separated from syntax and morphology since they are integrated parts of the speaker-hearer's competence.

Generative phonology seeks to establish an underlying representation of a whole sentence and map it on to a pronunciation through a sequence of rules. The underlying representation consists of knowledge of which the speaker is aware, and the rules are the speaker's unconscious knowledge. For example, an English-speaker has an awareness of a word *team* consisting of phonemes in sequence /tiim/, and *steam* consisting of /stiim/. The speaker unconsciously applies a rule which makes the /t/ of *team* aspirated but not the /t/ of *steam*.

Some rules are optional. Consider the following pieces of utterances:

I hope this won't disappoint you.
We don't want to leave without you.
But you must remember . . .

In all of these (and many more possible utterances) the word *you* follows a word which ends with *t*. A speaker may pronounce the sequence as *t* plus *y* or as *ch* – what we will represent hereafter as /č/. We can think of this as applying or not applying a rule which converts *t* + *y* into /č/. If a rule is optional for any speaker it naturally is different in its applications for different speakers.

Some rules are variable. There is a rule similar to the one above which changes *t* to *ch* when it is followed by *i* and another vowel; compare *suggest* and *suggestion*, *quest* and *question*. If the vowel following *i* is a stressed vowel, as in *Christianity*, *bestiality*, the rule may vary according to dialects. Some speakers have /t/ after /s/ in these words and others have a phoneme /č/.

One assumption of generative phonology is that all speakers of the language store essentially the same underlying representations for the morphemes that they know, and if they pronounce these morphemes differently the differences result from the application of different rules or the same rules in different orders. The implication of this assumption is troubling because in describing a language as widespread as English certain facts emerge which have to be described and yet which cannot be considered facts known, in any sense, by all speakers of the language. As we will see (chapter 4), different varieties of English have different vowel systems. Rules for placement of stress in English words are based, in part, on recognition of two kinds of vowels, but these two kinds of vowels are not truly distinct in any physical way for many speakers of the language.

Part of the speaker's knowledge is specific and part of it is general – rule-governed – but the boundary between the two is not at all clear. Our average speaker, let's say, knows the specific words *cat*, *dog*, *horse*, and *ox*. Knowledge includes, certainly, knowing what reference each has. Knowing each word and what it refers to is specific knowledge. The speaker can generalize, no doubt, that these are all related to a word *animal*. Whether the speaker has ever learned the word *noun* or not, he is aware that the words are used in similar ways in sentences. The speaker knows the fact that these words have a plural (not all languages make a distinction between singular and plural) and knows what the plural forms are for these four nouns. Knowledge of the plural form *oxen* is specific knowledge; no other English noun forms the plural in just this way. Knowledge of the plural forms *cats*, *dogs*, *horses* is general knowledge; it is the application of a rule. In speech *cat* and other nouns form their plural by adding a phoneme /s/, *dogs* is one of the nouns which have a final /z/ phoneme, and *horse* belongs to the group which add a whole syllable for the plural. We describe the complete rule in chapter 8. It is something which all speakers of English know but without knowing that they know it. When we learn a new noun, we form the plural automatically. Studies have shown that small children are able to apply this rule. No doubt about it, the rule is part of the competence of a speaker of English.

Now consider these pairs of words: *wise, wisdom; derive, derivative; Palestine, Palestinian*. We can recognize a rule here: when a suffix like *-dom, -ative,* or *-ian* is added to a word with a 'long I' in it, the 'long I' is converted to a 'short I.' This is a different kind of rule. It applies to words which have been formed in the past.

1.5 Summary

In any language there is variety, which can be discussed under two headings, variations among **users** and variations in **uses** of the language. Variations among users include geographic and social dialects, of which the former are of greater interest in this text. Variations in use include differences of **function**, differences of formality and politeness, and differences of tempo, all of which are intertwined. Language varieties based on such matters of use are called **registers**.

Geographic varieties of English result from a long history of regional differences in England itself; the slow development of a standard which, in its spoken form, is called **Received Pronunciation**; the political domination of Celtic-speaking countries by England from the beginnings of the Modern era; and the establishment of colonies overseas from the late sixteenth to the late nineteenth centuries.

It is useful to recognize the distinction between speech, an activity, and **language**, the code which makes communication possible through numerous speech acts. Language is the knowledge which speakers have and which makes communication possible; it is also an inheritance from the past. A language consists of a **lexicon**, a **phonology**, and a **grammar**. Phonology is the description of the sound system of a language, the link between speech and meaning. **Phonetics** is the science which studies speech sounds as sounds.

Although speaking is ordinarily a constant movement of the vocal organs, it is convenient to view speech as a **chain** composed of individual **segments** one after another. Each such segment is a composite of certain **articulatory features**. Some of these features serve to differentiate meanings in a language; such features are **distinctive** in that language. Features which are not distinctive are **redundant**. Segments which have the same distinctive features constitute a **phoneme** of the language. Phonemes combine in certain possible sequences to express **morphemes**, the units of meaning of the language. Phonemes contrast with one another to differentiate morphemes from one another.

Units of speech from smallest to largest are: **articulatory feature**, **segment**, **syllable**, **tone unit**, **utterance**, and **discourse**.

A **generative phonology** is part of a **generative grammar**, a view and theory of language which holds that a description of a language is a description of the language competence of a speaker of that language. Generative grammar considers phonology to be one component of a language and the description of phonology inseparable from the **grammar** and **lexicon**. Anything that is said in the language has an abstract **underlying form**. Various **rules** apply in a particular order to the underlying representation to produce the actual utterance. The rules supposedly encapsulate unconscious knowledge of the speaker, but there is a problem in distinguishing what parts of a person's knowledge are specific and what parts are general, rule-governed.

Notes

The distinction between users and uses of a language is from Halliday, McIntosh, and Strevens (1964).

Standard histories of the English language in Britain include Jespersen (1909–49) and Pyles (1971). At the present time there is no comprehensive study of what may be called World English; the closest approximations are anthologies such as Bailey and Görlach (1982) and Kachru (1982), which include sketches of English in countries where it has official, commercial, and/or educational uses but is not the native language of the general population, as well as descriptions of the English of the British Isles, Canada, the United States, the Caribbean, Australia, New Zealand, and South Africa. The pronunciation of English in native-speaker areas is the subject of Wells (1982).

The role of gestures, stance, and appearance in communication ('body language') has been the topic of various popular works and some serious studies; an example of the latter is Knapp (1972). The nature of non-verbal, vocal elements in communication (paralanguage) was explored in Trager 1949 and, more ambitiously, in Crystal and Quirk (1964).

For further description of dialect differences, regional and social, registers and ways of studying them see Fasold (1984) and Trudgill (1974).

The terms 'Standard British English' and 'Received Pronunciation' are not exactly identical. Dictionary-makers and grammarians of the eighteenth and later centuries, such as Johnson (1755) and Lowth (1762), are responsible for the establishment of a standard which, by and large, has been accepted as the 'correct' form of written English in Britain and, with various modifications, throughout the English-speaking world. 'Received Pronunciation' is the name for the way of speaking of the educated upper middle class in Britain. The term and the description of this speech came into existence in the early years of the twentieth century with the development of a science of phonetics.

2

Sound . . . and Voice

Essentially all the sounds that we hear are the result of vibrations in the air around us. In sections 2.1 to 2.5 we first consider some of the physical characteristics of such vibrations: why sounds differ in loudness and in pitch or tone, and how secondary vibration, resonance, is important.

For practical purposes we limit our study of speech to the sounds that are made when air is expelled from the lungs and is modified in various ways as it moves upward and out of the body. The vocal cords in the larynx provide the basic vibration in the air stream, which is further modified above the larynx in the vocal tract. There are two kinds of modification: the vocal tract can be shaped in different ways so that air vibrates in different patterns of resonance, or the air stream can be obstructed, wholly or partly, in different places. Obstruction and resonance can occur together (sections 2.6 to 2.9).

2.1 Hearing

'I hear something.' We speak of hearing as if it were something that we do, an action that we perform. Actually, hearing, like seeing, is not so much an action that we perform but rather something that happens to us, a stimulus that we receive and to which we react. When we hear something – when a door slams, a book falls to the floor, a plane passes overhead, or somebody calls our name – the air around us is disturbed. Something causes particles of air to move. These particles push against other particles of air, which in turn displace other particles, and so on in a 'domino' effect. Finally the particles of air which are next to our eardrums are subjected to a different pressure. The difference in pressure affects some tiny bones behind the eardrums; these bones cause changes of pressure in a liquid stored in the inner ear; and the different pressures in the liquid produce different nerve sensations, which are telegraphed to the brain. We hear.

Receiving these impressions from the world outside our skin seems to be purely passive, but it is not entirely so. Ordinarily we not only hear, we recognize what we have heard. We can distinguish the shattering of glass, the tearing of paper, the boom of an explosion, the pattering of rain, and many, many more sounds. In the storehouse of our memory we compare each new auditory experience with those we have previously recorded, and usually we find a match. Thus hearing is not entirely passive. Nevertheless, to understand what sound is, how sounds differ from one another, we have to focus on the activity of particles of air, not on the activity of the brain.

2.2 Energy, vibration, and medium

In order to produce sound, a physical system must include a source of energy and a vibrating body. When you slam a door, pluck a guitar string, or bounce a ball, you apply energy, or force, to a body which can move. The body does not merely move and stop; it moves back and forth, back and forth – it vibrates. The vibration is obvious in the guitar string and the bouncing ball. The vibration of the door when it closes may or may not be visible to us. There is another vibration which we never see. The movement of particles of matter (door, guitar, ball) is transmitted to the surrounding particles of air. Each air particle moves in response to the force that affects it, repeating the back-and-forth movement of the particle of matter that set it in motion. Each particle of air collides with another particle and sets it in the same vibratory motion. Each particle moves back and forth only a little, but altogether the surrounding particles move outward in the form of a wave. The original force is spread over a large distance.

We have mentioned three elements in the phenomenon of sound: an **initiator**, or source of energy, which causes the door to slam, the book to fall, and so on; a **medium**, the air through which the chainlike displacement happens; and a **receiver**, the ears and brain of the person who hears. Air is not the only possible medium for the transmission of sound. If you have had the experience of hearing voices while swimming under water, you know that water is a possible medium. You may also have had the experience of hearing through a wall of metal, plaster, or wood. And you may be aware that some 'primitive' peoples can hear animals moving in the distance by putting an ear to the ground. Metal, plaster, wood, earth, and water can be media for the transmission of sound, but generally all the sounds that we hear come to us through the sea of air in which we live.

Figure 2.1-a is a conventional way of representing the movement of a particle of air through space (the vertical dimension) over a period of time (the horizontal dimension). The particle, responding to whatever force has been applied to it, moves from point A to point X, then back to A (actually A_1 on the figure since a moment has passed); it then moves to point Y and returns to point A (here A_2 since another moment has elapsed), completing one cycle. Then another cycle begins. Any sound wave is made up of a number of such cycles. The number of cycles in a unit of time (usually one second) is called the **frequency** of that wave, and the amount of time for one cycle is the inverse, the **period** of the wave. Thus if a particle makes 100 cycles per second, its frequency is 100 cycles per second (also designated 100 Hertz, abbreviated 100 Hz) and its period is 1/100 of a second.

When a regular vibration continues for some time, the cycles are approximately even and the periods are equal. Such a wave is **periodic**. In contrast, an irregular vibration has unequal cycles and its wave is **aperiodic**. Not only is it irregular but it is also of short duration. The sound associated with a periodic wave is musical, whereas the sound associated with an aperiodic wave is noise. To use a rough analogy, a periodic wave is like the repeated bouncing of a spherical rubber ball, and the aperiodic wave is similar to what happens when you try to bounce a ball which is lopsided and too heavy.

2.3   The measurement of vibrations

Just as there are two dimensions, space and time, so there are two important measurements in the description of a sound wave. The maximum distance that a vibrating particle moves is called the **amplitude** of the wave. The line XX′ of figure 2.1-a indicates the amplitude of the sound produced by the particle of air (and its traveling companions) depicted here. The greater the force which produces the movement of the particle, the greater the amplitude of its displacement, and the louder the sound which results. We should have no difficulty in relating this statement to the world of our experience. We all know the difference between the loud sound caused by giving a forceful shove to a door and the mild click which results when the same door is given a gentle push.

The other measurement is frequency, which has already been mentioned. Different materials vibrate at different speeds; a particle of one kind of matter moves away and back to its starting point a certain number of times per second while a particle of another kind of matter moves a greater or lesser number of times in response to the same force. The greater the frequency of vibration, the higher the pitch of the resulting sound. Again, we know this from our common experience. Compare what happens when you slam a light-weight door in a plywood partition and what happens when you give an equal push to a heavy metal door in a concrete wall. In the first instance the vibration is rapid enough to be obvious; in the second case, so slow that it is imperceptible. Similarly, a guitar string under heavy tension vibrates faster and produces a higher-pitched hum than a string which is under less tension.

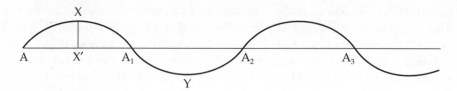

Figure 2.1-a

Figure 2.1-b

Figure 2.1-d

Figure 2.1-c

Figure 2.1-e

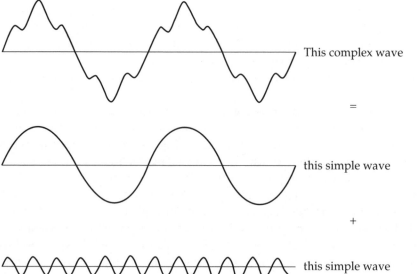

This complex wave

=

this simple wave

+

this simple wave

Figure 2.1-f

2A   Exercise: sound waves

(a) Figures 2.1-b and 2.1-c show sound waves with equal frequency but different amplitudes. Which is associated with the greater loudness?
(b) Figures 2.1-d and 2.1-e are waves of equal amplitude but different frequencies. Which is associated with the higher pitch?

Our discussion so far has been unrealistically simple. Any sound results not from a simple wave, such as figures 2.1-a to 2.1-e illustrate, but from a complex group of such waves. Take the example of the guitar string again. When the string is plucked, a certain amount of force is applied to one portion of the string, which is under a certain degree of tension. Other parts of the string are under different degrees of tension and receive smaller amounts of the force which moves the string. Consequently different parts of the string vibrate with different frequencies and different amplitudes, and so do the different bits of air which lie along the string. If you strike a chord on the guitar – that is, apply force to all the strings one immediately after the other – you produce a complex pattern of amplitudes and frequencies. Differences in complex patterns account for differences of quality in the sounds we hear. A complex wave can be broken down into a number of simple waves. This is illustrated in figure 2.1-f.

2.4   Resonance

An important part of the quality of a sound is due to a kind of secondary vibration called **resonance**. The classic demonstration of resonance is to strike a tuning fork and listen to its hum-m-m-m, then bring one end of the fork down onto a wooden table and change the metallic hum-m-m-m into a dull buzz-z-z-z. Particles of wood are set into vibration by the tuning fork. They resonate (re-sound) in response to the vibratory force of the tuning fork but they vibrate at their own frequencies.

When the strings of a guitar or violin vibrate, the box of the instrument picks up the vibration – it resonates. More importantly, the air inside the box also resonates. Different strings on the violin or guitar vibrate at different frequencies. The air inside the box vibrates at some of these frequencies but not others, so that it strengthens some of these frequencies and weakens others. The box of a violin, guitar, or other stringed instrument is a **resonance chamber**, and so is the area between the skins of a drum, the inside of an accordion or concertina, each pipe of an organ or calliope, and the tube of any wind instrument. If a resonance chamber strengthens some frequencies while weakening others, we say that it is resonant to those frequencies. The size and shape of a resonance chamber determine to which frequencies it is resonant.

2.5   Air in motion

Our discussion so far has been mostly concerned with sound created by percussion, force applied to some kind of matter, causing it to move and to displace particles of air. But air can itself be in motion and thus may be displaced by matter in its path, which also creates sound. We are all familiar with the sound of wind whistling through trees, or down an empty street between tall buildings, or through the slightly open window of a car speeding along a highway. We are also familiar with wind instruments like the flute, clarinet, saxophone, or organ. Each of these uses air which is blown or pumped into a resonance chamber – or, in the case of the organ, a set of resonance chambers. Some source of energy sends air into the tube(s), a reed furnishes the basic vibration, and differently shaped resonance chambers are created by stopping up different holes, as in a flute, piccolo, or harmonica, or by moving a slide in and out, as in a trombone.

When a sound is made by percussion, the length of the sound depends on the force used and the physical nature of the vibrating body. In other words, the **duration** of the sound is not independent of loudness (amplitude) and pitch (frequency). In contrast, when the flow of air produces a sound, the flow can usually be controlled so that duration varies independently. One can, for example, play notes on a flute which are long, loud, and low, or short, soft, and high, or short, loud, and high, and so on.

2.6   The human voice

Human speech is very much like the playing of a wind instrument. Different speech sounds, in any language, are made by moving a column of air through part of the upper body and creating various kinds of vibration and noise as the air moves. It is possible to use air that is drawn into the body from outside (try to say 'Yes' while inhaling). A more familiar way of using ingressive air for sound-production is to produce a click, such as the tongue-tip noise which we represent as *tsk-tsk*, or the clucking sound that is sometimes used in getting a horse to move. To produce such clicks we create a vacuum in the mouth, then open suddenly so that air rushes in. Another way of producing an air stream is to gather a quantity of air in the throat and then eject it all at once. In almost all of our speaking, however, we use a column of air which moves up from the lungs and out the mouth or the nose or both together, and we modify the air in its passage. Everything that we say about speech sounds from here on will assume the use of egressive lung air.

All of the vocal organs, shown in figure 2.2, have other functions – breathing, sucking, chewing, swallowing. The **lungs** expand and contract to bring in air or let it out. Air expelled from the lungs travels up the **trachea**, or windpipe. At the top of the trachea is a structure of cartilage known as the **larynx**, or voicebox. The primary vibration needed for speech is produced in the larynx by the **vocal cords**, which are described in the next section. Above

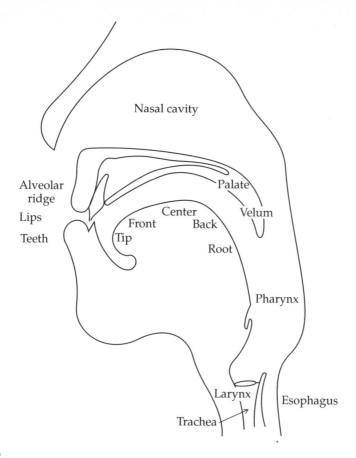

Figure 2.2

the larynx are three interconnected areas, the **pharynx**, the **nasal cavity**, and the mouth (or **oral cavity**) which serve as resonance chambers. The three together are called the **vocal tract**.

We can summarize the functions of these vocal organs this way: The lungs supply the basic force which is needed (**initiation**). The vocal cords furnish the basic vibration (**phonation**). The three resonance chambers are maneuvered in various ways to produce sounds of different quality (**articulation**). In general, variations in the force with which air is expelled from the lungs results in differences of intensity or loudness in speech sounds. Variations in the frequency of vibration of the vocal cords are responsible for variations in pitch, or tone. Variations in the shape of the vocal tract are related to different speech sounds. In theory, then, loudness, pitch, and articulation are separate from one another. In reality, these things go together. In an English utterance the parts which are more prominent than others are generally louder, higher in pitch, and have certain special articulatory characteristics. Most notably, the prominent parts have greater duration.

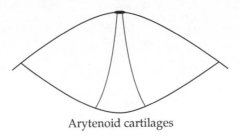

Arytenoid cartilages

Vocal cords open for normal breathing

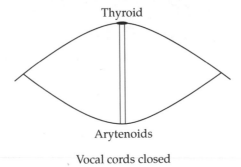

Thyroid

Arytenoids

Vocal cords closed

Figure 2.3

2.7   The vocal cords

Figure 2.3 shows the structure of the larynx in a simplified way. Within the larynx are two elastic bands of tissue, the vocal cords (or vocal bands, or vocal folds). These extend from the **thyroid** ('shield-shaped') **cartilage** in front – which, in the male, protrudes as the so-called Adam's apple – to the **arytenoid** ('ladle-shaped') **cartilages** in the back. The vocal cords are joined together at the thyroid cartilage but are attached separately to the two arytenoid cartilages, which can rotate and thus move the vocal cords apart or together. The opening between the cords is called the **glottis**. For ordinary breathing the glottis is wide open. For various purposes we can close the glottis, that is, bring the vocal cords together. We do this automatically when we swallow, so that food goes down the esophagus to the stomach and not into the trachea. The glottis also closes in order to lock air into the lungs so that our bodies can exert greater force, as in lifting a heavy object.

When they are neither fully open nor completely closed, the vocal cords are somewhat tense, and then the pressure of the outgoing air causes them to vibrate. The vibration is not audible; speech is produced above the larynx. As we produce a stream of speech, the vocal cords are sometimes vibrating, sometimes not vibrating. Speech sounds produced while the vocal cords are vibrating are **voiced**; those made without vibration are unvoiced, or **voiceless**.

If the cords are vibrating, they can be stretched to different degrees of tension, so that they vibrate at different frequencies, producing different pitches in the sounds articulated above the vocal cords. Speech has melody – different melodies or intonation patterns – as a result of these different frequencies of vibration.

How can you tell if a speech sound is voiced or voiceless? There are three good tests. Take the sound [z] as at the end of the word *buzz* and the sound [s] as at the end of the word *hiss*. Make a long [z-z-z] and a long [s-s-s] as you apply the tests.

(1) Put your thumb and fingers on your throat, on each side of the Adam's apple. You should feel vibration as you say one of these sounds, but not the other. (2) Cover your ears with your hands while making the two sounds. You should hear greater noise while making the sound that uses vibration in the larynx. (3) Try to sing up and down the scale while making each of these sounds. Singing means changing pitch, which means changing the frequency of vocal cord vibration. If the cords are vibrating, you can sing; if not, you can't.

By this time you should have decided – if you didn't already know – that [z] is voiced and [s] is voiceless. Try the same three tests with the [f] sound of *fife* and the [v] sound of *valve*. This test works well with fricative sounds like [s z f v] but it does not work well with stops such as the beginning and end of *pop* and *bob*.

2.8   The vocal tract

Air which leaves the larynx goes through the pharynx and then out through the nasal cavity or the oral cavity or both at the same time. Some speech sounds result from obstructing the flow of air somewhere in the pharynx or oral cavity. The obstruction may be partial, as in articulating the sounds [f v s z], or it may be complete, as in making the first and last sounds of *pop, bob, tot, dead*. Speech sounds which result from complete or partial obstruction are called **obstruents**; they are essentially noise, the result of aperiodic vibrations. Other, more musical speech sounds are called **sonorants**, or resonants; examples are the vowel sounds of the four words above and the consonants of *mill* and *run*. In the articulation of a sonorant the basic glottal vibration produced in the larynx is modified in the vocal tract. By changing the shape of parts of the vocal tract we create different resonance chambers so that different parts of the basic glottal vibration are strengthened while other parts are weakened.

The shape of the pharynx can be modified only slightly, either by raising the larynx or by retracting the root of the tongue – either of which makes the pharynx smaller. Changes in the shape of the pharynx have only minor importance in the production of English speech sounds.

The nasal cavity cannot be varied at all. It serves as a resonance chamber only if air is allowed to flow through it; speech sounds made with air not going through the nasal cavity have no nasal resonance. At the junction of the pharynx and the mouth there is a sort of trap door, the velic, the very end of the **velum** (see figure 2.2). The velic is lowered to permit the entry of air into the nasal cavity or raised to prevent it. Pronounce the word *mum* and prolong the final [m] sound. You are making a sound with egressive lung air, since it can be prolonged, and yet your lips are closed. Where is air escaping? Holding a finger in front of the nostrils will give the answer. And then, is [m] voiced or voiceless?

Of the three resonance chambers the mouth is the one which can be varied most. The jaw and tongue can be lowered and raised. The tongue may touch the roof of the mouth, stopping the flow of air (complete obstruction), or it may be positioned close to the roof of the mouth so that air moves through a narrow opening with friction or turbulence (partial obstruction). In a similar way the lower lip may cause complete or partial obstruction at the upper lip or upper teeth. The tongue, but not the lip, moves back and forth to cause obstruction, full or partial, in various parts of the mouth. Without any obstruction the tongue can assume different heights, producing resonance chambers of different size and shape. Moreover, the tongue can be curled in at the sides, or back at the tip; it can acquire a groove along the center line or instead maintain a flat surface. The lips can be stretched or rounded. All these ways of shaping the vocal tract are used in articulating speech sounds. In fact, all the sounds we shall study require some action or state in the mouth, with or without concomitant use of larynx, pharynx, and nasal cavity.

2.9   Kinds of speech sounds

As we talk, we constantly change the shape of the vocal tract, producing a stream of speech. We are likely to think that this stream of speech consists of one sound after another. In the word *mitt*, to use a very short example, we think that we articulate three distinct sounds in sequence, whch can be represented as [m], then [ɪ], and then [t]. This is true enough in terms of what the hearer perceives; it is not so accurate in terms of what the speaker does. The speaker's vocal organs do not assume one position, then another, and then another; they are in motion as long as an utterance lasts. Nevertheless, to describe speech we follow the perceptions of the hearer – we adopt the convenient fiction that any stretch of speech is like a chain with individual sounds, or **segments**, linked together. Each segment is different from any other segment because it is articulated with the vocal tract in one particular configuration: the lips are rounded or not, the tongue is low in the mouth or not, the vocal cords are vibrating or not, and so on. We call these different elements articulatory features. Each segment is a unique cluster of articulatory features. The segment [m] has certain features, [ɪ] has a different group of features, and [t] has a different combination of features. For instance, [m] is articulated with the vocal cords vibrating, the lips together, and air coming out of the nose. It is

voiced, **labial**, and **nasal**. There are other speech sounds which are voiced, like [v] and [z], others which are labial, like [b] and [p], and others, like [n], which are nasal, but only [m] is all three of these together. We may say that [m] is the intersection of three sets of articulatory features.

The most fundamental way in which speech sounds differ from one another is in the way the air stream is controlled. Control of the air stream is apparently the first thing that small children learn when they acquire their native language. Up to about the age of eight months an infant babbles – produces streams of speech sounds which are not really speech if 'speech' means use of a language code; but they are speech sounds in a physical sense, random products of the vocal apparatus as the child experiments with the noises it can make while breathing in and out. Babbling prepares the child for the next stage of linguistic growth, imitating the speech of adults and acquiring a vocabulary of single words.

At this stage of one-word utterances (one word, in the sense that the utterance cannot be broken into smaller parts that are recombined in different ways; something like *where-s-it* may be the child's way of asking the location of any thing or person or group of things or persons) the child's imitations do not usually sound very close to what older speakers say, but in two respects the child is generally quite accurate. The child recognizes syllables and it has some appreciation of prosody – the melodies of speech. If parents present the youngster with a one-syllable word ('doll,' 'milk,' 'bath,' 'ball,' to use English examples), the child's word is also a single syllable; if the adult model is two syllables ('water,' 'doggy,' 'baby,' 'bottle'), the child's rendition is also two syllables long. Apparently the child is equally sensitive to differences of loudness and pitch. It is likely to repeat the final part of Mother's utterances, everything from the last accented syllable to the end. If Mother says, 'Where shall we put this?' the child may say, in its own way, 'put this' with a rising pitch. Hearing something like 'Here's a nicer one,' the child may produce three syllables with falling pitch which somewhat echo 'nicer one.' So control of the air stream in making syllables and control of vocal cord vibration to produce some melodies seem to be the child's first speech acquisitions.

Each syllable which the child utters is likely to consist of two parts, closure and opening. The air stream is obstructed and then it flows freely; there is a consonant and then a vowel. Later, depending on what the child is imitating, some syllables will consist of closure, opening, and closure – consonant, vowel, consonant. The degree of closure and the amount of opening vary freely at first, and so does the place where closure is made, but eventually the child learns to control these manipulations and begins to sound like other members of the language community. Controlling the manipulations means learning to make different kinds of closure and opening and to make them in different parts of the vocal tract.

Different kinds of speech sounds, different manners of articulating, are different ways of manipulating the air stream. We recognize six kinds of speech sounds: **vowels**, **glides**, **nasals**, **liquids**, **fricatives**, and **stops**. Vowels and stops (the latter also called *plosives*) are completely different. Vowels are produced by allowing the air to flow freely, stops are made by complete obstruction of the air stream. Other kinds of speech sounds have some of the characteristics, or **features**, of vowels and some of the features of stops.

Stops and vowels differ from each other in four features:

1   A vowel is resonant, the result of periodic waves; when a vowel is articulated, particles of air vibrate in regular, repetitive patterns. A stop is essentially an instant of silence. If air particles are vibrating at all, there is no regular pattern. To express this difference we say that vowels are **[+ sonorant]** and stops are **[− sonorant]**.

2   A vowel is the center or **peak** of its syllable, more prominent than what precedes or follows in the syllable. When two or more adjoining syllables differ in loudness or pitch, the difference is in their respective vowels. In a two-syllable word like *baby* the first syllable is more prominent than the second, and that difference is due to the comparative prominence of their vowels. If the voice rises in saying 'Baby?' or instead falls and produces 'Baby!' – that is, whether the vocal cords increase or decrease their frequency of vibration – the change occurs in the vowels. Stops have no role in relative prominence or change of pitch. Thus we say that vowels are **[+ syllabic]** and stops are **[− syllabic]**.

3   When a vowel is articulated, air comes continuously out of the mouth. The nature of a stop is that air is stopped – prevented from escaping. We say that vowels are **[+ continuant]** and stops are **[− continuant]**.

4   When a stop is articulated, either the lower lip or some part of the tongue is in contact with some other part of the mouth – the upper lip or some part of the roof of the mouth. When a vowel is articulated, there is no interruption of the air stream. This distinction is captured with a feature [consonantal]. When there is some interruption of the breath stream, as there is for stops, the segment is **[+ consonantal]**. Vowels are **[− consonantal]**.

The other four classes of speech sounds, fricatives, nasals, liquids, and glides, are partly like stops and vowels but of course are also different from them and from one another. The four features, [sonorant], [syllabic], [continuant] and [consonantal], describe their similarities and differences.

Fricatives are segments like the [f v s z] of *feel, veal, seal, zeal*, respectively. They are articulated by squeezing the outgoing air stream between an articulator (the lower lip or some part of the tongue) and a point of articulation (the upper lip or some part of the roof of the mouth) so that turbulence or friction – rubbing – results. Fricatives are like stops in three features but differ in one. Like stops, they are the result of aperiodic vibration, therefore [− sonorant]; they require some interruption of the air stream, so they are [+ consonantal]; they are not typically the peaks of syllables and so are designated [− syllabic]. (There are marginal exceptions to the last statement: a hiss [s-s-s] and the interjection that we write *pst!* have a fricative as the peak of a syllable, but there are no English words with such syllables). Finally, unlike stops, fricatives are [+ continuant] since air is flowing continuously out of the mouth. Say *cup* and see if you can prolong the final sound; say *cuff* and hold the last sound as long as you can.

Nasals are segments like the [m] of *mitt* and the [n] of *knit*, sounds made by stopping the flow of air somewhere in the mouth but letting it exit through the nose. Nasals are musical – [+ sonorant] – as every singer and teacher of singing knows. Since the air stream is interrupted in the mouth, they are [+ consonantal]. Since air does not escape through the mouth, they are [– continuant]. (This is a matter of definition; [+ continuant] is defined to mean 'with air flowing out the mouth'; actually a nasal can be prolonged because air is flowing continuously through another exit. Say *come* and make the last sound continue as long as you have breath.) Last, we classify nasals as both plus and minus syllabic – [± syllabic]. They are usually not the peak of a syllable, but they can be, as in the word *kitten*.

Liquids include the [l] of *lead* and the [r] of *read*. In their articulation the tongue is raised, partly impeding the flow of air, but the tongue is shaped in such a way that air flows around it, creating particular patterns of vibration. Because of the impedance liquids are classed as [+ consonantal]; because of the periodic vibration they are [+ sonorant]; because air flows freely they are [+ continuant]. Finally, like nasals, they are [± syllabic] – usually not the peak of a syllable but sometimes the peak, as in *metal* and *manner*.

Glides include the [j] of *yet* and the [w] of *wet*, for example. Glides are like vowels except in one feature. Slow down the pronunciation of *yet* and *wet* until each word becomes two syllables, the first starting with a vowel like that of *tea*, the second word beginning with a vowel like that of *too*. A glide is like a vowel except that it does not have the prominence of a vowel, does not act as the peak of a syllable. Glides, then, are [– syllabic] but in other respects are like vowels: [+ sonorant], [+ continuant], [– consonantal].

Four features have been used to define six classes of speech sounds. The following chart summarizes them, with abbreviations of the feature names that will be used hereafter:

	SYL	CONS	CONT	SON
vowels	+	–	+	+
glides	–	–	+	+
liquids	±	+	+	+
nasals	±	+	–	+
fricatives	–	+	+	–
stops	–	+	–	–

Naturally each class is defined by a different cluster of pluses and minuses.

We have introduced the four features with emphasis on the six manners of articulation that they define. Let's recapitulate with emphasis on the features themselves.

A speech sound is [+ syllabic] if it is the most prominent segment of a syllable, the principal carrier of stress and pitch. Vowels are [+ syl] always, nasals and liquids may be [+ syl] but are more often [– syl], and other segments are [– syl].

A speech sound is [+ consonantal] if its articulation requires interruption of the breath stream, accomplished with the lower lip or some part of the tongue. Liquids, nasals, fricatives, and stops are [+ cons], vowels and glides are [– cons].

A speech sound is [+ continuant] if it is articulated with air flowing continuously out of the mouth. Vowels, glides, liquids, and fricatives are [+ cont], nasals and stops (which might be called 'nasal stops' and 'oral stops', respectively) are [– cont].

A speech sound is [+ sonorant] if its quality depends on the regular patterns of vibration of air particles within the vocal tract, so that some part of the vocal tract acts as a resonance chamber. Vowels, glides, liquids, and nasals are [+ son], stops and fricatives are [– son].

2B   Exercise: classes of sounds and features

Referring to the chart above, compare the classes of segments two by two:

(a)   Vowels and glides are alike in three features and different in one. In what feature do they differ?
(b)   In what feature(s) are liquids and nasals alike? In what do they differ?
(c)   How are fricatives and stops alike? How are they different?
(d)   How do stops and nasals compare (or differ)?
(e)   What difference is there between fricatives and liquids?
(f)   How similar, or how different, are vowels and stops?

2.10   Summary

Sound is the result of vibrations strong enough and near enough to affect our eardrums. In almost all of our usual experience the vibrations are transmitted through air (the medium), either because a moving body, the initiator, displaces particles of air or because air is in motion and is displaced by matter in its path or is channeled into some container. Displaced particles of air move back and forth, displacing other particles and causing them to repeat the same vibratory movement in a chain-like effect. The maximum distance that a particle moves in each direction from its starting point is the **amplitude** of the wave that it creates. The total distance from starting point to farthest distance in one direction to farthest distance in the other direction and back to the starting point is a **cycle**. The amount of time required for one cycle is a **period**. The number of cycles completed within a given period of time (usually one second) is the **frequency** of the vibration. Different vibrations have different amplitudes, the auditory correlate of which is difference in the **intensity** or **loudness** of the sounds produced; different vibrations also have different frequencies, and the corresponding sounds differ in **pitch**. Sounds may also differ in **duration**. Vibrating particles which move in regular cycles create **periodic** waves; those which move in irregular cycles, typically of short duration, create **aperiodic** waves.

Ordinarily sounds are associated with complex waves, various particles vibrating at different amplitudes and frequencies A complex wave can be analyzed as the sum of the component simple waves. Ordinarily, too, there is **resonance** associated with any vibration. Other particles of air in a **resonance chamber** vibrate in response to some initial vibration outside. A resonance chamber strengthens the initial frequencies to which it is resonant. The size and shape of a resonance chamber determine to which frequencies it is resonant; therefore a resonance chamber determines the **quality** of any sound which has resonance.

Speech is a function of the respiratory system of the human body. Almost always the initiator is air from the **lungs** which moves up the **trachea** and enters the **larynx**. Inside the larynx two bands of tissue, the **vocal cords**, when tense and partly closed, vibrate in response to the air from the lungs and provide **phonation**, the basic vibration for speech sounds. The quality of speech sounds is determined by the shape of the **vocal tract** above the larynx, where the vibrating air is modified in various ways. Differences in the force with which air is expelled from the lungs are responsible for differences in the intensity of speech sounds, and differences in the frequency of vibration of the vocal cords result in differences of pitch; however, the theoretical distinction between intensity and pitch is not always so clear-cut in actual language performance.

The vocal tract is conventionally divided into three interconnected areas, the **pharynx**, **nasal cavity**, and **oral cavity**, or mouth. Outgoing air must pass through the pharynx and from there through the nasal cavity or the oral cavity or both simultaneously. These areas, especially the mouth, are where specific articulations are accomplished by various modifications of the air stream. While such modifications take place in the vocal tract, the vocal cords vibrate or remain motionless, producing, respectively, **voiced** or **voiceless** sounds.

In our perception a stream of speech consists of **segments**, or individual sounds, one after another, though in the actual articulation there is no such clear segmentation. Although these segments are perceptive units, we describe them in articulatory terms; each segment is described as a cluster of **articulatory features**. Classification is most efficient if these features are **binary** in nature. Four such binary features express the ways in which the air stream is controlled. A segment is **sonorant**, the result of periodic vibration in the vocal tract, or not. It is **syllabic**, acting as the peak of its syllable, or not. It is **consonantal**, produced with some interruption of the air stream, or not. And it is **continuant**, made with air flowing continuously out of the mouth, or not. These four features, in various plus and minus combinations, serve to define six classes of segments: **stops, fricatives, nasals, liquids, glides,** and **vowels**.

Stops and vowels are entirely different in their defining clusters of features. Otherwise, any two of the classes share some features and differ in others.

2.11   Addendum: a note on redundancy

It was noted that some articulatory features are distinctive and others are redundant. This chapter has introduced four features for distinguishing classes of speech sounds. The next chapter introduces other features which distinguish segments of the same class from one another. Here, however, we need to recognize that even features which are distinctive in some areas may be used redundantly in other areas.

The way we have used four features – sonorant, syllabic, consonantal, and continuant – to designate six classes is somewhat redundant. Four features, with plus and minus values, would be enough to distinguish 16 classes ($2^4 = 16$), not just six. We can see this not only mathematically but by direct observation.

The feature [+ syllabic] is sufficient to designate the class of vowels; no other class has this feature. So the other features, [+ son, + cont, – cons], while they describe true facts about the pronunciation of vowels, have no role in telling how vowels are different from other classes of segments. For classification, one feature is distinctive, the other features are redundant. We can express this fact in a redundancy statement like this:

Whatever is [+ syl] is redundantly [+ son, + cont, – cons].

Or more briefly like this:

If [+ syl], then [+ son, + cont, – cons].

For glides we need two features together, [– cons] and [– syl], for a distinctive label. The feature [– cons] distinguishes vowels and glides together from other classes, and the feature [– syl] distinguishes glides from vowels. So the features [+ son] and [+ cont] are redundant. The redundancy statement:

If [– cons], [– syl], then [+ son, + cont].

2C   EXERCISE: REDUNDANCY STATEMENTS

What are the redundancy statements for nasals, liquids, fricatives, and stops?

2A   FEEDBACK

(a)   figure 2.1-b
(b)   figure 2.1-e

2B FEEDBACK

(a) Vowels are [+ syllabic], and glides are [– syllabic]. In the other three features they are alike. This means that glides are the equivalent of certain vowels in their articulation but not in their function within a syllable. A glide is never the peak of a syllable; a vowel always is.

(b) Liquids and nasals are [+ sonorant, + consoantal, ± syllabic]. Liquids are [+ continuant], nasals are [– continuant]. In other words, both classes have some interruption of the air stream but not so much as to prevent periodic vibration. With liquids air flows out from the mouth but not so for nasals.

(c) Fricatives and stops do not have periodic vibration, so they are [– sonorant]; both require interruption of the air stream, [+ consonantal]; and are not the peak of a syllable, [– syllabic]. Fricatives are made with air flowing out of the mouth, [+ continuant], but stops are not.

(d) Nasals and stops differ only in the feature [sonorant] and in the fact that nasals are sometimes syllabic. They are alike in being [+ consonantal] and [– continuant].

(e) The difference between fricatives and liquids is exactly parallel to the difference between nasals and stops. Fricatives are [– sonorant] and [– syllabic], liquids [+ sonorant] and sometimes syllabic. In the other two features they are alike.

(f) Vowels and stops are different in all four features.

2C FEEDBACK

Nasals:	If [+ son, – cont], then [+ cons, ± syl]
Liquids:	If [+ son, + cons, + cont], then [± syl]
Fricatives:	If [– son, + cont], then [+ cons, – syl]
Stops:	If [– son, – cont], then [+ cons, – syl]

Notes

For a more technical description of sound production see Lieberman (1977). For a more extensive treatment of the physiology of speech production see Ladefoged (1993, ch. 1), and Clark and Yallop (1995, ch. 2).

The features introduced here and in the next chapter are taken from Chomsky and Halle (1968).

Jakobson (1941) is a pioneering work, still valuable, in explaining how infants acquire the sound system of the language of the community into which they are born. Lenneberg (1967) is also a pioneer in stating that language acquisition is biologically determined to a large extent, something that a child does at the appropriate stage of maturation, much as it learns to sit up, crawl, walk, etc. when it is ready to do so. Clark and Clark (1977) and Dale (1976) contain good accounts of how a child acquires its native language.

3

Consonants

This chapter describes English consonants, specifically stops, fricatives, nasals, and liquids. The previous chapter explained that these phoneme classes are different manners of articulation, and we examined the features that make these classes different from one another. Here we are concerned with what the different stops, fricatives, and nasals are and what features distinguish the stops from one another, fricatives from one another, and so on. Three kinds of features are important for differentiating consonants:

voice – whether vocal cords are vibrating or not
tongue shape – whether the tongue has a flat surface, a groove along the center line, or is curled at the sides
articulator – whether the lower lip, tongue tip, tongue front, or tongue back blocks the air stream as it goes out

---

3A PRELIMINARY EXERCISE: IDENTIFYING CONSONANTS
BY MATCHING

(a) The words in the left-hand column below *begin* with 22 different consonants. The words in the right-hand columns begin with the same 22 consonants, but in a different order. Match each word on the left with the word on the right which has the same initial consonant (sound, not letter), and put the appropriate number in front of the word. An example is given.

1	bag	____ tomato	6	fan	____ guess
2	cat	____ Czech	7	gas	____ chef
3	cent	____ yacht	8	gem	____ dare
4	check	____ loose	9	leap	____ vote
5	dude	____ there	10	meek	____ kneel

11	nail	_2_	kite	17	thick	____	send
12	pain	____	holy	18	vest	____	rhyme
13	ptomaine	____	pest	19	weight	____	main
14	room	____	phone	20	whole	____	thin
15	shave	____	jest	21	young	____	boom
16	then	____	zest	22	zoom	____	wild

(b)   The words in the left-hand columns below *end* with 21 different consonants. The words in the right-hand columns have the same final consonants, but in a different order. Match each word on the left with the word on the right which has the same final consonant. An example is given.

1	both	____	love	12	pole	____	fade
2	car	____	rogue	13	rage	____	toll
3	clothe	_4_	dome	14	rich	____	daze
4	dumb	____	grub	15	rouge	____	lock
5	fate	____	smooth	16	rug	____	loss
6	globe	____	ridge	17	save	____	hope
7	graph	____	sane	18	sign	____	youth
8	lace	____	beige	19	soap	____	care
9	look	____	lung	20	tongue	____	ash
10	odd	____	gruff	21	wash	____	witch
11	phrase	____	eight				

(c)   This time match the *final* consonant of each word in the left-hand columns with the *initial* consonant of a word in the right-hand columns – if there is such a match. An example is given.

1	beige	____	pitch	12	maid	____	vain
2	breathe	____	team	13	meat	____	they
3	chip	____	kill	14	nave	____	zone
4	coach	____	bad	15	nose	____	mode
5	comb	____	dame	16	robe	____	name
6	cough	____	goal	17	rogue	____	lace
7	door	____	choke	18	rung	____	rake
8	face	____	jell	19	rush	____	yell
9	lane	_6_	fun	20	Ruth	____	wet
10	ledge	____	think	21	sail	____	head
11	lick	____	safe				____	shift

(d)   Two of the words in the left-hand columns have final consonants for which there is no match in initial position. What are the words?

(e)   Three words in the right-hand columns have initial consonants for which there is no match in final position. What are they?

3.1   The feature [consonantal]

Stops, fricatives, nasals, and liquids are all [+ consonantal]; in their articulation
the lower lip or some part of the tongue impedes the flow of air in some
way, in some part of the mouth. The four classes together are called **consonants**. Vowels and glides are articulated without such impedance; they are
[– consonantal]. For vowels and glides it is the shape of the oral cavity in
which air is flowing freely that determines the quality of the sound produced.
Glides are like certain vowels in their production, but they are like consonants
in the positions they occupy in syllables and larger units. The glides have been
included among consonants in the preliminary exercises above, but they are
discussed in the next chapter with vowels.

The four classes of consonants differ from one another in their manner
of articulation, specifically in whether or not the articulation is characterized
by periodic vibration of air particles and in whether or not the air stream is
escaping from the mouth during the articulation. In the previous chapter we
expressed these differences with the features [sonorant] and [continuant].

liquids	*nasals*	*fricatives*	*stops*
+ sonorant	+ sonorant	– sonorant	– sonorant
+ continuant	– continuant	+ continuant	– continuant

Liquids and nasals are 'musical' like vowels. Although the air stream is obstructed in some way, the vocal tract still acts as a resonance chamber in which
air particles flow in periodic waves. Obstruent consonants – fricatives and
plosives – are articulated with total or near-total obstruction of the air stream
so that resonance is minimal or absent. For liquids and fricatives air flows out
from the mouth during articulation; thus any of these consonants can be held
– continued – as long as the lungs provide air. Nasals can also be prolonged
since air escapes during their articulation, but through the nasal cavity alone.
(Some phoneticians use the term 'nasal stop.') A stop, since it involves
complete obstruction of the breath stream, is essentially an instant of silence.
A stop can be prolonged only in the sense that the silence is maintained for a
longer period of time.

Our next task is to investigate the differences within each of these classes.
What makes one stop distinct from another stop? How does a fricative, a
nasal, a liquid differ from other members of its class?

Here are the symbols for the consonants to be described, with an illustrative
word for each consonant:

Liquids	/l/ led /r/ red
Nasals	/m/ rum /n/ run /ŋ/ rung
Fricatives	/f/ fine /θ/ thin /s/ sue /ʃ/ mission
	/v/ vine /ð/ then /z/ zoo /ʒ/ vision

Stops   /p/ pill /t/ till /č/ chill /k/ kill
/b/ bill /d/ dill /ǰ/ Jill /g/ gill

To describe the articulation of a consonant is to tell what articulatory features are relevant. In general, three kinds of features are distinctive:

(a)   Differences in vocal cord action, or **voicing** – The vocal cords vibrate during some articulations and not during other articulations. Articulations with such vibration are voiced, or, in the notation of a binary system, [+ voice]. Consonants without vocal cord vibration are voiceless, or [– voice]. English stops and fricatives exist in pairs like /t, d/ or /s, z/ such that the two members of the pair are alike in all respects except that one is [– voice] and the other is [+ voice]. Therefore the feature [voice] is distinctive for stops and fricatives. On the other hand, all liquids and nasals are [+ voice], and voicing is not distinctive in these classes – it is not relevant for telling how one liquid differs from the other or one nasal from the other nasals.

Although we use the feature [voice], with plus and minus values, for both stops like /t, d/ and fricatives like /s, z/, it must also be noted that the feature is not identical in phonetic terms. In the articulation of /s/ as in *sue* and *loose* the vocal cords do not vibrate, whereas for the articulation of /z/ in *zoo* and *lose* they do vibrate. For the articulation of /t/ and /d/, as in *two* and *do*, the difference is not in vocal cord vibration during the articulation of these stops but rather in voice onset time. In the articulation of stops the air stream is held back, so that no vibration occurs. When the air stream is released at the beginning of *do*, for instance, vocal cord vibration begins almost immediately. When the release is made at the beginning of *two*, vibration does not come immediately. Instead, there is first an instant of aspiration – air is released between the closely positioned, but non-vibrating, vocal cords. Then vibration begins. So the 'voicedness' of a voiced stop and the 'voicelessness' of a voiceless stop are not so much in the actual articulation of the stops as in their environment.

(b)   Differences in **tongue shape** – The front part of the tongue, the blade, may be flat or it may be shaped so that it has a groove along the center line of the top surface, or it may be drawn in at the sides, or drawn back at the tip. To deal with these differences we recognize two features, [sibilant] and [lateral]. The feature [+ sibilant] indicates the presence of a groove, or slight trough, along the center line, and [– sibilant] means that there is no such groove. The feature [+ lateral] means that the tongue sides are curled inward, and [– lateral] indicates the absence of such curl. The feature [sibilant] is distinctive among fricatives and stops, the feature [lateral] indicates differences in the class of liquids. All nasal consonants are articulated with a flat tongue, so that these features are not distinctive for nasals.

(c)   Differences in **articulators** and **places of articulation** – In English the air stream may be obstructed, wholly or partially, by any one of four articulators:

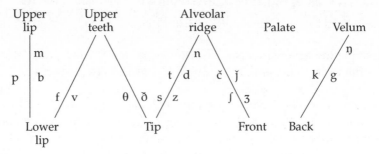

Figure 3.1

the lower lip;
the tip, or apex, of the tongue;
the front, or blade, of the tongue (the front third of the upper surface, excluding the apex);
the back, or dorsum, of the tongue (the back third of the upper surface).

These articulators may be said to lie along the lower edge of the oral cavity. Along the upper edge are the areas where the articulators make contact or near-contact:

the upper lip
the upper front teeth
the alveolar ridge, the hump behind the upper teeth
the (hard) palate, the area which is separated from the nasal cavity by a bony structure
the velum, or soft palate, the posterior area of the roof of the mouth with no bone above it.

The interplay of articulators with places of articulation is shown in the schematic diagram of figure 3.1. Compare figure 2.2. The lines connect articulators and places of articulation. Symbols are placed along the lines to show what articulator and what place of articulation are involved in the articulation of each consonant. Nasals are on the top line, stops on the second line, and fricatives on the third line. The place of articulation is not distinctive for liquids, so /l/ and /r/ are not in the diagram.

The positions of symbols along the lines indicate norms for articulation. As we will see, the place of articulation for any consonant (or any vowel) may vary somewhat according to what precedes and what follows.

3.2   Lip consonants (labials)

Five consonants are articulated with the lower lip:

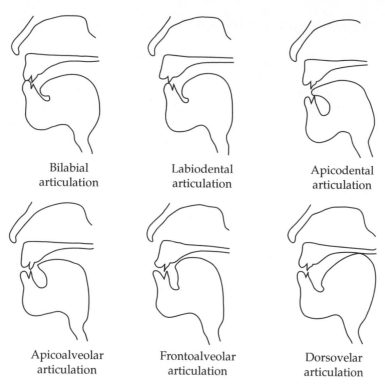

| Bilabial | Labiodental | Apicodental |
| articulation | articulation | articulation |

| Apicoalveolar | Frontoalveolar | Dorsovelar |
| articulation | articulation | articulation |

Figure 3.2

nasal /m/ as in *mat* /mæt/
stops /p/ as in *pat* /pæt/ and /b/ as in *bat* /bæt/
fricatives /f/ as in *fat* /fæt/ and /v/ as in *vat* /væt/.

The first three, /m p b/, are typically articulated by stopping the flow of air with the two lips pressed together (bilabial articulation). The fricatives /f v/ are made by resting the lower lip lightly against the upper teeth (labiodental articulation) and letting air flow out between lip and teeth. What makes /f/ and /v/ different from the other labial consonants is the fact that they are fricative, [+ continuant]. The small difference between bilabial and labiodental articulation is not contrastive. Labial fricatives are predictably labiodental, labial stops and nasal are typically bilabial (but see section 7.1a).

As you know, /p/ and /b/ differ in voicing, and the same is true for /f/ and /v/; /p/ and /f/ are [– voice], /b/ and /v/ are [+ voice]. The nasal /m/ is also [+ voice], but that feature is not distinctive for /m/ or other nasals. If English had both voiced and voiceless nasal consonants, as does the Welsh language, voicing would be distinctive for nasals just as it is for obstruents, but this is not the case.

3.3   Tongue-tip consonants (apicals)

The fricatives /θ ð/ are generally articulated with the tip of the tongue near or lightly touching the upper front teeth – generally at the cutting edge – so that air is squeezed out between tongue and teeth (apicodental articulation). For the nasal and oral stops /n t d/ the apex typically touches the alveolar ridge, stopping the flow of air at that point (apicoalveolar articulation). In the articulation of the fricatives /s z/ air is squeezed between the tip of the tongue and the alveolar ridge. (We say that the tongue-tip is the articulator for all the consonants discussed in this section, but for the fricatives /θ ð s z/ the articulator actually includes the area just behind the tip, as well. In fricative articulation the air stream moves over a comparatively long surface.) If we compare the fricatives /θ ð/ and /s z/, we discover another difference between the one set and the other. The apicodental fricatives are articulated with a flat tongue surface, whereas /s z/ are sibilant, produced with a groove or channel along the center line of the tongue surface. Sibilant fricatives are more audible than flat fricatives because the air stream is moving through a channel which has more depth than width. Compare the final sounds of *faith* /feiθ/ and *face* /feis/, *bathe* /beið/ and *bays* /beiz/. In our analysis of the English sound system we consider that the kind of friction is the feature that is truly distinctive:

/θ ð/ are [– sibilant], /s z/ are [+ sibilant]. The position of the tongue-tip is not distinctive.

3B   QUESTIONS ABOUT FEATURES

(a)   How do /t/ and /d/ differ? /θ/ and /ð/? /s/ and /z/?
(b)   Is /n/ [+ voice] or [– voice]? Is this feature distinctive for /n/?

3.4   Tongue-front consonants (laminals)

The consonants /č ǰ/ are called **affricates**. An affricate is a combination of stop and fricative. To produce the first and last consonants of *church* /č з rč/ and *judge* /ǰ ʌ ǰ/, for instance, the tongue-front, with a groove along the center line, makes contact with the alveolar ridge or the area just behind it, stopping the flow of air; then the tongue is lowered and air passes along the groove creating friction. If the tongue-front does not make contact but is positioned near the alveolar ridge, only friction or turbulence occurs. This is what happens in the articulation of /ʃ/ and /ʒ/. Compare /č/ and /ʃ/, as in *witch* /wɪč/ and *wish* /wɪʃ/; compare /ǰ/ and /ʒ/, as in *pledger* /'plɛǰər/ and *pleasure* /'plɛʒər/. All four have the same articulator, the front of the tongue. Fricatives /ʃ ʒ/ are produced with air flowing continuously out from the mouth; they are [+ continuant]. For /č ǰ/ the air stream is first interrupted, then allowed to exit through a narrow channel. Since air does not escape continuously during the articulation, /č ǰ/ are counted as [– continuant]. Though /č ǰ/ differ from /p b t d k g/ in being affricates rather than plain stops, they are classified as stops.

Like /s z/, /č ǰ ʃ ʒ/ are [+ sibilant]. These six are the only sibilant consonants in English. Of course /č/ and /ʃ/ are [– voice], /ǰ/ and /ʒ/ [+ voice].

3.5 Tongue-back consonants (dorsals)

There are three consonants articulated with the back, or dorsum of the tongue:

nasal /ŋ/ as in *lung* /lʌŋ/
stops /k/ as in *luck* /lʌk/ and /g/ as in *lug* /lʌg/

We make closure between the dorsum and the velum (soft palate), or a little more forward, the back part of the hard palate, so that air is stopped. Like other stops, /k g/ make a pair which differ only in voice – [– voice] and [+ voice], respectively. Like other nasals, /ŋ/ is [+ voice].

3.6 Summary chart

Altogether we have used a system of seven features to classify 18 English consonants, the stops, fricatives, and nasals. For one feature, the articulator, we recognize a four-way distinction here: *l*(ip), *t*(ip), *f*(ront), and *b*(ack). The other six features are binary, with plus and minus values.

	SYL	CONS	CONT	ART	VOI	SIB
p	–	+	–	l	–	–
b	–	+	–	l	+	–
f	–	+	+	l	–	–
v	–	+	+	l	+	–
m	±	+	–	l	+	–
t	–	+	–	t	–	–
d	–	+	–	t	+	–
θ	–	+	+	t	–	–
ð	–	+	+	t	+	–
s	–	+	+	t	–	+
z	–	+	+	t	+	+
n	±	+	–	t	+	–
č	–	+	–	f	–	+
ǰ	–	+	–	f	+	+
ʃ	–	+	+	f	–	+
ʒ	–	+	+	f	+	+

k	–	+	–	b	–	–
g	–	+	–	b	+	–
ŋ	±	+	–	b	+	–

3C   QUESTIONS ABOUT FEATURE DIFFERENCES

Referring to the chart above, what is the only difference between

(a) /p/ and /b/?   (e)   /b/ and /m/?
(b) /d/ and /ð/?   (f)   /n/ and /ŋ/?
(c) /b/ and /v/?   (g)   /s/ and /ʃ/?
(d) /ð/ and /z/?   (h)   /f/ and /θ/?

In what feature(s) does /d/ differ from

(i) /t/?   (l)   /n/?
(j) /b/?   (m) /g/?
(k) /ð/?   (n)   /z/?

Finish these statements of proportion:

(o) /p/ is to /b/ as /t/ is to ___ .
(p) /č/ is to /ʃ/ as /ǰ/ is to ___ .
(q) /b/ is to /m/ as /d/ is to ___ as ___ is to /ŋ/.
(r) ____ is to /s/ as /v/ is to /z/.
(s) Of the four articulators used in English, more consonants are articulated
     with the _____ than any of the others. Fewest consonants are articu-
     lated with the _____ .

3.7   Articulators or points of articulation?

The description of consonants used here differs in two ways from what
you may find in some other phonology books. For one thing, our description
is based on the articulators – lower lip or tip, front, and back of tongue.
Many phonologists describe the same consonants on the basis of the point
of articulation – usually the upper lip (*labials*), the upper teeth or alveolar
ridge (*dentals* or *alveolars*), the hard palate (*palatals*), and the velum (*velars*).
It seems more accurate to classify these consonants with respect to the articulator rather than the point of articulation because the point of articulation
can vary quite a bit whereas the articulator does not (see chapter 7, Consonant
and Vowel Variation). Furthermore, the term *palatals* is not entirely accurate
for the consonants /č ǰ ʃ ʒ/ since these are articulated with the front of the
tongue in conjunction with the alveolar ridge, rather than with the palate.

Nevertheless, the terms based on place of articulation are traditional and frequently used, so that one needs to be familiar with any classification which has such a basis.

Secondly, some books dealing with the phonology of English, having established four points of articulation (as above), introduce a pair of binary features to produce a more elegant classification. Labial consonants and dental/alveolar consonants are all articulated at the alveolar ridge or more forward, whereas velar and, supposedly, palatal consonants are articulated behind the alveolar ridge. If one takes the alveolar ridge as an arbitrary dividing line in the mouth (comparable to the meridian of Greenwich as an arbitrary dividing line for demarking east and west longitude on the face of the earth), labial and dental/alveolar consonants are designated [+ anterior] and palatal and velar consonants are [− anterior].

Another binary feature is needed to distinguish labial and velar consonants from those made more toward the center of the mouth, the dental/alveolars and palatals. Notice that there is something in common between articulation at the lip area and articulation at the back of the mouth; the oral cavity has the shape of a long tube, interrupted at one end − the labial end − or the other − the velar end. In contrast, for the articulation of a dental/alveolar or a palatal consonant the tip or front of the tongue is raised, dividing the oral cavity into two areas of different size, one in front and one in back of the body of the tongue. The distinguishing feature is named [coronal] after the bone in the skull which lies above this part of the mouth. Dental/alveolar and palatal consonants are [+ coronal], and labial and velar consonants are [− coronal].

Here, then, is the scheme for classifying stops, fricatives, and nasals by point of articulation with binary features:

LABIAL	*DENTAL/ALVEOLAR*	*PALATAL*	*VELAR*
+ ant	+ ant	− ant	− ant
− cor	+ cor	+ cor	− cor
p b	t d	č ǰ	k g
f v	θ ð	ʃ ʒ	
	s z		
m	n		ŋ

Note that the classification is the same four-way division that we have introduced. Only the names are different.

3.8   The feature [lateral]

In chapter 2 liquids, the consonants which begin the words *led* and *red*, for instance, were shown to be

± syllabic
+ consonantal
+ continuant
+ sonorant

We can now add two other features which the liquids share: they are [+ voice] and [– sibilant].

How do /l/ and /r/ differ from each other? Phonologists who use the features [anterior] and [coronal], as described above, say that /l/ is [+ anterior] and /r/ is [– anterior] since /l/ is sometimes articulated with the tip of the tongue on the alveolar ridge and /r/ is never articulated so far forward. However, both consonants are articulated in different parts of the mouth; neither the articulator nor the place of articulation is truly distinctive for these two consonants. What distinguishes them from each other is the shape of the tongue. One of them, /l/, is articulated with the sides of the tongue curled in and air escaping over the sides. We say that /l/ is [+ lateral].

For /r/ the tongue is also curled but in a different way; the whole body of the tongue is pulled back and bunched up, with a slight groove in the very tip – not a groove along the center line of the surface, which would make it a sibilant. Typically, there is also some rounding of the lips. Instead of pulling the tongue back and humping it up, some speakers turn the tongue-tip backward; hence the term 'retroflex' has been used by some phoneticians, but this name is not appropriate for the most usual articulation. Various appropriate names might be used to describe the physical facts of articulation. To place /r/ in a system of distinctive features it is enough to say that it is [– lateral].

3.9   Summary

Of the six classes of phonemes four of them, stops, nasals, fricatives, and liquids, are alike in being [+ consonantal]. Within each of these classes phonemes are distinguished from one another by three other kinds of features: **voice**, **tongue shape**, and **articulator**. English stops and fricatives exist in pairs such that one member of each pair is [+ voice], articulated with vocal cords vibrating, and the other [– voice], articulated without such vibration. This feature is not distinctive for nasals and liquids, which are all [+ voice].

We recognize two special kinds of tongue shape. For one of these, designated [+ sibilant], there is a groove along the center line of the tongue through which the air stream travels. Six consonants, /s z ʃ ʒ č ǰ/, are [+ sib], and all other English phonemes are [– sib]. The other special tongue shape is indicated with the feature [+ lateral], an articulation in which the sides of the tongue are drawn inward. In English only the liquid /l/ is [+ lat].

There are four articulators, the lower lip and three parts of the tongue – tip, front, and back – lying along the lower edge of the oral cavity. Each articulates in conjunction with some point of articulation along the upper edge of the cavity. The following chart names the articulators and for each gives the general adjective, and then the more precise terms which designate articulator and point of articulation.

Lip   labial   bilabial, labiodental
Tip   apical   apicodental, apicoalveolar
Front   frontal   frontoalveolar, frontopalatal
Back   dorsal   dorsopalatal, dorsovelar

(The front of the tongue is also called the *blade*, for which the Latin equivalent is *lamina*. Hence some phoneticians use the adjective *laminal* and the prefix *lamino-* in place of *frontal* and *fronto-*, respectively.)

Rather than describing feature content this way, with the names of four articulators, some phonologists prefer to recognize two features, **[anterior]** and **[coronal]**, based on divisions of the oral cavity. The correspondence in classifying is like this:

labial   [+ anterior, – coronal]
apical   [+ anterior, + coronal]
frontal   [– anterior, + coronal]
dorsal   [– anterior, – coronal]

The consonants /č/ and /ǰ/ are phonetically different from other stops; they are **affricates**, produced by first stopping the flow of air, then letting it flow out through a slight opening so that friction or turbulence results – a stop with fricative release.

The two sets of obstruents, /p t č k f θ s ʃ/ and /b d ǰ g v ð z ʒ/, differ in that the first are voiceless, [– voice], the second group are voiced, [+ voice]. So far as fricatives are concerned, 'voiceless' means that the vocal cords are not vibrating and 'voiced' means that they are vibrating during the articulation. For stops the difference between voicelessness and voicedness is not necessarily in the articulation but in what follows. For example, after the release of the initial stops in *buy, die, guy* the vocal cords vibrate immediately; following the release of the initial stops in *pie, tie, kind* there is a delay in the onset of vibration, a period of **aspiration**, in which air is squeezed between motionless vocal cords.

3D   EXERCISE: PRACTICE WITH SYMBOLS

Each word below has three consonants separated by two vowels (CVCVC). Write the symbols for the three consonants. The first is done as an example.

cherub   č-r-b   thistle   ptomaine
garage   havoc   possess
Philip   jealous   gingham
receipt   package   righteous
machine   Kenneth   sheriff
budget   disease   nothing

behave	cynic	shebang
Janice	sugar	vision
butcher	rhythm	cattle
nickel	button	cousin

3A   FEEDBACK

(a)

1	bag	13	tomato	12	pain	20	holy
2	cat	4	Czech	13	ptomaine	12	pest
3	cent	21	yacht	14	room	6	phone
4	check	9	loose	15	shave	8	jest
5	dude	16	there	16	then	22	zest
6	fan	7	guess	17	thick	3	send
7	gas	15	chef	18	vest	14	rhyme
8	gem	5	dare	19	weight	10	main
9	leap	18	vote	20	whole	17	thin
10	meek	11	kneel	21	young	1	boom
11	nail	2	kite	22	zoom	19	wild

(b)

1	both	17	love	12	pole	10	fade
2	car	16	rogue	13	rage	12	toll
3	clothe	4	dome	14	rich	11	daze
4	dumb	6	grub	15	rouge	9	lock
5	fate	3	smooth	16	rug	8	loss
6	globe	13	ridge	17	save	19	hope
7	graph	18	sane	18	sign	1	youth
8	lace	15	beige	19	soap	2	care
9	look	20	lung	20	tongue	21	ash
10	odd	7	gruff	21	wash	14	witch
11	phrase	5	eight				

(c)

1	beige	3	pitch	12	maid	14	vain
2	breathe	13	team	13	meat	2	they
3	chip	11	kill	14	nave	15	zone
4	coach	16	bad	15	nose	5	mode
5	comb	12	dame	16	robe	9	name
6	cough	17	goal	17	rogue	21	lace
7	door	4	choke	18	rung	7	rake
8	face	10	jell	19	rush	__	yell
9	lane	6	fun	20	Ruth	__	wet
10	ledge	20	think	21	sail	__	head
11	lick	8	safe			19	shift

(d) beige, rung
(e) yell, wet, head

3B FEEDBACK

(a) The first member of each pair is [– voice], the second [+ voice].
(b) /n/ is [+ voice] but the feature is not distinctive since there is no nasal
     consonant in English which is [– voice].

3C FEEDBACK

(a) –/+ voice   (e) –/+ sonorant
(b) –/+ continuant   (f) tip/back
(c) –/+ continuant   (g) tip/front
(d) –/+ sibilant   (h) lip/tip

(i) –/+ voice   (l) –/+ sonorant
(j) tip/lip   (m) tip/back
(k) –/+ continuant   (n) –/+ continuant,
                                 –/+ sibilant

(o) /d/   (p) /ʒ/
(q) /n/ /g/   (r) /f/
(s) tip; back

3D FEEDBACK

cherub	č-r-b	thistle	θ-s-l	ptomaine	t-m-n
garage	g-r-ʒ, g-r-ǰ	havoc	h-v-k	possess	p-z-s
Philip	f-l-p	jealous	ǰ-l-s	gingham	g-ŋ-m
receipt	r-s-t	package	p-k-ǰ	righteous	r-č-s
machine	m-ʃ-n	Kenneth	k-n-θ	sheriff	ʃ-r-f
budget	b-ǰ-t	disease	d-z-z	nothing	n-θ-ŋ
behave	b-h-v	cynic	s-n-k	shebang	ʃ-b-ŋ
Janice	ǰ-n-s	sugar	ʃ-g-r	vision	v-ʒ-n
butcher	b-č-r	rhythm	r-ð-m	cattle	k-t-l
nickel	n-k-l	button	b-t-n	cousin	k-z-n

Notes

The features used here are, with one exception, those introduced in Chomsky and
Halle (1968) and which are widely accepted. The exception is the feature [sibilant],
which ought to be justified on both phonetic and phonological grounds. The phonetic
realizations of the phonemes /s z ʃ ʒ č ǰ/ are all articulated with a groove along the

center line of the tongue, a tongue shape not used for any other articulation in English. Phonologically these consonants form a natural class: regular nouns ending with these consonants form the plural number, for example, in the same way and differently from other nouns; see chapter 8.

See Ladefoged (1993, ch. 3), and Roach (1991, chs. 4, 6, and 7), for slightly different treatments of English consonants.

4

Vowels and Glides

In describing English consonants we needed to tell how each consonant is articulated and what features distinguish one consonant from another. As we saw, there are some possible differences in the approach to description: more emphasis may be put on the articulator or on the place of articulation. Some descriptions use single symbols for the affricates /č/ and /ǰ/, as we do, while others use a two-letter symbol for each, /tʃ/ and /dʒ/. However, these variations are small.

It is different with vowels. There are several analyses which linguists have made of English vowels. The different analyses recognize different numbers of vowels, they use different symbols and combinations of symbols to represent them, and they use different terms to describe them. What is regarded as a simple vowel in one analysis, for example (and symbolized with a single letter), may be treated as a diphthong in another analysis (and represented with a sequence of two symbols). One unfortunate consequence of these different analyses is that some people assume that the description and symbols which they learned first are the only 'correct' ones.

Why are there such different analyses of English vowels? For two reasons: (1) Different dialects of English have somewhat different systems of vowels; these differences are not big enough to prevent English-speakers from different parts of the world from understanding one another but they are enough to be noticeable, and the differences make our task of description more difficult than the description of consonants. (2) Different linguists give more importance to different features – physical features like length, tongue movement, tenseness, or differences in the kinds of syllables in which vowels occur. These are the issues we explore in this chapter.

4A   PRELIMINARY EXERCISE

(a)   In the first column below each word consists of a consonant followed
by a vowel. (You may have learned to call some or all of these vowels
'diphthongs.' That is a description based on phonetic features, which we
will examine later. Right now we are concerned only with identifying
the different vowel-units of English, whether they are to be counted as
diphthongs or simple vowels.) In the second column the same eight vowel-
units appear again, in a different order, in words which end with one
consonant. The third column has words with the same eight vowel-units,
re-arranged, followed by two consonants. Identify the vowels of column
II and column III by matching with those of column I.

I		II	III	
1	see	____ loaf	____ wild
2	may	____ lake	____ point
3	lie	____ shout	____ boost
4	raw	____ bruise	____ fiend
5	go	____ like	____ pound
6	toy	____ neat	____ range
7	cow	____ hawk	____ bolt
8	shoe	____ coin	____ haunt

(b)   The six words in column IV, below, contain vowels which do not ordinarily occur at the end of a word. They may be followed by one consonant,
as in column IV, or two consonants, as in column V, and sometimes by
three consonants (e.g. *tempt, midst*). Match the words of column V with
those of column IV.

	IV	V	
(a)	pit	____ husk
(b)	pet	____ fox
(c)	pat	____ rest
(d)	put	____ wolf
(e)	putt	____ sift
(f)	pot	____ fact

4.1   Dialect differences

Do *lock* and *log* have the same vowel sound?
Do *pat* and *bad* have the same vowel?
Are *cot* and *caught* homonyms?
Do *bomb* and *balm* sound the same?
Does *pork* rhyme with *fork*?
Does *hurry* rhyme with *furry*?

Any native speaker of English has an immediate answer for each of these questions, but in each case there are other speakers who give the opposite answer. Whereas there is general uniformity in English consonants, there are interesting differences in the vowels. The differences are of three kinds: in the **inventory** of vowels, in their **incidence**, and in their pronunciation, or **phonetic realization**. When we compare the speech of people from different parts of the English-speaking world, we easily notice differences of pronunciation but there are probably differences of inventory and incidence that we do not recognize.

The inventory of vowels is the number of vowel phonemes which contrast with one another – which are capable of differentiating words. Chapter 3 dealt with the inventory of English consonants. To know the vowel inventory of a language or of a single dialect we have to find out how many distinctive vowels (that is, vowels which are capable of distinguishing one meaning from another) occur in the same or approximately the same phonetic environment. The total number of such distinctive units is the inventory of vowel phonemes in that language or that dialect. Different dialects of English have different vowel inventories. Here are three examples: Most speakers of English pronounce some words with the vowel of FOOT and others with the vowel of BREW; in Scotland, however, all such words are pronounced with the vowel of BREW—there is no FOOT-vowel, and that makes one vowel less in the inventory of Scottish English than in other dialects. In the north of England words like FOOT and words like NUT, which elsewhere have different vowels, are spoken with the vowel of FOOT; we may say that there is no NUT-vowel as there is in other dialects. In most of Canada and much of the United States LAW and LOCK (or *caught* and *cot*) are pronounced with the same vowel, though they represent large groups of words which are differentiated by other speakers. Whenever a group of people have two vowel phonemes corresponding to a single vowel phoneme for another group of people, the two groups have a difference of inventory.

The term *incidence* refers to the occurrence of particular vowels in particular sets of words. Speakers of different dialects may have the same number of vowels available for making distinctions but use them in different sets of words. For example, some speakers of English pronounce *father*, *rather*, and *lather* so that they rhyme, all having the same vowel in the first syllable. Other speakers rhyme *father* and *rather* but pronounce *lather* with a different vowel in the first syllable. Still others pronounce *rather* to rhyme with *lather* but have a different first vowel in *father*. The following chart shows how the words are pronounced in the three dialects:

Dialect A	**Dialect B**	**Dialect C**
father, rather, lather	father, rather	father
	lather	rather, lather

How these three words are pronounced is a trivial matter in itself, but it illustrates a much bigger matter. There are whole sets of words like *half*, *laugh*, *glass, bath* which are pronounced with different vowels by different speakers of English – differences in the incidence of the vowel phonemes they have.

Finally, to understand differences of phonetic realization, it would help if we could all hear a number of people from different parts of the English-speaking world pronounce the word *house*. We could say that they all pronounce the 'same' vowel, and they use it in essentially the same large class of words, but their ways of rendering the vowel are quite different, differences in articulatory features – the positions and movements of tongue and lips.

4.2   Vowel features

All vowels are:

[+ syllabic], capable of carrying stress and pitch
[– consonantal], made without impeding the air flow
[+ continuant], articulated with air going continuously out from the mouth
[+ sonorant], made with regular patterns of vibration
[+ voice], produced with vocal cords vibrating
[– sibilant], produced with a flat tongue surface

What are the articulatory features which make vowels differ from one another? Several kinds of features need to be considered:

(1)   Vowels differ from one another in **quality**. Quality is determined by the shape of the resonance chamber, which in turn depends mainly on the position of the tongue. The blade or the dorsum of the tongue may be positioned at different heights. Following a general convention, we recognize three degrees of height and label them High, Mid, and Low. To a lesser extent the shape of the oral cavity, and therefore the quality of a vowel, depends on the shape of the lips – whether they are more rounded or more spread.

(2)   Vowels can differ in **length**. To be sure, any vowel can be stretched out or clipped short; in this sense length depends on the importance of a word in an utterance and on the habits of the speaker. In describing vowels we are less concerned with this kind of variation and more concerned with determining whether some vowels are typically shorter than others – whether two vowels which are fairly similar in quality also differ in length. The vowels of *feet* and *fit*, for example, are somewhat similar in quality but the first is typically longer than the second. However, we consider the difference in quality more important than the difference in length.

(3)   Vowels differ in **complexity**. This is the familiar distinction between a simple vowel, or monophthong, and a compound vowel, or diphthong. For a simple vowel, tongue and lips remain relatively stable throughout the articulation. A diphthong is made with tongue (and lips) moving. For English it is

possible to recognize three kinds of diphthong: those made with front of tongue moving upward, symbolized in our phonetic descriptions with a raised [ⁱ] after the vowel, those made with back of tongue moving upward, indicated with a raised [ᵘ], and those in which the tongue moves toward a mid-central position, symbolized with a raised [ᵊ].

(4)   There may be a difference in **tenseness**. Muscles in the lips and, more importantly, in the tongue can be tightened or relaxed. You can feel the muscles in the root of the tongue by putting your fingers where chin and neck come together and thus compare the tension in different vowel articulations; compare the vowels of *feet* and *fit*, for example. Tenseness alone, however, does not create an audible difference.

Different descriptions of English vowels have treated these features in different ways. Any description of the vowels of English (or of any language) has to recognize differences of *quality*, but with other kinds of features there is redundancy. The facts of articulation for the different vowels in different dialects are much too complex to consider these labels truly descriptive.

Quality, length, and complexity are physical characteristics of vowels. Another characteristic of vowels is their **occurrence**. In English some vowels occur with a consonant following or without a consonant following, for example, the vowel of *feet* and *fee*. Other vowels never occur in a one-syllable word without a consonant following, for example the vowel of *fit*. We call the first kind **free vowels** and the second kind **checked vowels**.

4.3   A general inventory and particular inventories

To describe the most widely spoken dialects of English and to explain how they resemble and differ from one another we need to set up an inventory of vowels which is larger than the inventories of most dialects. Our inventory contains 24 vowels, as described below. (The term 'vowel' is used here as a cover term for what may be a simple vowel, a diphthong, or even a triphthong). These 24 vowels can occur in monosyllabic words or in the stressed syllable of words of more than one syllable. The next chapter deals with vowels in unstressed syllables.

For reasons which will become clear later, we divide these 24 vowels into three groups:

    6 checked vowels
    9 free vowels
    9 R vowels

We use a key word for each of the 24.

The six checked vowels are the ones illustrated in the following key words, with our vowel symbol following:

	Front		*Back*	
High	CHICK	/ɪ/	FOOT	/u/
Mid	STEP	/ɛ/	NUT	/ʌ/
Low	BAT	/æ/	LOCK	/ɒ/

These vowels are called 'checked' because in one-syllable words such as these they are always followed by one or more consonants. There is no word which begins like *chick* or *nut*, for instance, and ends with the vowel. These are the vowels which formed part (b) of the preliminary exercise 4A.

The three vowels illustrated in the left-hand column are articulated in the front of the mouth, those in the right-hand column farther back; and in each column the topmost vowel is articulated with the tongue (front or back) high in the mouth, the second one somewhat lower, and the third one with the tongue low in the mouth.

The nine free vowels are illustrated by these key words, with our symbol – always two letters – following:

	Front		*Back*			
High	TREE	/ii/	BREW	/uu/		
Mid	DAY	/ei/	TOE	/ou/		
Low	SPA	/aa/	LAW	/ɔɔ/		
	TIE	/ai/	TOY	/oi/	NOW	/au/

These are the vowels of part (a) of Exercise 4A. They occur in open syllables, as in these key words, and also in syllables closed by one or more consonants; e.g. *treat, date, tight, calm, voice, brood, toast, noun, lawn.*

The nine R vowels are illustrated by these key words, again with symbols following:

	Front		*Back*			
High	EAR	/ir/	TOUR	/ur/		
Mid	CHAIR	/er/	DOOR	/or/		
			FUR	/ɜr/		
Low	STAR	/ar/	WAR	/ɔr/		
	FIRE	/air/	SOUR	/aur/		

Dialects of English are either 'rhotic' or 'non-rhotic' according to whether the words above are pronounced with or without a frictionless continuant [r]. RP and all of south-eastern England, Australia, New Zealand, South Africa, and, variably, the southern United States and eastern New England are non-rhotic. Northern and western England, Scotland, Wales, Ireland, Canada, and most of the United States are rhotic, and there are groups of 'r-ful' speakers in areas which are generally non-rhotic, or 'r-less.'

In non-rhotic dialects no [r] is pronounced, in words like these, if the vowel is final or followed by a consonant. If any of these vowels is followed by a vowel, [r] is pronounced. This happens within a word (e.g. *serious, glory, starry*)

	Front	Central	Back
High	i		(u)
	ɪ	ɨ	(ʊ)
Mid	e	ə ɚ	(o)
		ɜ ɝ	
	ɛ	ʌ	
Low	æ	ɐ	(ɔ)
	a	ɑ	(ɒ)

Figure 4.1   Phonetic chart for vowels, showing the quality (tongue height and tongue advancement) associated with each symbol; parentheses indicate lip rounding.

and when a word with a final R vowel is closely linked to a following word which begins with a vowel, as in *The car is here, near a bank, war and peace.* This phenomenon is known as 'Linking R.'

4.4   Phonetic descriptions

The Phonetic Chart (figure 4.1) contains symbols which we need to refer to later in this section. Each symbol stands for a vowel-like articulation; its place in the chart indicates the tongue height – high, mid, or low – and tongue advancement – front, central, or back. Symbols in parentheses represent rounded vowels. This chart is for very precise descriptions.

Figures 4.2 a–g show our key words in their relative positions on the same kind of charts. These charts are less precise because they apply to all dialects

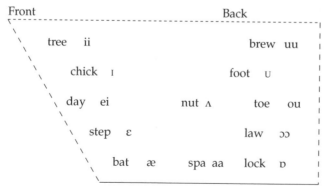

Figure 4.2-a   The relative positions of 12 vowels (the front line slants because the tongue draws back as it goes down).

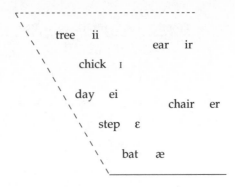

Figure 4.2-b Front vowels

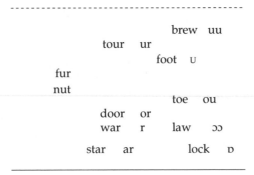

Figure 4.2-c Back vowels

Figure 4.2-d Diphthongal /ei/ and /ou/

Figure 4.2-e /ir/, /er/, and /ur/ in non-rhotic dialects

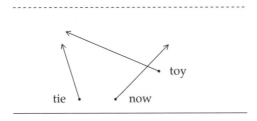

Figure 4.2-f Diphthongal /ai/, /au/, /oi/

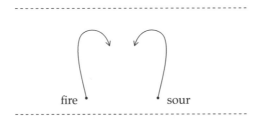

Figure 4.2-g /air/ and /aur/ in non-rhotic dialects

of English. The next paragraphs give phonetic descriptions of the 24 key words, with reference to the charts and with examples for practice.

TREE – Articulated by all speakers in the high-front area; in some dialects there is length but no movement of the tongue – [iː]; for other speakers the front of the tongue moves upward, [iⁱ], though of course there is not a great distance for it to move.

   Practice: sleep beat teach week seed siege league beef teeth niece leave tease dream green seal east fiend field 'evil 'easy 'reason 'demon a'gree be'lieve pro'ceed ma'chine re'peal

CHICK – A short, lax high-front unrounded vowel [ɪ]; in South Africa the vowel is high-front only in the environment of a frontal or dorsal consonant (e.g. *chick, wish, fig, bridge*); in other environments it is high-central [i] (*tip, build, sit*); in New Zealand the high-central vowel is the norm in all positions of occurrence.

   Practice: bit hip rich sick crib lid ridge dig stiff myth hiss fish give fizz hymn chin sing fill limp lint nymph silk build list 'ticket 'liver 'mission 'city 'silver de'pict di'stinct

EAR – In Ireland and Scotland /ir/ has the vowel of TREE followed by a consonant /r/; in most of North America the vowel is like that of CHICK with a consonant /r/. In RP and other non-rhotic dialects the vowel is that of

CHICK followed by a glide to mid-central posiiton [ɪ°]. See figure 4.2-a.
  Practice: fear beard fierce 'serum 'dreary 'hero
  sin'cere ap'pear inter'fere

DAY – Generally articulated with the tongue-front moving upward from the
mid-front position [eⁱ]; in northern England, Scotland, Ireland, and variably
elsewhere the vowel is long but nongliding [eː]; in Cockney and Broad
Australian the beginning is lower mid-central [ʌⁱ].
  Practice: tape bait cake blade rage vague safe faith face
  save bathe raze beige name lane mail paint change 'paper
  'bacon 'wager 'favor 'ancient de'lay pa'rade de'bate com'plain
  ar'range

STEP – A short, lax, mid-front unrounded vowel [ɛ], without great variation.
  Practice: bet wretch check ebb led ledge egg clef Beth less
  flesh gem bell hemp rent friend help melt theft chest next
  'ready 'jelly 'never 'pleasure 'any di'rect e'vent con'tempt

CHAIR – In Ireland and Scotland the vowel is that of DAY, in North America
the vowel of STEP, followed by a consonant [r]. In non-rhotic dialects the
vowel of STEP with a mid-center off-glide, [ɛ ə]
  Practice: fair scarce stairs 'area 'dairy ca'nary a'ware com'pare

BAT – A low-front unrounded vowel; in North America it is higher and
sometimes diphthongal, [æ°] or [æⁱ]; in Britain lower and farther back.
  Practice: map match tack grab lad badge tag math cash ham
  man gang shall lamp ant bank hand fact tax 'matter
  'salad 'travel 'packet 'traffic col'lapse at'tract ca'nal

BREW – Articulated in the high-back area or more forward; just as TREE may
be long or have upward movement of the tongue-front, so BREW may be long
or have upward gliding of the tongue back, [uː] or [uᵘ].
  Practice: loop boot Luke rude fugue proof Ruth truce prove
  smooth groom prune tool wound boost 'pupil 'ruby
  'lucid 'nuisance 'fusion re'view a'muse ap'prove

FOOT – A short, lax, high-back vowel with weak rounding [ʊ]; in Scotland
and northern Ireland words which elsewhere have the FOOT vowel have the
BREW vowel instead.
  Practice: put look good puss bush full wolf 'bullet
  'pudding 'cushion 'sugar 'woman

TOUR – In Ireland and Scotland the vowel of BREW, in North America the
vowel of FOOT, followed by consonant [r]; in non-rhotic dialect the vowel of
FOOT followed by a centering offglide, [ʊ°] (see figure 4.2-e).

Practice: cure 'tourist 'mural 'curious in'surance en'dure
de'tour ma'ture ob'scure se'curity

TOE – Generally articulated with the tongue back moving upward; in RP and
the southern hemisphere the vowel begins from a mid-central position, [ɜᵘ], in
North America from a mid-back position, [oᵘ]; in Scotland and Ireland and
variably elsewhere the vowel may be mid-back long, with no gliding, [oː].
  Practice: hope boat coach yoke robe ode vogue loaf rove both
  dose dome roll bolt fold coast 'over 'ocean 'shoulder
  'poster be'low e'rode re'voke ap'proach con'trol

NUT – A short, lax unrounded vowel with considerable variation in quality; in
northern England those who do not speak RP are likely to have no distinction
between the vowels of FOOT and NUT; in Scotland and much of Canada and
the United States the vowel is higher mid-central [ʌ], in RP and the southern
hemisphere it is more open, a lower mid-central [ɐ].
  Practice: cup luck rub mud fudge rug muff fuss rush
  love fuzz rum run rung dull lump hunt funds lunch lunge
  chunk pulse bulge 'button 'sudden 'luscious 'onion a'bove
  in'duct cor'rupt

FUR – In rhotic dialects this vowel is a mid-central, slightly rounded, comparatively long vowel articulated with the tongue drawn back and with a
groove in the very tip; what is viewed as a sequence of vowel + R is actually
an r-colored vowel – the groove and tongue-retraction are present throughout
articulation. In non-rhotic dialects the vowel is equivalent except that there is
no lip-rounding and, more to the point, there is no groove or retraction.
  Practice: chirp shirt church work berg bird urge surf birth
  nurse curve firm burn curl 'murder 'further 'circus 'virtue
  'person 'turtle 'perfect re'serve di'vert con'firm re'hearse

LAW – A long rounded low-back vowel.
  Practice: bought hawk broad sauce cause dawn fall bald salt
  false paunch 'daughter 'autumn 'author ap'plaud

SPA – A low-back unrounded vowel.
  Practice: palm calm 'father fa'cade

LOCK – In England, including RP, in Scotland, and the southern hemisphere
a low-back, weakly rounded short vowel [ɒ]; in Ireland and North America a
low-central or low-back unrounded vowel [ɑ]. For many Canadians and Americans the vowels of LOCK and STAR are identical except for the following /r/
in the latter.
  Practice: stop pot crotch rob rod lodge bomb doll fond solve
  fox prompt 'body 'stocking 'profit 'bother 'comet 'folly
  'wander a'dopt con'coct

DOOR, WAR – The distinction between these is not maintained in all dialects, though it is heavily used in dialects which retain the distinction. Where the distinction holds, the vowel of DOOR can be equated with that of TOE and the vowel of WAR with that of LAW, in both cases followed by a sonorant consonant in rhotic dialects [ɔ r] or a centering offglide in non-rhotic ones [ɔə]. In rhotic dialects which do not have this distinction the articulation may range between [o] and [ɔ] but is likely to be nearer the latter, [ɔ]. Rhotic dialects are also likely to have the more open vowel, followed by centering offglide [ɔə] or simple length [ɔː], in free variation or with the offglide in open syllables, the long vowel in closed ones. In non-rhotic dialects DOOR, WAR, and LAW may have the same vowel, or the first two may have a centering offglide and LAW a long vowel.

> *Practice* (DOOR): bore   fort   porch   pork   board   forge   forth
> borne   'portal   an'gora   'choral   'floral   'glory   'story   me'morial
> ex'plore   ig'nore   re'port   di'vorce
> (WAR): fork   short   warn   horn   morning   George   wart   swarm
> horse   form   born   'Lawrence   'order   'corner   'normal

STAR – A long, unrounded low-central or low-back-central vowel. In non-rhotic dialects it is equivalent to the vowel of SPA; in rhotic dialects it differs from that vowel only in the presence of the sonorant consonant at the end.

> *Practice*: harp   heart   march   dark   hard   large   scarf   hearth   farce
> marsh   carve   charm   yarn   'farther   'armor   'target   'partial
> 'sergeant   'marvel   re'mark   de'part   di'scard

TIE – A variety of articulations, mostly beginning in the low area, low-central or somewhat more forward or somewhat more back, followed by upward movement of the tongue front – [aⁱ, a<ⁱ, a>ⁱ]; many Londoners, South Africans, Australians, and Americans in the South and South Midland have little or no tongue movement – [aː] – when the vowel is final or followed by a voiced consonant, e.g. *why, wide*; some Americans and practically all Canadians have a mid-central beginning point, [ɐⁱ] before a voiceless consonant, e.g. *white, type, bite, like*.

> *Practice*: bribe   bride   life   rice   drive   rise   chime   fine   tile
> pint   find   child   Christ   'fiber   'tiger   'hyphen   'silent   de'ny
> u'nite   col'lide   ar'rive   de'sign

FIRE – Like the diphthong of TIE followed by a consonant [r] in rhotic dialects; in non-rhotic dialects it is a triphthong – the tongue moves from low-front towards a high-front position, then to a central position (see figure 4.2-g); this triphthong may be reduced to a diphthong, [aə].

> *Practice*: sire   tired   'iron   'diary   'fiery   'siren   'pirate   en'tire
> in'spire

TOY – Begins in the low-back area or somewhat higher, with upward movement of the tongue front, [ɔⁱ].

Practice: boy void voice noise coin coil point moist 'oyster 'poison 'doily em'ploy ex'ploit ap'point a'void re'joice

NOW – A variety of articulations, mostly beginning in the low area, low-front or low-central, with upward movement of the tongue back – [æ^u, a^u]; those who have a mid-central beginning point for the vowel of TIE have a similar beginning for NOW, [ɐ^u] – that is, whenever this diphthong occurs before a voiceless consonant.

Practice: bout couch loud gouge mouth house rouse down owl count pound ouce lounge 'powder 'fountain 'trousers 'council al'low de'vout a'mount sur'round pro'nounce

SOUR - In rhotic dialects like the diphthong of NOW followed by a consonant [r]; in non-rhotic dialects a triphthong involving movement of the tongue from low- towards high-back position and then to mid-central.

Practice: hour flower 'dowry de'vour

4.5   The vowel inventories of specific dialects

Most varieties of English have fewer than the 24 vowel phonemes of our general inventory. We now consider vowel inventories of some of the principal dialects of the language. We begin with one which does have the full inventory of 24.

Inventory 1 (rhotic):   Ireland

TREE/EAR	CHICK		FOOT	BREW/TOUR
DAY/CHAIR	STEP	FUR	HUT	TOE/DOOR
	BAT	SPA/STAR	LOCK	LAW/WAR
TIE/FIRE		TOY		NOW/SOUR

All 24 of our vowel distinctions are maintained in Irish English. The R-vowels are pronounced with a sonorant consonant. The R vowels have generally the same quality as free vowels, and the forward slash separates each R vowel from the free vowel which is closest to it; the EAR vowel has the same quality as the vowel of TREE, CHAIR the same as DAY, FIRE the same as TIE, and so on.

The English spoken in Scotland is almost identical with that of Ireland, so far as number of vowel contrasts is concerned. The one exception is that words of the FOOT class have the vowel of the BREW class. The English of the north of England is similar but with another difference: the vowel of NUT is the same as the vowel of FOOT.

The next inventory indicates the vowel contrasts in a broad variety of dialects: in the south of England, including RP and Cockney, in South Africa, New Zealand, and Australia. Within this range of dialects there are big differences of pronunciation – between Cockney and RP, for instance – but the vowel system is essentially the same.

Inventory 2 (non-rhotic):   RP, Australia, New Zealand, South Africa

TREE	EAR	CHICK		FOOT	BREW	TOUR
DAY	STEP		FUR		NUT	TOE
BAT	SPA = STAR				LOCK	LAW = DOOR = WAR
TIE	FIRE		TOY		NOW	SOUR

The sets represented by EAR, CHAIR, and TOUR have centering diphthongs [iᵊ, tʃ, ɛᵊ, tuᵊ]; FUR and STAR words have long vowels [fɜː, staː, wɔː], the latter being identical with SPA. Among older speakers of RP LAW may have a long vowel, [ɔː] and WAR a centering diphthong, [ɔᵊ]; among younger speakers these are identical.

Inventory 3 (rhotic):   'General North American'

TREE	CHICK/EAR			FOOT/TOUR	BREW
DAY	STEP/CHAIR	FUR	HUT		TOE/DOOR
	BAT		SPA = LOCK/STAR		LAW/WAR
TIE/FIRE		TOY	NOW/SOUR		

This inventory is the system of vowels in varieties spoken by many Americans and Canadians. The system shown here has DOOR pronounced with approximately the vowel of TOE, followed by /r/, and WAR articulated with the vowel of LAW, plus /r/. An increasing number of North Americans, like speakers of English represented in Inventory 2, have no such distinction, so Inventory 3 can be modified for such speakers with the notation DOOR = WAR. Unlike most other varieties of English the LOCK vowel is identical with the SPA vowel, as shown here, or with the LAW vowel (so: LOCK = LAW), or all three of these groups of words have the same vowel (SPA = LOCK = LAW). STAR has the same vowel followed by /r/. For most North Americans the EAR vowel is nearer to CHICK than to TREE, CHAIR more like STEP than DAY, TOUR more similar to FOOT than to BREW.

Eastern New England and the American South are variably rhotic. EAR, CHAIR, and TOUR are nearer in quality to the free vowels, TREE, DAY, and BREW, respectively, with a centering offglide. STAR and WAR may also, especially in the South, have a centering offglide. Otherwise these dialect areas differ in only minor ways from the above.

4.6   The incidence of vowels

As noted in section 4.2, English dialects differ in the occurrence of vowels in certain specific sets of words. What these occurrences are can best be understood by looking at some historic facts.

The following words, all spelled with the letter *a*, were pronounced with the same vowel phoneme until about the seventeenth century. Let's call it 'short A.'

nap hat dance command craft bath class father palm want
water fall salt

And all of the following words had the same vowel, a different vowel phoneme that we may call 'short o.'

top hot bomb pond bother log long soft moth loss

The following words were pronounced with a diphthong AU, perhaps close to what is now heard in the word *house*:

law pause dawn laundry sausage

In about the seventeenth century the diphthong AU became a simple low-back vowel. At about the same time the short A vowel and short O vowel 'split,' coming to be pronounced in very different ways in different environments – before /l/, after /w/, before voiceless fricatives, before some combinations of nasal + obstruent, and so on. Some of the allophones of short A became identical with some allophones of short O; some allophones of short A and some allophones of short O became identical with the reflex of the diphthong AU, but the details differ from dialect to dialect.

Consider the original short A words, above. The words *nap* and *hat* now have the low-front BAT vowel in all dialects, and *fall* and *salt* have the low-back LAW vowel for all speakers of English. In many dialects *father* and *palm* have the low-central vowel of SPA. The words *dance, command, craft, bath, class* represent parts of the vocabulary which may have the vowel of BAT or that of SPA. *Water* and *want* may have the SPA vowel, the LAW vowel, or the LOCK vowel. The line of words representing the original short O may be pronounced all with the same vowel, or those on the right side with the vowel of LAW and those on the left with the LOCK vowel. Finally, the stressed vowel of polysyllabic words like *sausage* and *laundry* has, in some varieties of the language, become like LOCK and thus different from the LAW vowel of monosyllabic words with the original AU.

All these matters make it somewhat awkward to describe English vowels, but they have little or no effect on communication.

4B PRACTICE WITH TRANSCRIPTION

(a) The following monosyllabic words are in our transcription. Write each
     one in the usual orthography.

(i)	/fɪt rɪč kɪn gɪft brɪsk ʃɪp
(ii)	lɛǰ rɛst θrɛd brɛθ ǰɛm ðɛn
(iii)	kæt čæp gæs stæk θæŋks ðæt
(iv)	fʊl bʊk gʊd pʊʃ sʊt wʊlf
(v)	kʌt sʌm lʌv brʌʃ flʌd θrʌst
(vi)	nɒt tɒp flɒk skɒč dɒǰ bɒks
(vii)	biik tiim fiist liif kwiin riič
(viii)	meik trein beis čeinǰ seif veig
(ix)	suup truuθ čuuz muuv fjuum kjuub
(x)	roul poust mould ðouz čouk houp
(xi)	lɔɔ brɔɔd čɔɔk gɔɔz θɔɔt sɔɔs
(xii)	bait daim čaild straid wain θraiv
(xiii)	ʃaut paund mauθ gauǰ haus naun
(xiv)	point čois soil hoist void ǰoi
(xv)	čirz sfir bird pirs klir nir
(xvi)	fer skers prer sterz skwer rer
(xvii)	hɜrt wɜrk vɜrb čɜrč ɜrθ nɜrs
(xviii)	gard marč čarǰ harθ karv harʃ
(xix)	kɔrk kwɔrt ʃɔrt nɔrθ wɔrn tɔrč
(xx)	wair taird spair airn kwair/

(b) Transcribe the one-syllable words below, using our set of consonant and
     vowel symbols.

(i)	plea	(ii)	list
	please		chip
	pleased		shift
	lease		thin
	least		thing
(iii)	wake	(iv)	wretch
	vague		stretch
	rage		wedge
	grave		jest
	space		dress
(v)	track	(vi)	lock
	hatch		ox
	gasp		drop
	raft		bomb
	badge		romp

(vii)	youth	(viii)	wood
	use (noun)		should
	use (verb)		pull
	Luke		look
	Ruth		bush
(ix)	ghost	(x)	luck
	those		numb
	oath		thus
	rose		crutch
	vogue		judge
(xi)	hawk	(xii)	moist
	cause		choice
	fault		coins
	stalk		Lloyd
	broad		poise
(xiii)	rise	(xiv)	rouse
	grind		ground
	chime		crouch
	knife		spout
	jive		loud

(c) English has fairly numerous sets of homophones, or homonyms, like *pale* and *pail* or *cite, site,* and *sight*. Since they are pronounced the same, they are transcribed the same way in a phonological transcription: in our system /peil/ for the first set and /sait/ for the second. Each of the following transcriptions represents a set of homophones – two unless otherwise noted. See if you can write the words that are represented.

/sii/	/sɛl/
/biit/	/miit/ (3)
/breik/	/nait/
/loud/	/jouk/
/streit/	/vein/ (3)
/faul/	/plein/
/hjuu/	/rait/ (3)
/wiik/	/hiil/
/biic/	/seil/
/lɛd/	/piis/
/mein/	/meil/
/sou/ (3)	/piik/ (3)
/swiit/	/ræp/
/greit/	/steik/
/dæm/	/tou/
/dir/	/her/
/fɜr/	/bor/

(d)   Another kind of homophonous set is seen in the words *tax* and *tacks*, or *find* and *fined*. In each case the two words are phonologicallly identical – they sound the same – but are morphologically different – they are different in word formation. We can show the morphological difference in our phonological representation. We write /tæk#s/ for *tacks* and just /tæks/ for *tax*, /fain#d/ for *fined* and /faind/ for *find*. The symbol # indicates that what follows is a suffix, and of course the symbol has no pronunciation.

In the following pairs of homophones, one of the two words has a suffix, which is always one of four consonants, /t d s z/; the other word has the same final consonant, but it is not a suffix. Identify the words.

/deiz, dei#z/	/praid, prai#d/
/čeist, čeis#t/	/rouz, rou#z/
/trækt, træk#t/	/læps, læp#s/
/čuuz, čuu#z/	/toud, tou#d/
/bænd, bæn#d/	/nouz, nou#z/

4.7   The glides

The initial phonemes of *yet* and *wet* are classified as glides or semiconsonants They differ from vowels in being [– syllabic] and are like vowels in these features:

[– consonantal]
[+ continuant]
[+ sonorant]
[– sibilant]

The glides /j/ and /w/ are the non-syllabic equivalents of the vowels /ɪ/ and /ʊ/, respectively. So they are both [+ voice, + high], and /j/ is [+ front, – round], /w/ [– front, + round].

The classification of /h/ is a greater problem. The initial sound of *head* is articulated by bringing the vocal cords close together and forcing air between them while they are, ordinarily, not vibrating. Thus from one point of view /h/ is a voiceless fricative like /f θ s ʃ/. However, it differs from these fricatives in two respects: the friction is produced in the larynx, not in the mouth; and it has no voiced counterpart as the oral fricatives do. Ordinarily voiceless, it may be voiced when it occurs between vowels, as in *ahead*.

From another point of view, if we examine a set of words like *he, hay, hat, hawk, hope, hoot*, we see that /h/ is articulated with the same tongue position and lip shape as the vowel that follows. From this point of view, /h/ is the voiceless equivalent of whatever vowel comes next, and this is one reason for considering it a glide – a vowel-like phoneme which does not function as a vowel. Another reason is that it occurs, like /j/ and /w/, only in syllable-initial position; it is [– syl] like /j/ and /w/. Unlike them it is [– voice]. Otherwise it has no distinctive features; it is neither [+ high] nor [+ low], neither [+ front] nor [– front], neither [+ round] nor [– round].

4C   PRACTICE WITH PHONEME CLASSES

Fifteen words are written below. Each word appears twice, first in the conventional spelling and then re-spelled in our phoneme notation. Under each phoneme symbol write the initial letter of the class to which that phoneme belongs – V(owel), G(lide), L(iquid), N(asal), F(ricative), or S(top). Use V for a checked vowel, V: for a free vowel, and VR for an R vowel. The first three words are done as examples.

shrimp	/ʃrɪmp/	*chain*	/čein/	*dwarf*	/dwɔrf/
	FLVNS		SV:N		SGVRF
quilt	/kwɪlt/	gland	/glænd/	muse	/mjuuz/
breathe	/briið/	junk	/jʌŋk/	flesh	/flɛʃ/
stark	/stark/	woods	/wʊdz/	length	/lɛŋθ/
strange	/streinǰ/	clown	/klaun/	mirth	/mɜrθ/

4D   EXPLORING MATTERS OF VOWEL INCIDENCE

Sort out the following words according to the vowel phoneme which you have in the stressed or only syllable, putting all the words with one vowel phoneme in one group, those with a different vowel in another group, and so on. The sorting is to be done on the basis of your pronunciation, not what a dictionary says. You may finish with as few as two groups or as many as five.

ham   hack   wax   swamp   squad   last   lost   clause   psalm   coffee
August   after   example   often   lot   collar   caller

4.8   Summary

The description of English vowels is complicated by the fact of dialect differences among speakers of the language. A fairly obvious difference is in pronunciation, or **phonetic realization** of the vowels. More subtle differences exist in the **inventories** of vowel phonemes and their **incidence** of occurrence. We have used, first, a **general inventory** of 24 vowel phonemes, divided into six **checked vowels**, nine **free vowels**, and nine **R vowels**. The inventories of specific dialect areas are described in relation to this general inventory; specific inventories are often smaller than the general inventory since a distinction which exists in some parts of the English-speaking world is not maintained by other speakers – and the general inventory includes, essentially, all vowels distinguished in any dialect area. We have recognized **rhotic** and **non-rhotic dialects**; in the former the R vowels are pronounced with constriction – the phoneme /r/ – following the vowel; in the latter there is no /r/ unless a vowel follows immediately.

The existence of the linking R is due to something that happened in history. In the dialect of south-eastern England during the early modern period the consonant /r/ ceased to be pronounced when final or preconsonantal (e.g. *car, cart*) but was retained when intervocalic (e.g. *carry*). Intervocalic retention applied not only within words but also to closely linked words in phrases, like those illustrated above. Linking R is usual in most non-rhotic dialects, but not in the American South; speakers there have no [r] in *the car* nor in *The car is here*, for example. Some readers will claim that DOOR and WAR have the same vowel, others will say that WAR rhymes with STAR, and some may claim that EAR and CHAIR rhyme. It is just these dialect matters that lead us to present a general inventory.

An interesting extension of linking R is called 'intrusive R,' from a historical point of view. In non-rhotic dialects *war* rhymes with *law*, *star* with *spa*, and *odor* with *soda*. Quite naturally, if *war* and *odor* 'acquire' an [r] in such groups as *war and peace*, *The odor is bad*, the same treatment can result for *law-r-and order* and *The soda-r-is bad*. Differences of incidence reflect historic facts. The most complex differences of incidence concern the low vowels, which at an earlier time underwent various changes. An original 'short A' came to have quite different pronunciations in different positions of occurrence, and an original 'short O' likewise acquired different positional variants. Some allophones of short A became identical with some allophones of short O and with the reflex of the diphthong AU, but the results were different in different dialects.

Vowels differ from one another in several kinds of features, the most important of which is **quality,** determined by the size and shape of the oral chamber in which particles of air are vibrating. Traditionally, vowel quality has been described through a matrix of two dimensions, **tongue height (high, mid, low)** and **tongue advancement (front, central, back)**, with the additional feature of **lip shape (rounded, unrounded)**. Vowels also differ in **length (long, short)**, **complexity (monophthong, diphthong)**, and **tenseness (tense, lax)**. Comparing the checked vowels, as a group, with the free vowels, as a group, we can say that checked vowels are short, monophthongal, and lax, while free vowels are long or diphthongal and tense, but the details differ so greatly from dialect to dialect that these categories are not used in this book.

The glides /j/ and /w/ are the [– syllabic] counterparts of [+ high] vowels; /j/ is [+ front], /w/ [– front].

The phoneme /h/ is not like any other English phoneme. It is a sort of voiceless vowel occurring only at the beginning of syllables, and we classify it as a glide.

4A FEEDBACK

(a)   *II*   *III*   (b)   *V*

5	loaf	3	wild		e	husk
2	lake	6	point		f	fox
7	shout	8	boost		b	rest
8	bruise	1	fiend		d	wolf
3	like	7	pound		a	sift
1	neat	2	range		c	fact
4	hawk	5	bolt			
6	coin	4	haunt			

4B FEEDBACK

(i)   fit   rich   kin   gift   brisk   ship
(ii)   ledge   rest   thread   breath   gem   then
(iii)   cat   chap   gas   stack   thanks   that
(iv)   full   book   good   push   soot   wolf
(v)   cut   sum/some   love   brush   flood   thrust
(vi)   not   top   flock   Scotch   dodge   box
(vii)   beak   team   feast   leaf   queen   reach
(viii)   make   train   base   change   safe   vague
(ix)   soup   truth   choose   move   fume   cube
(x)   roll/role   post   mold   those   choke   hope
(xi)   law   broad   chalk   gauze   thought   sauce
(xii)   bite   dime   child   stride   wine   thrive
(xiii)   shout   pound   mouth   gouge   house   noun
(xiv)   point   choice   soil   hoist   void   joy
(xv)   cheers   sphere   beard   pierce   clear   near
(xvi)   fare/fair   scarce   prayer   stairs   square   rare
(xvii)   hurt   work   verb   church   earth   nurse
(xviii) guard   march   charge   hearth   carve   harsh
(xix)   cork   quart   short   north   warn   torch
(xx)   wire   tired   spire   iron   choir/quire

(b)

(i) /plii	(ii) lɪst	(iii) weik	(iv) rɛč
pliiz	čɪp	veig	strɛč
pliizd	ʃɪft	reiǰ	weǰ
liis	θɪn	greiv	ǰɛst
liist	θɪŋ	speis	drɛs

(v)   træk   (vi)   lɒk   (vii)   juuθ   (viii) wʊd
        hæč   ɒks   juus   ʃʊd
        gæsp   drɒp   juuz   pʊl
        ræft   bɒm   luuk   lʊk
        bæǰ   rɒmp   ruuθ   bʊʃ

(ix)   goust   (x)   lʌk   (xi)   hɔɔk   (xii)   moist
        ðouz   nʌm   kɔɔz   čois
        ouθ   ðʌs   fɔɔlt   koinz
        rouz   krʌč   stɔɔk   loid
        voug   ǰʌǰ   brɔɔd   poiz

(xiii) raiz   (xiv)   rauz
        graind   graund
        čaim   krauč
        naif   spaut
        ǰaiv   laud/

(c)

see, sea   sell, cell
beat, beet   meet, meat, mete
brake, break   night, knight
load, lode   yolk, yoke
strait, straight   vain, vein, vane
foul, fowl   plane, plain
hue, hew (Hugh)   right, rite, write (wright)
week, weak   heal, heel
beach, beech   sail, sale
lead, led   peace, piece
main, mane   mail, male
so, sew, sow   peak, peek, pique
sweet, suite   rap, wrap
grate, great   stake, steak
dam, damn   toe, tow
deer, dear   hair, hare
fir, fur   boar, bore

(d)

daze, days   pride, pried
chaste, chased   rose, rows
tract, tracked   lapse, laps
choose, chews   toad, towed
band, banned   nose, knows

4C   FEEDBACK

shrimp	/ʃrɪmp/	chain	/čein/	dwarf	/dwɔrf/	
	FLVNS		SV:N		SGVRF	
quilt	/kwɪlt/	gland	/glænd/	muse	/mjuuz/	
	SGVLS		SLVNS		NGV:F	
breathe	/briið/	junk	/jʌŋk/	flesh	/fleʃ/	
	SLV:F		SVNS		FLVF	
stark	/stark/	woods	/wʊdz/	length	/lɛŋθ/	
	FSVRS		GVSF		LVNF	
strange	/streinǰ/	clown	/klaun/	mirth	/mɜrθ/	
	FSLV:NS		SLV:N		NVRF	

4D   FEEDBACK

There is no right answer. One way of describing the possible distribution of these words into vowel categories is to say that:

   ham, hack, wax   have /æ/, the vowel of BAT;
   after, example, last   may have the same vowel;
   and the other words may not have that vowel.

If the other words fall into three groups, a possible distribution is:

   psalm   collar   caller
          lot   clause

with the remaining words in the *collar* group or the *caller* group or divided among the two.

Notes

The three kinds of difference in phonological systems of the dialects of a single language – inventory, incidence, and phonetic realization – were first sketched by Troubetzkoy (1939).

   The use of key words to designate the vowels of English derives from Wells (1982). For more detailed descriptions of phonetic realizations of vowel phonemes than are given here Wells should be consulted.

   Giegerich (1992, ch. 3) presents comparative sketches of vowel systems of different English dialects, with emphasis on 'Southern British Standard,' 'Scottish Standard,' and 'General American.'

5

Syllables and Stress

Phonemes in sequence form syllables. Syllables in sequence differ in intensity (or loudness), in pitch (or tone), and in duration – some syllables are comparatively strong and others are weak. Syllable strength depends on several things: what vowel it has, whether it is the stressed syllable of a word, and whether it is the accented syllable of a tone unit. This chapter deals with the structure of English syllables and the patterns of strong and weak syllables in words and in tone units.

5.1 Syllables

Every English word consists of at least one syllable, and many words have two, three, four, or more syllables. The syllable is a unit that is hard to define with scientific rigor but fairly easy to recognize. Anyone can tell the number of syllables in, for example, *cat, delay, wonderful, geography*, and *metamorphosis*, (though we may not agree on the number of syllables in *girl, mile, sour*, and certain other words), but no one knows just what physical action of the speaker creates a syllable.

In discussing syllables we are concerned with two kinds of facts, the structure of a syllable and the relative prominence of syllables when two or more occur in sequence.

Every syllable has a structure, a sequence of some of the phonemes of the language. The syllable *cat* consists of the phonemes /k/, /æ/, and /t/ in that order; the syllables *act* and *tack* have the same three phonemes but in different sequences. In discussing syllable structure we want to tell not merely the structures of specific syllables; we want to describe what general structures are possible for English syllables and what structures are impossible. For example, can there be syllables like /ktæ/ or /tkæ/ or /ætk/? Different languages have different kinds of syllable structure. Describing the possible syllable structures is part of describing the sound system of a language.

Every English syllable has a center or **peak**, an element which is [+ syllabic]. As we have seen, all vowels are [+ syllabic] by definition. In addition, the sonorant consonants /m, n, l, r/ become syllabic in certain positions, as described in section 5.8. Thus every word, phrase, or sentence has as many syllables as it has syllabic elements, and vice versa.

The peak may be preceded by one or more non-syllabic elements, which constitute the **onset** of the syllable, and it may be followed by one or more non-syllabic elements which constitute the **coda**. The peak and coda together are called the **rhyme**. In *cat* the onset is /k/, the rhyme is /æt/, the peak is /æ/, and the coda is /t/; in *tree* the onset is /tr/, the peak is /ii/, and there is no coda – or the coda is zero, so that peak and rhyme are the same; the word *ax* has a zero onset, the peak is /æ/, and the coda is /ks/, so that the rhyme is equivalent to the whole syllable. These three syllable structures can be shown as follows:

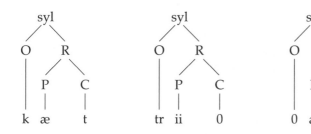

More will be said about syllable structure in the next section of this chapter. First, however, we need to take up the matter of relative prominence of syllables in sequence, in a word or in a tone unit.

Every utterance consists of at least one tone unit, and every tone unit consists of at least one syllable. If there are two or more syllables, one of them is more prominent than the other(s). In a brief utterance of one tone unit such as

Pat took ten **books**.

the syllable *books* is likely to be most prominent, indicated here with bold type. We call this prominence the **accent** of the tone unit. The syllable *books* has the accent, or is the accented syllable. However, a speaker can create certain effects – transmit certain subtle meanings – by accenting a different word:

Pat took **ten** books.
Pat **took** ten books.
Pat took ten books.

In chapter 9 we discuss what these different meanings are.

Accent is primarily a change of pitch. In a statement *Pat took ten* **books**, the pitch falls – the frequency of vibration of the vocal cords decreases – as the vowel of the accented syllable is articulated. In a question, *Pat took ten* **books?**, at least in one possible way of asking, the pitch rises in the same place – the vocal cords increase their frequency of vibration. Along with the change of pitch there is typically a greater intensity, more force with which air is expelled from the lungs, and greater length, or duration, in the vowel and other sonorant elements of the accented syllable. Using a binary system we say that the accented syllable is [+ accent] and an unaccented syllable is [– accent].

If an accented word is polysyllabic, the accent is associated with one particular syllable of the word, the syllable which is stressed, or has **stress**. If we replace *books* in our example with *papers* and keep the accent on the last word, the first syllable of the word bears the accent; if we replace with *reviews* and keep the accent there, the second syllable of *reviews* is accented. The word 'paper is stressed on the first syllable, and re'view is stressed on the second syllable, indicated here with the raised tick. Stress is the property of a word, just as accent is the property of a tone unit. In every polysyllabic word the stress is, with some exceptions, fixed on a particular syllable; thus, 'Patrick, Pa'tricia, re'quest, de'liver, 'seven, e'leven. Stress is, then, the potential for accent. If a word is accented within a tone unit, its stressed (or only) syllable is the accented syllable of the tone unit. Of course, a word pronounced alone constitutes a tone unit by itself, and its stressed or only syllable is accented.

Using a binary system we say that some syllables are [+ stress] and others [– stress]; a syllable which is [+ stress] may be [+ accent] or [– accent].

In a tone unit every major word (roughly, every noun, verb, adjective, and adverb) has a stress, indicated below with a raised tick before the stressed syllable, and one word has accent as well as its own stress.

    'Pat 'took 'ten '**books**.
    Pa'tricia re'quested 'seven re'**views**.
    'Patrick de'livered e'leven '**pa**pers.

When a syllable is stressed but not accented, it does not have a change of pitch. It may be spoken at a slightly higher pitch than an unstressed syllable, and it has greater length and intensity; stressed syllables are relatively stronger and longer, unstressed syllables weaker and shorter. The greater strength of a stressed syllable is noted in, among other things, the aspiration of voiceless stops. Compare the aspirated /p/ [pʰ] of 'Pat, 'Patrick, and the first consonant of 'paper with the unaspirated /p/ in Pa'tricia and the second consonant of 'paper. The weakness of an unaccented syllable is observed in, among other things, its vowel. The first and last syllables of Pa'tricia have a schwa, /ə/, a vowel which does not occur in stressed syllables. The same vowel occurs in the unstressed syllables of 'paper and 'seven, and perhaps in the first and last syllables of re'quested. The succession of strong and weak syllables in English utterances is responsible for a kind of rhythm which is called stress timing (chapter 9).

The two kinds of facts, syllable structure and syllable prominence, are thus interrelated. The structures of stressed and unstressed syllables differ in certain small ways. Some elements can occur only as the peaks of unstressed syllables, not as the peaks of stressed syllables, and some phonemes have different pronunciations in stressed and unstressed syllables. Syllable structure and syllable prominence are interrelated in another way: the onset of an unstressed syllable is generally less precise than the onset of a stressed one. Consider the words *de'pend* and *'deepen*. In *de'pend*, with a stressed second syllable, it is easy to recognize where the first syllable ends and the second syllable begins. In the word *'deepen*, in which the first syllable is stressed, the syllable division is not so obvious. The coda of the first syllable and the onset of the second syllable are not clearly separated; the /p/ may belong to the first syllable or to the second. This 'fuzziness' or ambiguity in some syllable boundaries is part of the English sound system.

5.2   Syllable structure

Every language has phonemes, and every language has its own common patterns in which phonemes are arranged to form syllables and the syllables are arranged to form larger units. In some languages all syllables consist of one consonant followed by one vowel (CV), so that no word has a cluster of consonants or of vowels; any word has the form CV, or CVCV, or CVCVCV . . . , depending on how many syllables it has. In English there are never more than two vowels in sequence in a single word (as in *neon, poet, cruel, radio*), but clusters of two, three, or more consonants are fairly common: *prescribe, district, splints, tempts*, for example. Still, not just any two, three, or more consonants can cluster. There are definite limits, or **constraints**, on co-occurrence. **Phonotactics** is the part of phonology which studies and describes such constraints. Phonotactics is the topic of chapter 6, in which the structures of polysyllabic words are examined. In this section we want to treat only the possible structure of a single syllable.

In the exercises of chapter 4 you designated certain words in a special way by writing the class name (**Vowel, Glide, Liquid, Nasal, Fricative,** or **S**top) to which each phoneme of a word belongs; thus *shrimp* /ʃrɪmp/ was designated FLVNS, and *quilt* /kwɪlt/ was shown as SGVLS. Designations like these are called **canonical forms**. We can recognize the canonical form of a syllable, a morpheme, or a word; of course, an item like *shrimp* or *quilt* is at the same time a single syllable, a single morpheme, and a single word. Canonical forms enable us to describe the possible shapes of syllables, morphemes, and words in a language and to compare the shapes of two or more words or syllables. Canonical forms can be indicated with full information about classes (V, G, L, N, F, S) or by just indicating Vowels and Consonants; *neon* and *poet*, for instance, both have the canonical form CVVC; *plant* and *cramp* are both CCVCC, or, more specifically, SLVNS (stop, liquid, vowel, nasal, stop). For a polysyllabic word the canonical form must include an indication of stress. The words *comic* and *bucket* have the same canonical form, 'CVCVC, and *arrest* and *event* share the canonicl form V'CVCC. In English a canonical form CVC, as in *bed, nut, sack, love,* is obviously more common than CVCV'VCV, as in *tapioca.*

We start by investigating the canonical forms of some one-syllable words. We limit our investigation to words which consist of just one morpheme, without a suffix. Words with non-syllabic suffixes, like *warm-th* /wɔrmθ/, *tempt-s* /tɛmpts/, and *grasp-ed* /græspt/ end with unusual clusters of consonants. No word without a suffix has such clusters of consonants as /-rmθ/ or /-mpts/ or /-spt/. Clusters like these are considered separately, in chapter 7.

A word of one syllable has one vowel, of course. The vowel may be initial in the word (e.g. *and*); it may be preceded by one consonant (e.g. *band*), two consonants (e.g. *bland*), or three consonants (e.g. *strand*), but no more. In a word without a suffix the vowel may be final (e.g. *go*), or followed by one consonant (e.g. *goat*), two consonants (*toast*), or three consonants (*corpse*), but no more. All the possibilities for a monosyllabic, monomorphemic word can be expressed in this formula:

$$C_0^3 \quad V \quad C_0^3$$

That is, the peak consists of one vowel, the onset may be zero to three consonants, and the coda may consist of zero to three consonants.

5A EXPLORING SYLLABLE ONSETS

Here are 25 one-syllable words:

> act bald blame chain clay crisp dog drip dwarf edge faith flaw grasp home ice lend ox screw skin snow splint spring squaw stretch twin

(a) Which words have a zero onset?
(b) Which have an onset of one consonant (C-)?
(c) Which have an onset of two consonants (CC-)?
(d) Which have an onset of three consonants (CCC-)?
(e) In words with a CCC- onset, what is the first consonant?

5A FEEDBACK AND COMMENT

(a) act, edge, ice, ox
(b) bald, chain, dog, faith, home, lend
(c) blame, clay, crisp, drip, dwarf, flaw, grasp, skin, snow, twin
(d) screw, splint, spring, squaw, stretch
(e) /s/

These words show only a sample of the consonants which can occur in initial position. We can see, however, that initial clusters of two consonants fall into several specific types:

1   certain consonants followed by /l/ (Cl-): blame, clay, flaw
2   certain consonants followed by /r/ (Cr-): crisp, drip, grasp
3   certain consonants followed by /w/ (Cw-): dwarf, twin
4   /s/ followed by certain consonants (sC-): skin, snow

Initial clusters of three consonants are essentially combinations of type (4), above, with types (1), (2), and (3):

sCl-   splint
sCr-   screw, spring, stretch
sCw-   squaw

5B   EXPLORING SYLLABLE CODAS

Here are 25 more words:

bee   cast   corpse   dog   false   hemp   joke   lynx   nose   opt   owe prompt   pulse   quartz   scab   silk   spark   squirt   stand   task traipse   verb   young   world   zoo

(a)   Which words have a zero coda?
(b)   Which have a one-consonant coda (-C)?
(c)   Which have a -CC coda?
(d)   Which have a -CCC coda?

5B   FEEDBACK AND COMMENT

(a)   bee, owe, zoo
(b)   dog, joke, nose, scab, young
(c)   cast, false, hemp, opt, pulse, silk, spark, squirt, stand, task, traipse, verb
(d)   corpse, lynx, prompt, quartz, world

A variety of single consonants can occur as the coda, only a few of which are illustrated here. Clusters of two consonants in final position are of these types:

1   /l/ followed by certain consonants (-lC): false, silk
2   /r/ followed by certain consonants (-rC): spark, squirt, verb
3   a nasal consonant followed by certain other consonants (-NC): hemp, stand
4   less commonly, clusters of stops and of stop and fricative: opt, cast, task, traipse

Clusters of three consonants generally consist of a liquid or a nasal followed by two stops or a stop and a fricative: corpse, lynx, prompt, quartz, world.

These different combinations of consonants are dealt with in more detail in chapter 6.

5.3 Strong and weak syllables

The stressed vowel of a polysyllabic word can always be identified with the vowel of some monosyllabic word, one of the 24 keywords that were introduced in chapter 4. For example, the stressed vowel of *aroma* is the same as the vowel of TOE, and the stressed vowel of *cinema* is the same as the vowel of CHICK. To identify unstressed vowels is not always so easy. The most common unstressed vowel is the schwa, /ə/, which occurs in the first and third syllables of *aroma*. The schwa also occurs in the third syllable of *cinema*. The vowel in the second syllable of *cinema* may be /ə/ or a higher vowel /i/, depending on who is speaking.

Numerous English words contain one strong syllable (containing the stressed vowel) and one or more weak syllables, as in these examples:

S w	*w S*	*S w w*	*w S w*
salad	balloon	bulletin	remember
measure	command	Canada	contagious
value	result	elephant	develop
yellow	supply	harmony	annoyance

In long words there may be two strong syllables. Of course, only one of the strong syllables is the stressed syllable.

s w S	*S w s*	*S w s w*	*s w S w*
engineer	architect	architecture	California
lemonade	elevate	elevator	elevation
understand	modify	modifying	understanding

There may be two weak syllables in succession in the interior of a word.

s w w 'S w	*s w w 'S*	*s w w 'S w w*
modification	Senegalese	eligibility

Before the stressed syllable there are never more than two weak syllables in succession. Thus, if the stressed syllable is the fourth syllable of the word, either the first syllable is strong, as in

s w w 'S w   modification

or the second syllable is strong, as in

w s w 'S w   hallucination

After the stressed syllable there may be two weak syllables, as in some of the examples above. There may be three weak syllables, but only in words with certain endings.

```
'S  w  w  w        candidacy  gentlemanly  hesitancy
w  'S  w  w  w      impenetrable
```

A tone unit may thus contain four kinds of syllables:

(a) a syllable which is accented, [+ accent] (and also [+ stress] and [+ strong]);

(b) one or more syllables which are [+ stress] (and also [+ strong]) but [– accent];

(c) one or more syllables which are [+ strong] but [– stress] (and therefore [– accent]);

(d) one or more syllables which are weak, [– strong] (and therefore [– stress] and [– accent]).

To put it another way, these four kinds of syllables are related in a hierarchy which can be represented this way:

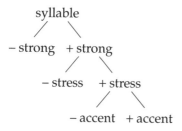

Let's illustrate with a simple sentence that is one tone unit.

```
           Patrick   understood   Patricia.
strong     s  –      s    –    s     –  s  –
stress     s  –      –    –    s     –  s  –
accent     –  –      –    –    –     –  S  –
```

Of course, the accent can be moved to the stressed syllable of *understood* or to the stressed syllable of *Patrick*.

Note: the accented syllable is stressed but only one stressed syllable is accented. All stressed syllables are strong but not all strong syllables are stressed. A weak syllable cannot be stressed and therefore cannot be accented.

There are several ways of indicating the relative strength of syllables in a word. Most dictionaries use a heavy slanting accent mark *after* the stressed syllable and a lighter accent mark after any other strong syllable, like this:

ar′chitect′ en′gineer′   el′eva′tor el′eva′tion

Phoneticians and phonologists have long used a different system, with a raised tick *before* the stressed syllable and a lowered tick before any other strong syllable:

'archi,tect ,engi'neer   'ele,vator ,ele'vation

Another system used by some linguists puts an acute accent (´) above the vowel of the stressed syllable and a grave accent (`) over the vowel of another strong syllable:

árchitèct   ènginéer   élevàtor   èlevátion

These are different ways of marking syllables but they are based on the same principle – that syllables have different amounts of strength or intensity. Metrical Phonology proposes a different idea: strength or intensity is not something that can be quantified. Strength and weakness are relative to each other. Metrical Phonology recognizes another prosodic unit between syllable and tone unit, the **foot**. A foot consists of two syllables, one strong and the other weak. A word with two syllables contains one foot, a four-syllable word has two feet, and so on. A word may contain one extra syllable. The words *engineer* and *architect* both consist of a foot plus an extra syllable, and in both words the foot consists of a strong syllable followed by a weak syllable. In *engineer* the extra syllable is strong relative to the foot; in *architect* the foot is strong and the extra syllable is weak. *Elevator* and *elevation* have four syllables each, therefore two feet, each consisting of a strong syllable and a weak one. In *elevator* the first foot is stronger than the second; in *elevation* the second foot is stronger than the first.

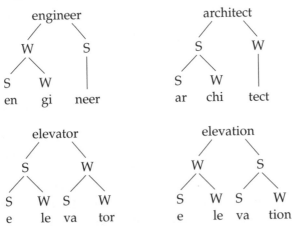

We will have more discussion of Metrical Phonology in chapter 12.

5.4 Syllable division

Syllable division is not an easy topic in English. Some languages are spoken with syllable timing (see chapter 9), so that all syllables are almost equally loud and equally long. English has stress timing: certain syllables are louder and longer, others are softer and shorter. In a language with syllable timing it is fairly easy to say where each syllable begins and ends. In English the beginning of a strong syllable is clear, but it is not easy to tell where a weak syllable begins unless it is the initial syllable of the word.

A dictionary provides information about the way a *written* word should be syllabified – where it can be divided in case a writer has to put part of the word on one line and the rest on the next line. The dictionary indicates syllable division according to certain conventions which have been used by printers since the eighteenth century. These conventions are based on two principles: (1) recognition of prefixes and suffixes, which are not divided (*mis.treat, un.able, free.dom, work.ing*); (2) different treatment according to whether the vowel letters A, E, I (or Y), O, and U are 'long' or 'short' – that is, whether they represent free vowels or checked vowels, respectively. If the vowel is 'long,' it ends the written syllable and the next consonant letter goes in the following syllable, but if the vowel is 'short,' the next consonant letter goes with the preceding vowel letter. Thus, in writing we are supposed to divide words into syllables this way:

ra-di-um, fla-vor	but	rad-i-cal, sav-age
le-gal, me-di-um	but	leg-a-cy, med-i-cine
fi-nal, ri-val	but	fin-ish, riv-er
co-pi-ous, so-lo	but	op-er-a, sol-id
pu-pil, stu-dent	but	pun-ish, stud-y

Note that the first principle takes precedence over the second; we write, for example, *fad-ing, writ-er*, not *fa-ding, wri-ter*.

This is the way written words are divided into syllables, but it is not the way spoken words are divided. Various people, including some linguists, have been misled by the printers' conventions and think that, for example, the first syllable of *final* is *fi-* /fai/ and the first syllable of *finish* is *fin-* /fɪn/. The fact is that, in speech, a single consonant between a strong vowel – any strong vowel – and a weak vowel is **ambisyllabic**: the consonant does not clearly belong to either the strong syllable or the weak syllable. There is no clear syllable break. We represent the syllable division this way:

Similarly, when consonant clusters like *pl-, dw-, gr-, st-* (clusters which occur word-initially) are between vowels, the first consonant is ambisyllabic:

In these examples the intervocalic consonant, or the first consonant of an intervocalic cluster, is ambisyllabic because it comes between a stressed vowel and an unstressed one, or between two unstressed vowels. When a consonant, or a cluster like *st-, dr-*, etc. comes before the vowel of a strong syllable, whether stressed or not, the consonant or the cluster is clearly in the strong syllable: *re'peat, de'clare, de'stroy, 'pene,trate.* Compare *'deepen* and *de'pend*, the noun *'record* and the verb *re'cord*.

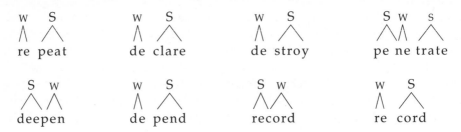

What are the rules for dividing English words into syllables?

1 If two vowels occur in sequence, the syllable break is between the vowels (V.V): *ne.on, cha.os, cru.el(ty), bi.o(logy), re.a(lity)*. As we have noted before, the first of the two vowels is always a free vowel. (We indicate the syllable division with a dot.)

2 If one consonant occurs between two vowels and the second vowel is strong, whether stressed or not, the consonant is part of the second syllable: *re.'pent, va.'ca(tion), ('pe)ne.trate, ('lon)gi.tude*.

   If one consonant occurs between a strong vowel and a weak vowel, the consonant is ambisyllabic; we represent this with the symbol ˆ before the ambisyllabic consonant: *'coˆpy, 'moˆdel, 'leˆvel*. When a single consonant occurs between two weak vowels, it may be ambisyllabic: *'ciˆneˆma, 'poˆsiˆtive*, or it may go in the syllable with the second weak vowel: *'ciˆne.ma, 'poˆsi.tive*.

3 If two vowels are separated by a consonant cluster, syllable division depends on what consonants are in the cluster. If the cluster is of the type that can occur word-initially (sC-, Cr-, Cl-, Cw-, sCr-, etc.) and the following vowel is strong, the whole cluster is part of the syllable with the strong vowel: *Pa.'tri(cia), de.'cline, re.'quire, di.'stress, su.'spect* (verb).

   If the second vowel is weak, the first consonant of the cluster is ambisyllabic: *'saˆcred, 'proˆblem, 'proˆbaˆbly, ca. 'taˆstro.phe, 'suˆspect* (noun).

4 If the consonant cluster is one that cannot occur in initial position, the consonants are divided in such a way that the second syllable begins with a consonant or a consonant cluster which can occur initially: *'can.dy, 'at.las, 'shel.ter, 'em.blem, 'pan.try, 'car.pen.ter*. Note that two consonants which are in the same syllable if they are word-final (e.g. *wind, shelve*) go into separate syllables if they occur word-medially: *'win.dow, 'sil.ver*.

In chapter 6 we examine various consonant clusters. In chapter 8 we consider some more variable kinds of syllable division.

5.5 Suffixes and stress

When a prefix or suffix of Old English origin is added to a word, it has no effect on the position of stress, for example:

'neighbor 'neighborly 'neighborhood
'thoughtful un'thoughtful un'thoughtfulness

In contrast, words of Greek, Latin, or French origin often show a change of stress when an affix is added or changed:

'origin o'riginal origi'nality
'photograph pho'tography photo'graphic

As a result, a vowel that is stressed in one word becomes unstressed in a related word and the vowel is reduced, and a reduced vowel in one word may become stressed in a related word. Compare the first vowel in *origin* and *original*, the second vowel in *photograph* and *photography*.

5C EXERCISE ON STRESS IN RELATED WORDS

In the following pairs of words put a capital S under the stressed syllable of each word and put a small s under each strong syllable that is not stressed.

Examples: Canada Canadian   Japan Japanese
                 S   S   S   s   S

(a) atom atomic   (g) compose composition

(b) define definition   (h) continent continental

(c) melody melodic   (i) modify modification

(d) parent parental   (j) origin original

(e) terrify terrific   (k) invite invitation

(f) ambiguous ambiguity   (l) combine combination

5.6 Compounds and some other words

A compound word consists of two (or possibly more) simple words, each of which has its own stress as an independent word. Many compounds are stressed on the first word, and the stressed vowel of the second word is strong but unstressed. Some examples:

'keyhole   'stoplight   'motorcycle   'air conditioned
  S   s   S   s   S w s w   S   w   s w

ex'pressway   'wastebasket   'Main Street   com'puter screen
 w   S   s   S   s w   S   s   w   S w   s

A smaller number of compounds are stressed on the second word.

apple 'pie   kitchen 'sink   Fifth 'Avenue
 s   w   S   s   w   S   s   S w w

A few compounds are stressed differently by different speakers of English.

'ice cream   *or*   ice 'cream   'week end   *or*   week 'end
 S   s   s   S   S   w   s   S

In a number of words which were once compounds the vowel of the second part has been reduced to schwa, /ə/ ('*breakfast*, '*cupboard*), and many words that were originally compounds are no longer recognizable as such ('*nostril*, '*sheriff*, '*stirrup*, '*window*). In British English this sort of reduction has gone farther than in North American English: *nobody* and *strawberry*, for instance, have a full vowel in the next to last syllable in North America; in Britain and the southern hemisphere they are apt to have /ə/ or to lose the vowel altogether and become two-syllable words. Compare typical British and American pronunciations of the following words, which are not compounds:

	British	American
ceremony, difficulty	S w w w	S w s w
necessary, territory	S w w w	S w s w
	or S w w	
Lancaster, Rochester	S w w	S s w

(a)   The words below are all spelled with -*man* as the second element. Some of the words are full compounds; -*man* is a strong syllable with the vowel /æ/. Other words are reduced compounds; -*man* is a weak syllable with /ə/. Which are the full compounds? (We may not all agree.)

businessman   chairman   fireman   foreman   gentleman   layman
madman   mailman   marksman   midshipman   patrolman
policeman   postman   salesman   seaman   watchman   workman

(b)   Similarly, written words in which -*land* is the second element include true compounds, with /æ/ in the second element, and reduced compounds, with /ə/. Which of the following are true compounds?

> highland   lowland   woodland   hinterland   dreamland
> wonderland   England   Scotland   Ireland   Poland   Switzerland
> Greenland   Newfoundland   Swaziland

(c)   English has a few nouns like the words in the first line below and numerous adjectives like those in the second line. In one group the syllable written -*ful* is strong and has the vowel /ʊ/. In the other group that syllable is weak and has /ə/. Which group has the strong final syllable?

> armful   bowlful   cupful   handful   spoonful
> cheerful   graceful   hopeful   peaceful   thoughtful

(d)   There are more than a thousand verbs in English with the written ending -*ate*. With few exceptions they are stressed on the third syllable from the end, the antepenult, and the last syllable, the ult, is strong, /-eit/: '*elevate, in'timidate, re'ciprocate*. In adjectives and many nouns with this ending the antepenult is stressed and the ult is weak, /-ət/. Compare the verb *graduate* and the noun *graduate*, the verb *moderate* and the adjective *moderate*.

Examine each word in the following list. Put a letter after the word to tell if it is a verb (V), a noun (N), or an adjective (A) – or some combination of these. If a noun has /ei/ instead of /ə/ in the last syllable, note it.

adequate	educate	obliterate
advocate	elaborate	obstinate
affectionate	estimate	passionate
affiliate	illiterate	penetrate
alternate	immediate	percolate
candidate	impersonate	predicate
considerate	intimate	separate
delegate	marinate	stimulate
duplicate	moderate	subordinate

(e)   Each of the following written words represents two spoken words, a noun and a verb, pronounced differently by most speakers. How do the pronunciations differ?

> compliment   document   experiment   implement   ornament
> supplement

5.7   Identifying the vowels of weak syllables

In weak syllables there is often a variation in what vowel is pronounced. For example, the first syllable of *believe, defend, pretend, review* may have /ə/ or a high-front vowel, /ii/ or /ɪ/. Perhaps many speakers vary their pronunciation depending on how fast they speak. Here are some examples of variation in weak syllables:

Initial pretonic syllable

/ii/, /ɪ/, /ə/	believe depend enough prefer remain
/ei/, /ə/	fatality vacation
/uu/, /ʊ/, /ə/	July Louise musician nutritious
/ou/, /ə/	Korea morale obey opinion protect

Medial posttonic syllable

/ɪ/ or /ə/	candidate colleges furniture latitude
/ʊ/ or /ə/	argument document masculine popular

5E   EXERCISE AND COMMENT: FINAL /I, U, O/

Consider vowels in word-final position.

(a)   Is the vowel in the last syllable of these words /ii/ or /ɪ/?

city   easy   happy   silly   study

(b)   Do these words end with /uu/ or /ʊ/ – or /ə/?

continue   issue   sinew   value

(c)   All of the following words can be pronounced with final /ou/. Some of them are pronounced with final /ə/ by some speakers; the others are always pronounced with /ou/. Which are which?

arrow   auto   fellow   follow   motto   photo   potato   yellow

COMMENT

(a)   First of all, there is no possible contrast between /ii/ and /ɪ/ in word-final unstressed position, so that speakers vary. The vowel is short and lax like /ɪ/ but may be higher, like /ii/. Some speakers feel they pronounce the same two vowels in words like *city* and *silly*; other speakers say they pronounce the same vowels in words like *easy* and *needy*.

Since there is no contrast, we say that the potential contrast of /ii/ and /ɪ/ is **neutralized** in this position.

(b) Similarly, there is no possible contrast between /uu/ and /ʊ/ in this position and pronunciations vary. The potential contrast is neutralized in word-final, unstressed position.

(c) *Arrow, fellow, follow, potato,* and *yellow* are pronounced with /ə/ by some people. The other words are not.

5F EXERCISE AND COMMENT: /I, U/ BEFORE VOWELS

What is the second vowel of these words?

(a) radio   medium   video   stadium
(b) annual   usual   graduate   manual

COMMENT

When two unstressed vowels occur in sequence, the first is a high vowel, either high-front as in group (a) or high-back as in group (b). Do the words in group (a) have /ii/ or /ɪ/ in the second syllable? Do the words in group (b) have /uu/ or /ʊ/ in the second syllable? Once again, there is neutralization.

5G EXERCISE AND COMMENT: CONTRAST OF /ə/ AND /ɪ/

Some speakers make a contrast between *roses* and *Rosa's*, between *rushes* and *Russia's*. The vowel /ɪ/ or something like it occurs in *roses* and *rushes* and the other two words have /ə/ in the second syllable. If you make such a contrast, you can easily tell which of the following words have /ɪ/ and which have /ə/ in the second syllable.

careless longest bucket atlas chicken human manage salad
sandwich orange polish music stomach gallop Philip native
building

COMMENT

For those who make a distinction *atlas, human, salad, stomach,* and *gallop* have /ə/ in the last syllable and the other words have /ɪ/. For many other speakers there is no difference; *chicken* and *human* have the same last vowel and *roses* and *Rosa's* are homophones. A contrast that exists in some dialects is neutralized in other dialects. If there is no contrast, there may be variation – one vowel occurring before certain consonants and the other vowel before other consonants. Typically, this means that /ɪ/ occurs before coronal and dorsal consonants, as in *sandwich, orange, manage, polish, music,* and *building,* while /ə/ occurs before other consonants.

5.8   Syllabic consonants

In the pronunciation of the word *button* the tongue-tip touches the alveolar ridge for the [t], blocking the flow of air through the mouth, the velic is closed, blocking the flow of air through the nose, and the vocal cords are not vibrating. Then the velic opens and the vocal cords vibrate while the tongue remains against the alveolar ridge. A syllabic consonant [n̩] is articulated without the tongue moving from the position of [t]. There is no vowel between [t] and [n]. Syllabic [n] is frequent in English, mostly after coronal consonants /t d s z č ǰ ʃ ʒ/, as in *button, wooden, listen, cousin, kitchen, virgin, motion, vision*. Syllabic [m̩] and [ŋ̩] are less common. The former may be heard in a phrase like *keep 'em* [kiipm̩] or a rapid pronunciation of *open* [oupm̩]. The latter may occur in, for example, *looking good* [lʊkŋ̩ gʊd] or a rapid pronunciation of *I can go* [ai kŋ̩ goʊ]. All these examples have a nasal consonant which is **homorganic** with the preceding obstruent – that is, made with the same articulator, lip, tongue-tip, or tongue-back. The articulator remains in place while the air stream finds a new outlet, through the nasal cavity. No vowel is articulated but the duration of the nasal consonant is the same as that of a vowel. It takes as long to say *button* and *listen*, for example, as *buddy* and *issue*.

The liquid consonants /l/ and /r/ may be syllabic, as in *total* [toutl̩] and *bitter* [bɪtr̩], respectively, or there may be a schwa between the last two consonants. In such words as *girl, file, foul, fire, hour* we may find a problem in telling how many syllables there are because the final /l/ or /r/ may be syllabic or not. Pronunciations vary with speakers or, for a single speaker, with tempo.

Syllabic consonants occur only in unstressed syllables. What is phonetically a syllabic consonant may vary with a sequence of /ə/ and the corresponding non-syllabic consonant. A syllabic consonant is to be interpreted phonologically as /ə/ plus a consonant. Thus *button* is phonetically [bʌtn̩] and phonologically /'bʌtən/; *battle* is phonetically [bætl̩] and phonologically /'bætəl/. These words have the same canonical form as *bullet* and *gallop*, for instance – CVCVC.

5H   PRACTICE WITH SYLLABIC CONSONANTS

You may pronounce a syllabic /n/ [n̩] in some or all of the following:

cotton	maiden	Britain	sudden	nation
kitten	beaten	brighten	mutton	patient
lesson	prison	reason	present	caution
didn't	wasn't	wouldn't	doesn't	imagine
botany	monotony	fascinate	president	erosion
coat 'n' hat	bread 'n' butter			

When /t/ or /d/ occurs before syllabic /n/, the syllable division is after /t/ or /d/: *kitten* ['kɪt.n̩], *didn't* ['dɪd.n̩t].

In words like the following, in which the consonant before /n/ is labial or dorsal, there is a /ə/ between that consonant and /n/.

wagon   common   second   even
bacon   open   toughen ribbon

The following contain an apical consonant followed by a syllabic /l/, [l̩]:

whistle petal   saddle candle
muscle muzzle   little catalog

What'll we do?   Wait'll the boss sees this.

After labial and dorsal consonants there is a schwa between that consonant and /l/, as in the following:

ripple   double   pickle   evil

In the following words we may say there is a syllabic /r/:

better   ladder   cover   dinner
coward   commerce lantern drunkard

Actually, what is pronounced in the last syllable is a vowel with 'r-coloring'. The tongue is in the same position as for the articulation of a schwa, /ə/, but it is retracted somewhat and there is a slight groove in the tip. Compare the ending of *manner* and *manna*. In the pronunciation of both words there is a single phonetic segment after /n/. That segment is a schwa in *manna* and a schwa with tongue retraction and tongue-tip groove for *manner*. The usual phonetic symbol for this segment, [ɚ], recognizes it as a vowel, but we may also consider it a syllabic consonant with the symbol [r̩] because in English it is comparable to syllabic /n/ and syllabic /l/. Of course, speakers who do not pronounce a final /r/ have a schwa in both *manna* and *manner*.

5.9   Summary

In a tone unit of more than one syllable one of the syllables is more prominent than the other(s) because it is the place where the melody or intonation changes; it is the **accented syllable**, [+ accent]. The accented syllable and perhaps other syllables are **stressed syllables**, [+ stress], having greater intensity and duration than syllables which are [– stress]. Typically every major word in a tone group has one stressed syllable. Finally, stressed syllables and some unstressed syllables are **strong**, [+ strong], and other syllables are **weak**, [– strong]. A syllable that is [+ strong] is potentially [+ stress] and therefore potentially [+ accent]. Long English words have an alternation of strong and weak syllables.

In describing syllables by their position in a word or longer form we speak of **initial, medial,** and **final** syllables. To describe position with respect to the tonic syllable we use the labels **pretonic** and **posttonic**.

Every syllable has a **peak**, an element which is [+ syllabic]. Consonants which precede the peak constitute the **onset** and consonants which follow the peak form the **coda**. Peak and coda together make up the **rhyme**.

The consonants and vowels of a language occur in certain kinds of sequences and not others. Statements about what sequences may or may not occur are called **constraints**. The full description of constraints is called **phonotactics**.

In English consonants that occur between a strong vowel and a weak vowel or between two weak vowels are **ambisyllabic**. One vowel, the schwa /ə/, occurs only in weak syllables. The sonorant consonants /m n l r/ can be phonetically syllabic in weak syllables.

Full **compound words** are composed of two independent words, each of which has at least one strong syllable. Most of them are stressed on the first word but others are stressed on the second word.

5C   FEEDBACK

(a)   atom   atomic
    S   S

(b)   define   definition
     S   s S

(c)   melody   melodic
    S   S

(d)   parent   parental
    S   S

(e)   terrify   terrific
   S s   S

(f)   ambiguous   ambiguity
   s S   s   S

(g)   compose   composition
      S   s   S

(h)   continent   continental
   S   s   S

(i)   modify   modification
   S s   s   S

(j)   origin   original
 S   S

(k)   invite   invitation
  s S   s   S

(l)   combine   combination
   S   s   S

5D   FEEDBACK

(a)   Answers may vary. The words *businessman* and *mailman* have a full vowel /æ/ in the last syllable, and *madman* may also have /æ/. The other words generally have /ə/.

(b)   The words *hinterland, dreamland, wonderland,* and *Swaziland* have /æ/ in the last syllable; *highland, midland, England, Poland, Switzerland,* and *Greenland* have /ə/; *lowland* and *woodland* are pronounced with /æ/ or /ə/; *Newfoundland* has three accepted pronunciations: /'n(j)uufəndlænd, 'n(j)uufəndlənd, n(j)uu'faundlænd/.

(c)   The nouns with -*ful* are true compounds and have a strong last syllable with /ʊ/. The adjectives have a weak final syllable with /ə/.

(d)

adequate A	educate V	obliterate V
advocate V,N	elaborate V,A	obstinate A
affectionate A	estimate V,N	passionate A
affiliate V,N	illiterate A,N	penetrate V
alternate V,N,A	immediate A	percolate V
candidate N*	impersonate V	predicate V,N
considerate A	intimate V,A,N	separate V,A
delegate V,N*	marinate V	stimulate V
duplicate V,N,A	moderate V,A	subordinate V,N,A

The nouns marked N* may have /ei/ or /ə/ in the last syllable; other nouns and all adjectives have /ə/; all verbs have /ei/.

(e)   Verbs ending in -*ment* have a strong syllable with the full vowel /ɛ/; the corresponding nouns have a weak final syllable, with /ə/.

Notes

Work dealing with the syllable in (English) phonology is extensive but has been produced in a relatively short period of time. They include: Bailey (1968, 1980), Bell and Hooper (1978a, 1978b), Fallows (1981), Hoard (1971), Malmberg (1955), O'Connor and Trim (1953), Pulgram (1970), Rudes (1977), Vennemann (1972).

Roach (1991, ch. 8) gives a different description of the English syllable. For a treatment of prosody and syllables in a variety of languages see Ladefoged (1993, ch. 10).

6

Phonotactics

In chapter 5 we examined the structure of a one-syllable, one-morpheme word, observing that such a word has one vowel and it may begin with zero, one, two, or three consonants and may end with zero, one, two, or three consonants. In this chapter we explore and describe how consonants and vowels occur in longer words. We will be concerned with what consonants can occur together initially and finally and between vowels and what sequences of vowels and consonants are possible.

The description which follows deals especially with the **constraints** on the occurrence of consonants: certain sequences of consonants are possible in English words and other sequences do not occur. To a large extent the patterns which occur and the constraints on what does not occur are obvious and easily stated. Near the end of the chapter, however, we take note of some facts which don't fit the patterns or which can be interpreted in different ways.

6.1 Word-initial position

The first (or only) vowel of a word may be preceded by:

(0) Zero (that is, the vowel may be initial):

apple elephant eager oblige...

(1) Any single consonant except /ʒ/ or /ŋ/*:

bell package mellow wild vest fat...

 * Neither /ʒ/ nor /ŋ/ occurs initially in native English words, but /ʒ/ does occur in words borrowed from other languages. Various names, especially, are

known to speakers of English, such as *Giselle, Zhivago, Gitane*. There are no such words with initial /ŋ/.

(2) Certain clusters of two consonants, which we need to classify further. There are strong constraints on what kinds of consonants can occur together. The next problem begins with an exhibit of the types of consonant clusters, with examples. Then there are questions to be answered about the words in the exhibit.

6A PROBLEM: INITIAL CLUSTERS

First, here is the exhibit:

(i)   Cr- (consonant + /r/)

       pray   brave   train   drain   craze   graze
       frill   thrill   shrill

(ii)   Cl- (consonant + /l/)

       play   blade   clay   glaze
       flay   slay

(iii)   Cw- (consonant + /w/)

       twin   dwindle   quit   Gwen
       thwart   swim
       whistle

(iv)   sC- (/s/ + consonant)

       spy   sty   sky
       sphere
       smile   snow

And here are the questions. Assume that the exhibit contains all the examples needed for answering the questions.

(a)   In the sequences designated Cr-, do both voiced and voiceless stops occur before /r/?
(b)   Do both voiced and voiceless stops occur before /l/?
(c)   Do the sibilant stops (affricates), /č/ and /ǰ/, occur initially before the liquids /r/ and /l/?
(d)   Do voiced and voiceless fricatives occur before /r/?   before /l/?
(e)   In the sequences Cw-, which stops and fricatives occur before /w/?

(f)   When two glides occur together initially, the first is /h/ and the second is /w/, as in *whistle, wheel, white, which*, but not all speakers pronounce an /h/ in these words; for them the words begin with /w/. The matter is dealt with further in the section 'Feedback and Discussion', below.

All other initial clusters of two consonants have the fricative /s/ followed by a stop, a fricative, or a nasal.

(g)   The only stops which can follow initial /s/ must be voiceless and non-sibilant, specifically, ____ , ____ , and ____ .

(h)   The only fricative which is found in second position in an initial consonant cluster is ____ , occurring only in a few words of Greek origin (and always spelled 'ph').

(i)   Which nasal consonants can follow initial /s/?

6A   FEEDBACK AND DISCUSSION

(a)   Both voiceless and voiced stops occur initially before /r/.
(b)   Both voiceless and voiced stops occur initially before /l/.
(c)   /č/ and /ǰ/ do not occur in that position.
(d)   Only voiceless fricatives occur initially before /r/ and before /l/.
(e)   /t d k g θ s/

Summarizing a little, we see that only these stops and fricatives occur initially before /r l w/:

/p b f t d θ s ʃ k g/

but /s/ does not occur before /r/, /t d θ ʃ/ do not occur before /l/, and /p b f ʃ/ do not occur before /w/. The occurring clusters can be plotted like this:

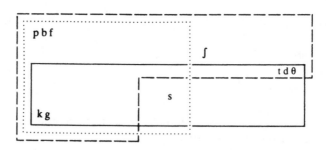

The solid line encloses the obstruents which occur initially before /w/, the dotted line encloses those which occur initially before /l/, and the dashed line those which occur initially before /r/.

(f)   Those who pronounce /h/ in *wheel* and other 'wh' words have a contrast between *which* /hwič/ and *witch* /wɪč/, *whine* /hwain/ and *wine* /wain/. Those who don't pronounce /h/ before /w/ (quite possibly the majority of the world's English-speaking population) have no such distinction. Even those who have /hw/ in *when, where,* etc. are likely to 'drop' the /h/ in certain contexts. Consider the two sets below. In which set would /h/ more likely be lost?

When did they leave?	...	the day when they left
What does he want?	...	don't know what he wants
Where is it?	...	find out where it is

The /h/ is more likely to be 'kept' when such words are at the beginning of an utterance, as in the examples on the left and to be omitted when the words are in the interior of an utterance, as on the right.

(g) /p t k/
(h) /f/
(i) /m n/

To summarize some more, we see from these statements that if an obstruent (S or F) and a sonorant (N or L or G) occur together at the beginning of a word, the obstruent precedes the sonorant; in other words, the sonorant is on the 'inside' position, next to the first vowel (or only vowel) of the word. Using the symbol # at the left to represent word-beginning, we have:

$$\#\quad \text{obstruent}\quad \left\{\begin{array}{l}\text{nasal}\\\text{liquid}\\\text{glide}\end{array}\right\}\quad \text{vowel}$$

This is a **scale of sonority**: a vowel is the most sonorant of all speech sounds, and sonorant consonants are more sonorant than obstruents. In English, nasal, liquid, and glide are mutually exclusive in pre-vowel position; they do not occur in sequence; if one of them occurs here, the others do not. We will find that this is a little different in post-vowel position. (And see the note about /j/ in section 6.2.)

(3) Initial clusters of three consonants are of the following types:

(i) sCr-

     spry   street   scream

(ii) sCl-

     splendid   sclerosis

(iii) sCw-

     squint

Here the initial fricative is always /s/; the second consonant is a voiceless stop, /p t or k/; the third consonant is /r l or w/. We can see that the 3-consonant clusters originate, so to speak, by putting together the type sC-, where C has to be /p/, /t/, or /k/, with types Cr-, Cl-, and Cw-, in which /p/, /t/, or /k/ has to be compatible with /r/, /l/, or /w/. Since there is no initial */pw-/ or */tl-/, there is no initial */spw-/ or */stl-/.

6.2   A note regarding /j/

Consider the following words:

> puny   beauty   fuse   muse   view   cue   hue   spew   skew
> tube   duty   new   suit   student

Words like these begin with one or two consonants followed by the glide /j/. In the preceding section we dealt with the glide /w/ in initial clusters like *twin* and *swim*. Why not treat the glide /j/ at the same time and list the initial clusters in which /j/ occurs? The answer is that there is a difference between /w/ and /j/. When /w/ occurs in an initial cluster, it may be followed by various vowels, as in *sweet*, *twin*, *dwarf*, *quote*, just as /r/ and /l/ in initial clusters can be followed by various vowels. However, when /j/ occurs in an initial cluster, as in the examples above, it is always followed by the vowel /uu/. We notice also that, unlike /w/, /r/ and /l/, /j/ occurs after the nasal /m/ (*music*) and the voiced fricative /v/ (*view*). For these reasons some linguists prefer to consider the whole sequence /juu/ a single vowel-unit.

The words in the second line above bring us to a dialect difference. These words have an apical consonant or consonants in initial position. For some speakers such words as *stew*, *student*, *tube*, *Tuesday*, *tune*, *due/dew*, *duty*, *new*, *nude* begin with /stjuu-, tjuu-, djuu-, njuu-/. Others – the great majority of Irish, Canadians, and Americans – pronounce such words without a /j/: /stuu-, tuu-, duu-, nuu-/. Some – but very few – of those who have a /j/ after /t d n/ may also pronounce a /j/ after initial /s/ as in *suit* and *super*.

Does /j/ occur after /č/ and /ǰ/, as for example in *chew* and *juke*? In most parts of the English-speaking world the question is irrelevant. In Britain some regional dialects make a distinction between *choose* and *chews*. The former is /čuuz/ and the latter is /čjuuz/, [tʃⁱuːz] or /čiwz/ [tʃiᵘz]. For other dialects of English, which have no such distinction, the question of whether or not there is a /j/ after initial /č/ (and /ǰ/) is a moot one.

6.3   Contrast and variation

A phoneme is a unit of sound which has different pronunciations (is manifested by different segments) in different positions of occurrence. In some cases the variability is due to what comes before or after the phoneme. As we have seen, for example, the vowel of *home* is nasalized (because /m/ follows) while the vowel of *hope* is not nasalized; the first consonant of *too* is likely to be pronounced with rounded lips and the first consonant of *tee* with stretched lips because the speaker anticipates the articulation of the vowel which follows. This kind of variability will be treated in chapter 7. But variability is also due to another factor, the amount of 'room' there is for the phoneme. The sketch below is supposed to represent in a crude way the inside of the mouth and the approximate distance of the initial consonants from one another in the mouth.

FRONT			BACK	
pay, bait	take, date	chase, jade	Kate, gate	
pray, brave	train, drain		craze, grave	
play, blame		claim, glaze		

Before a vowel, as shown in the first line, there are four pairs of stops. Each pair has its own 'territory.' A stop can be articulated at different points within that territory but it cannot 'intrude' into the territory of a neighbor. (Actually, of course, the labial stops cannot be articulated anywhere except at the lips.) Before /r/, as the second line shows, there are only three of these pairs of stops. Consequently, the non-labial ones have more room in which to be articulated. Note your pronunciation of the initial stops of *take*, *date* and *train*, *drain*. You may find that your pronunciation of /t/ and /d/ are farther back before /r/. The third line indicates that there are only two pairs of stops which occur initially before /l/ – only one non-labial pair. Many speakers have a more forward /k/ and /g/ before /l/ than in the other types of initial position.

6.4 Word-final position

The last (or only) vowel of a word may be followed by:

(0)   Zero (that is, the vowel may be word-final)

   no   day   agree   supply   soda . . .

(1)   Any single consonant except /h/

   nap   cub   room   leaf   believe . . .

(2)   Certain clusters of two consonants; the exhibit below sorts these clusters by type and gives relevant examples. Questions follow.

6B   QUESTIONS: FINAL CLUSTERS

Here is the exhibit for final clusters:

(i)   -rC

> harp   verb   hurt   word   arch   urge   work   berg
> wharf   carve   birth   force   harsh
> harm   barn
> curl

(ii)   -lC

> help   bulb   belt   weld   belch   bulge   milk
> shelf   delve   filth   pulse   Welsh
> film   (kiln)

(iii)   -NC (nasal + consonant)

> lamp   ant   hand   lunch   sponge   bank
> nymph   month   rinse   lens

(iv)   -FS (fricative + stop)

> lisp   list   risk

(v)   -SF (stop + fricative)

> lapse   spitz   fox   adze

(vi)   -SS (stop + stop)

> apt   act

6B   QUESTIONS

(a)   If a final consonant cluster consists of an obstruent (S or F) and a sonorant (L or N), the _____ precedes the _____ ; that is, the _____ is in the 'inside' position, next to the (last) vowel.

(b)   If the sonorant consonant is a nasal, it is **homorganic** with the following obstruent; that is, it is produced with the same articulator as the obstruent. This means that before the labials /p/ and /f/ only ____ occurs; before dorsal /k/ only ____ occurs; and before other consonants the nasal is ____ . If the sonorant is a nasal, the only voiced obstruents which follow are /d/ and /ǰ/, as in *land* and *sponge*. Other voiced obstruents do not occur in this position. Words like *climb* and *thumb* were once pronounced

with a final /b/; compare the words *clamber* and *thimble*, originally related words, where the /b/ is not final and still survives. Similarly, words
like *hang* and *long* once had a final /g/; compare *finger* and *linger*, where
the /g/ survives in medial position. In words like *hang* and *long* the final
/g/ is still present in the speech of some people, but it has disappeared in
most dialects of English. If the sonorant is a liquid, either /l/ or /r/, it
may be followed by other voiced obstruents – see -rC and -lC, above –
but these are relatively rare.

(c) If two sonorants occur together in final position, can both be nasals?

(d) Can both be liquids? If so, in what order do they occur?

(e) When two obstruents occur together in final position, they may be fricative
+ stop (FS), stop + fricative (SF), or two stops (SS), but two fricatives do
not occur finally unless one of them is a suffix (e.g. *cuff-s*, *breath-s*). The
word *adze* (homophonous with *add-s*) is exceptional: it ends with the voiced
consonants /dz/. All other final clusters of two obstruents are _____ .

6B FEEDBACK AND DISCUSSION

(a) The sonorant precedes the obstruent; that is, the sonorant is in the inside
position.

(b) Only /m/ occurs before /p/ and /f/; only /ŋ/ occurs before /k/; before
other consonants the nasal is /n/.

(c) If a word ends with two sonorants, the two sonorants will not both be
nasal; there is no final cluster of the type -NN. The spelling of *damn*,
solemn, etc. shows that a cluster of /m/ and /n/ once occurred in final position, but no longer; compare *damnation* and *solemnity*, where the cluster
is not final.

(d) Two liquids can occur word-finally; /r/ must precede /l/.

(e) Except for *adze* all final clusters of two obstruents are voiceless. Note also
that every such cluster contains /s/ or /t/, and perhaps both of them.

From the sequences described above we can establish another scale of
sonority. Moving away from the vowel, which is the most sonorous of speech
sounds, there is a general sequence like this (where #, at the right end, marks
the end of a word):

vowel   r   l   nasal   obstruent   #

/r/ may precede /l/; either of them can come before a nasal; and any of these
three occurs before an obstruent – but of course not all four occur together
since there is a constraint against more than three final consonants. Indeed,
there are further constraints on what the three final consonants may be, which
we examine in the next section.

(3) Three consonants in a cluster; the types and examples are shown in the
next exhibit.

6C   CLUSTERS OF THREE CONSONANTS

Here is the exhibit:

(i)   three obstruents – stop, fricative, stop (SFS)

> text   midst

(ii)   nasal + two obstruents

> NSS: prompt   distinct
> NSF: glimpse   jinx
> NFS: against   amongst

(iii)   liquid + stop + fricative (LSF)

> corpse   quartz

(iv)   two liquids + stop (LLS), with only one example: world

QUESTION

The word *world* is the only example of a 3-consonant cluster in which all three consonants are voiced. In all other such clusters the last two consonants are _____ obstruents. Furthermore, either /____ / or / ____ / occurs in every such cluster, and perhaps both of them.

6.5   Word-medial position

Between two vowels in a word there may be from zero to four consonants. The number of possible consonants is greater than in word-initial or word-final position, and the number of types of clusters is also larger. Since medial clusters are between two vowels, we also need to consider how they divide between syllables. What can occur between two vowels in a word?

(0)   Zero (no consonant at all). In this case the first vowel must be a 'free' vowel since it ends a syllable.

> neon   poet   coward   giant

(1)   Any one consonant. Most consonants occur between a stressed vowel and an unstressed vowel (where the consonant is ambisyllabic) and also between an unstressed vowel and a stressed vowel (where the consonant belongs to the same syllable as the stressed vowel).

p	'copy	re'pel	b	'rabid	de'bate
t	'metal	re'tain	d	'medal	a'dore
č	'hatchet	a'chieve	ǰ	'rigid	re'ject
k	'wicker	de'cay	g	'wagon	be'gin
f	'coffin	af'fair	v	'cover	a'vert
θ	'author	me'thodical	ð	'weather	—
s	'message	mas'sage	z	'razor	re'serve
ʃ	'mission	ma'chine	3	'measure	re'gime
m	'common	a'muse	n	'dinner	de'ny
l	'rally	re'ly	r	'berry	pa'rade

There seem to be no words with medial /ð/ before a stressed vowel, but this is probably due to the fact that the consonant /ð/ is rather rare in any position.

The nasal /ŋ/ is also rare; it occurs between a stressed vowel and an unstressed one (and only in a few words like *gingham*) but not before a stressed vowel.

The glides /j w h/ are just the opposite. In medial position they occur only before stressed vowels: *be'yond, a'ware, pro'hibit*. Such words as *bias* and *coward* might be interpreted as /'bajəs 'kawərd/, with /j/ and /w/ followed by an unstressed vowel but this implies a syllable division /'ba.jəs, 'ka.wərd/. It seems more accurate to regard these words, and others like them, of course, as having complex vowels /ai/ and /au/ which end their syllables: /'bai.əs, 'kau.ərd/. In other words, the first syllable of *bias* sounds like the word *by* and the first syllable of *coward* sounds like *cow*. Even before a stressed vowel the front glide may be part of the preceding vowel unit, as in *Toyota* /toi'outə/. /h/ does not occur medially before an unstressed vowel; the word *vehicle* is either /'viiəkəl/ or /'vii,hɪkəl/ – compare *vehicular* /vii'hɪkjulər/, where /h/ is in the stressed syllable.

(2)   There may be two consonants. We divide them into two groups.

(a)   clusters of the types which also occur word-initially; when they occur between a stressed vowel and an unstressed one, the first consonant is ambisyllabic; when they occur between an unstressed vowel and a stressed one, the whole cluster is in the same syllable as the stressed vowel.

'whisper	'master	'whiskey		de'spair	di'sturb	e'scape
'April	'citrus	'Audrey	'sacred	de'press	pro'tract	se'crete
'problem	'necklace (/'nɛklis/)			su'blime	se'clude	
'awkward	'Edward			re'quire		

(b)   clusters which do not occur word-initially; the syllable division is between the two consonants, no matter which is stressed.

'cap.tain 'tip.sy 'doc.tor 'can.dy 'tem.per 'pan.ther 'ran.cid
'car.pet 'mur.der 'sel.dom 'ar.my 'har.ness 'hel.met 'ear.ly
dic'ta(tion) con'demn im'pel in'sist sur'pass per'tain

The words above have consonant clusters in medial position which also occur finally in other words: *captain* has the same cluster as *apt*, *candy* has the same cluster as *hand*, *carpet* has the same cluster as *harp*, and so on. But medial clusters are more numerous and more varied than those which occur initially and finally. Consider these different types:

(i)   two obstruents of which one or both are voiced

        rugby   husband   obtain   subside

(ii)   two voiceless obstruents, not including /s/ or /t/ (Remember that one
        or both of these occur in almost every final cluster of obstruents.)

        napkin   option   fracture

(iii)   two fricatives

        esthetic   asphalt   diphtheria   (/dɪf'θiriə/ or /dɪp'θiriə/)

(iv)   an obstruent and a nasal

        acme   acne   arithmetic   dogma   magnet

(v)   a voiced fricative and a liquid

        gosling   every (/'ɛvri/)

(vi)   /t d θ/ followed by /l/

        butler   maudlin   athlete

(vii)   a nasal plus a voiced obstruent other than /d/ and /ǰ/ (Remember that
        these are the only voiced obstruents after a nasal in final position.)

        timber   finger   Denver   clumsy

(viii) a sequence of two nasals, or a nasal and a liquid

        enmity   amnesia   only   Henry

(ix)   /l/ before /r/ or /w/

        already   always

(x)   any consonant followed by /j/ when /j/ is not followed by /uu/

        onion   failure

In all these cases syllable division is between the two consonants.

(3)   three consonants, which can be divided into groups:

(a)   clusters which also occur initially; the first consonant must be /s/

        mistress   resplendent   distress

(b)   clusters which do not occur initially, and which can be subdivided:

     (i)   clusters in which the syllable division is after the first consonant
             (C.CC)

             an.thra(cite)   bel.fry   coun.try   pil.grim   pam.phlet

     (ii)   clusters in which syllable division is after the second consonant
             (CC.C)

             ant.ler   emp.ty   func.tion

     (iii)   clusters in which the second consonant, always /s/, may be
             ambisyllabic

             capˆstan   inˆstant   parˆsley   textile /tɛkˆstail/

6D   QUESTION: MEDIAL CLUSTERS

The type of cluster illustrated in (i), above, is probably more common than the
types in (ii) and (iii). In type (i) what kind of consonant is the middle one of
the three? What kind of consonants are the first and third, the ones next to the
vowels?

---

(4)   Four consonants; the second consonant is always /s/

      instrument   obstruct   express /ɛksprɛs/   exclaim /ɛkskleim/

Here /s/ is ambisyllabic in *instrument*, where the stressed vowel precedes; in
the other three words /s/ begins the stressed syllable.

6E PRACTICE: DIVIDING INTO SYLLABLES

Divide the following words into syllables.

pansy	doctor	sulfur
skeptic	ethnic	hatred
magnolia	orchestra	influenza
oxygen ('ɒksɪʤən)	technique	hypnosis
synthesis	spasmodic	linguistics

6.6 Borrowed words

In this chapter we have examined the patterns in which consonants go together in English words. But we should note that, as language changes over a period of time, word patterns are among the things that change. A thousand years ago English (in the form called Old English) had such words as *hnutu* 'nut,' *hrof* 'roof,' *cnawan* 'to know,' *fneosan* 'to sneeze,' with clusters of consonants which no longer occur in English words. At some time in history the first consonant in clusters like *hn-*, *hr-*, *kn-* became silent, and the cluster *fn-* changed to *sn-*.

A language can acquire new phoneme patterns, mostly by borrowing words from another language or other languages. In the English of today we find words, including names, borrowed from other languages, which have uncommon sequences of consonants, e.g. *schwa*, *shtick*, *Schlitz*, *tsunami*, *pueblo*. Can you think of others?

So we need to observe that, although there are general patterns in which consonants go together, there are also innovations in the patterns. Patterns do not remain static.

6.7 Omission and insertion of a consonant

In this chapter clusters of consonants have been presented as though they are invariable, but that is not really the case. The word *English*, for instance, may have the medial cluster /-ŋgl-/ but it may also be pronounced with just /-ŋl-/. When two morphemes come together in a word, as in *kindly* or *windmill*, new clusters of consonants are created – in these examples /-ndl-/ and /-ndm-/. Often such clusters are simplified – in these two examples by loss of /d/ in the middle of the clusters. We deal with more kinds of consonant-dropping like these in chapter 13. Here we want to deal with some instances of what may be called variable clusters. Consider the consonant clusters in these words:

dreamt tempt hamster Hampshire warmth Thompson redemption

Is there a /p/ in these words? It won't do to say that some of the words have a /p/ and others do not. It is more accurate to say that each word may or may not be pronounced with the voiceless stop that is made by bringing the lips together. In each word there is a voiced labial nasal, /m/, and there is another consonant which is voiceless, non-labial, and non-nasal. Between the two there may be a transitional /p/ which shares some of the features of the consonants on each side.

m	*(transition)*	*t, s, θ, ʃ*
+ voice	(– voice)	– voice
+ nasal	(– nasal)	– nasal
labial	(labial)	non-labial

The Old English word *aemtig* has become Modern English *empty*. Textbooks on the history of the English language sometimes cite this as a case of epenthesis, the insertion or addition of a consonant, in this case /p/. But was anything really added? In Old English, as in Modern English, there was no possible contrast between a cluster /-mt-/ and a cluster /-mpt-/. The only change is a matter of interpretation.

In a similar fashion, the following words contain the voiced dorsal nasal /ŋ/ and some voiceless non-dorsal, non-nasal consonant. Is there or isn't there a /k/ between them?

thanks   linked   defunct   puncture   function

Again, there is no contrast between such sequences as /ŋks/ and /ŋs/, /ŋkt/ and /ŋt/, /ŋkč/ and /ŋč/, /ŋkʃ/ and /ŋʃ/.

When we consider apical clusters, however, we find a different situation. Is there a contrast between /ns/ and /nts/?

prince – prints   tense – tents   sense – cents
correspondence – correspondents

Some speakers do, and others do not, make a distinction. For those who make such a distinction *prince* ends with /ns/ and *prints* ends with /nts/. Notice that /ns/ occurs within morphemes and /nts/ only across a morpheme boundary: /print # s/, etc.

6.8 Limits on vowel occurrences

However many vowels there are in English, or in any variety of English, they are not used as extensively as they might be. Theoretically, if a common canonical form for words is CVC, as in *cat, bed, lip, seem, shake*, etc., one might expect that all consonants would occur in initial position, all consonants would occur in final position, and all vowels in between. We have already seen that there are limitations on the consonants in initial and final position, and we shall now see that there are strong constraints on vowel occurrences. It happens that essentially all vowels can occur after all initial consonants but not all occur before all final consonants. For example, before final /ŋ/ or /ŋk/ there are only four possible vowels in native English words, illustrated by:

sing sang song sung
pink rank honk dunk

Foreign names like *Jung* or *Soong* or an odd interjection like *boing* or *oink* are exceptions to this statement, but they are the only kinds of exceptions. Native English words with final /ŋ/ or /ŋk/ can be preceded by only four vowels.

In itself this constraint is a trivial matter, of course, but such constraints affect the number of possible vowel contrasts which exist, and these contrasts have an effect on what people pronounce and, as we will examine in chapter 8, on what people have to perceive. With respect to pronunciation, what is the vowel of *sing*, for example? Is it the same as the vowel of *seat* or the vowel of *sit*? Different speakers will give different answers to the question, and why not? If there is no contrast between these two vowels before /ŋ/ – no possible contrast in meaning between something like /siiŋ/ and something like /sɪŋ/ – then there is obviously more room for variation in what is pronounced.

Before tongue-tip consonants in word-final position it is easy to find examples of a large number of different vowels. We illustrate with final /t d n s l/:

ii	beat	bead	bean	niece	feel
ɪ	bit	bid	bin	miss	fill
ei	bait	wade	bane	mace	fail
ɛ	bet	wed	Ben	mess	fell
æ	bat	bad	ban	mass	pal
ɒ	pot	rod	don	moss	doll
ɔɔ	taut	laud	dawn	sauce	ball
ʌ	putt	mud	dun	muss	dull
ou	boat	mode	bone	dose	bowl
ʊ	put	good	—	puss	full
uu	boot	food	boon	moose	fool
ai	bite	bide	dine	nice	file
au	bout	loud	down	mouse	foul
oi	Hoyt	void	coin	voice	foil

As we have seen, not all of these distinctions are maintained in all dialects.

The pronunciation of vowels before postvocalic /l/, as in *feel, field, bolt,* requires some special comment here. The checked vowels /ɪ ɛ æ ʊ ʌ ɒ/ sound approximately the same before /l/ as before other consonants, and the same is true of the low back /ɔɔ/. The high and mid free vowels, however, have, for most speakers, a slight centering offglide in this position. Compare the pronunciation of these vowels before /l/ and before /t/:

feel, field	[fiəl(d)]	feet	[fiⁱt]
fail, failed	[feəl(d)]	fate	[feⁱt]
pool, pooled	[puəl(d)]	toot	[tuᵘt]
bowl, bold	[boəl(d)]	boat	[boᵘt]

For some speakers words like *pool, bowl* become two-syllable pronunciations and thus rhyme with *cruel, Noel,* and the like.

The vowels designated /ai, au, oi/ vary dialectally before /l/ as elsewhere. For each there is a one-syllable and a two-syllable pronunciation:

file	[faⁱl], [faəl]	or	[faⁱəl]
foul	[faᵘl]	or	[faᵘəl]
foil	[fɔᵊl]	or	[fɔⁱəl]

When /l/ follows a free vowel and is itself followed by a vowel, as in the next group of words, there is no offglide. The /l/ may be more 'clear' or more 'dark,' depending on dialect.

feeling failing pooling holy calling silent howling toilet

Since some vowels have quite different allophones before final /l/ and in final position, there are possible audible differences in such examples as these:

sea lion	[.. iⁱlaⁱ ..]	seal island	[.. iᵊlaⁱ ..]
too lofty	[.. uᵘl ..]	tool office	[.. uᵊl ..]
Am I late	[.. aⁱleⁱt]	Aisle Eight	[aᵊleⁱt]

6.9   Free vowels and checked vowels

When we turn to other final consonants and consonant clusters we see that constraints can be best stated with reference to the two groups of vowels, the checked ones which typically occur in closed syllables, /ɪ ɛ æ ʊ ʌ ɒ/, and the free vowels which occur in closed and open syllables, /ii ei ai oi uu ou au aa ɔɔ/.

Free vowels occur before single consonants but only before a limited number of consonant clusters (within a single morpheme). The consonant clusters are /nt nd st ld nǰ/, as in:

paint pint point count
fiend find wound pound
feast chaste Christ moist joust boost boast
field wild bold
change lounge,

and less commonly before other clusters, such as /ps/ in *traipse*, /ks/ in *coax*, and /lt/ in *bolt*.

Just as there are constraints on what vowels may occur before certain consonants and consonant clusters, there are constraints on what consonants may occur after certain vowels, notably /ai au oi/. The vowel /oi/ occurs in final position (e.g. *toy*) and it may be followed by a consonant but there are only six consonants – all coronal consonants – which occur: /t/ (*exploit*), /d/ (*void*), /s/ (*voice*), /z/ (*noise*), /n/ (*coin*), and /l/ (*coil*); and two clusters, /st/ (*moist*) and /nt/ (*point*). There is no word which ends with /-oip/ or /-oič/ or /-oik/, for instance. Consonants which occur after /oi/ are all tongue-tip consonants. The constraint may be expressed in this formula:

Given: o i C (C) #
$$\qquad\qquad\quad \downarrow\quad \downarrow$$
Then: tip tip

6F **INVESTIGATING SOME CONSTRAINTS**

There are similar, but less rigid, constraints on the occurrence of consonants after /ai/ and /au/.

(a) Consider these 36 theoretically possible word-endings (/ai/ and /au/ plus 18 consonants). See if you can think of a word for each of these endings. If you can't think of one fairly quickly, the sequence probably doesn't occur.

-aip	-ail	-aup	-aul
-aib	-aič	-aub	-auč
-aif	-aiĭ	-auf	-auĭ
-aiv	-aiʃ	-auv	-auʃ
-aim	-aik	-aum	-auk
-ait	-aig	-aut	-aug
-aid	-ais	-aud	-aus
-aiθ	-aiz	-auθ	-auz
-aið	-ain	-auð	-aun

(b) What kind(s) of consonants occur after /au/?

Before most clusters of two or more final consonants only the checked vowels occur. The high-back vowel /ʊ/ is relatively rare, so that there are not usually more than five vowels occurring before most clusters of consonants. Some examples:

/-mp/	limp	hemp	camp	bump	stomp
/-pt/	crypt	inept	apt	corrupt	adopt
/-kt/	strict	sect	act	conduct	concoct
/-lf/	sylph	shelf	Ralph	gulf	golf

There are also five vowels contrasting before the next set of consonant clusters, but here /æ/ is replaced by /aa/ in RP and other dialects.

/-ft/ lift left draft tuft soft
/-sk/ risk desk mask dusk mosque

Before other clusters it may be hard to find even five vowels contrasting. Consider:

/-mf/ nymph
/-ts/ blitz
/-lǰ/ bilge bulge
/-lč/ filch belch mulch
/-lp/ help scalp pulp
/-lk/ milk elk talc sulk
/-lθ/ filth wealth
/-ls/ else pulse false
/-lʃ/ welsh
/-lb/ bulb

The set of vowels in English is not used to the potential limits.

6.10 Functional loads

One consequence of these limitations is a difference in the **functional load** of certain vowel contrasts. If we try to find minimal pairs for the high-back vowels /uu/ and /ʊ/, as in *pool* and *pull*, *suit* and *soot*, or even near-minimal pairs like *food* and *good*, we won't easily succeed. On the other hand, for the high-front vowels /ii/ and /ɪ/ there are numerous minimal pairs: *week/wick, team/Tim, reap/rip, seal/sill, beach/bitch*, etc. The contrast of /uu/ and /ʊ/ has a low functional load, and that of /ii/ and /ɪ/ has a high functional load.

Because the contrast of /uu/ and /ʊ/ has a low functional load, there is variation among speakers in the choice of one or the other of these vowels. The words below are pronounced by some people with the vowel of *food*, by others with the vowel of *good* – and they don't necessarily all have the same vowel for a given speaker or group of speakers.

root roof hoof hoop coop room broom

6.11 Summary

Speech is, in a way, a sequence of openings and closings of some part of the vocal tract, so that sequences of consonant, vowel, consonant, vowel (like the word *banana*) are perhaps the most fundamental kind of word pattern. Many languages, English among them, have patterns of consonant co-occurrence which are considerably more complex, but still there are constraints on what may occur. While the listing of such occurrences seems to be a matter of tedious detail, the *types* of occurrence are relatively few. People who know the language have a (largely unconscious) awareness of these patterns, which facilitates their perception and comprehension of what they hear. Students of English who come from different language backgrounds may have different amounts of difficulty in acquiring the pronunciation of certain sequences of English phonemes and speakers of English may have similar problems in learning another language.

In part, sequences of consonants follow a **scale of sonority**. Before the first (or only) vowel of a word two consonants are most likely to be obstruent + sonorant (e.g. /pr-, tw-, gl-, sn-/); if two obstruents occur, the first must be /s/; if three consonants occur, the first is /s/, the second /p t or k/, the third /r l or w/. In final position the sequence is sonorant + obstruent (e.g. /-mp, -rk, -ld/); if two sonorants co-occur, /r/ precedes /l/ and either may precede a nasal; if two obstruents co-occur, they are both voiceless and include either /s/ or /t/; sequences of three consonants show the same general kinds of constraints. In medial position more clusters and more kinds of clusters occur, but the same general limitations are seen: two obstruents usually agree in voice; in clusters of three consonants, the middle one is typically an obstruent while the first and third – the ones next to vowels – are sonorants.

As with other language matters, the phonotactics of English consonants is not static. There are variant ways in which certain clusters are actually pronounced, especially where no contrast is involved. And there are some novel clusters in recently borrowed words. There are likewise constraints on the occurrences of vowels. From a theoretical point of view these constraints mean that potential contrasts are not exploited as much as they might be; certain vowel contrasts have a low **functional load** while other contrasts have a high functional load. The limitations on contrasts also account for certain vowel variations among speakers. One particular constraint among vowels is seen in the distinction between **free vowels** and **checked vowels**. The former occur in word-final position and when followed by single consonants and a very small number of possible consonant clusters. The latter do not occur finally but can be followed by single consonants and consonant clusters.

6C   FEEDBACK

Voiceless obstruents   /s/ or /t/

6D   FEEDBACK

The middle consonant is an obstruent, the first and third are sonorants.

6E FEEDBACK

The most likely syllable divisions are these:

'pan.sy (/.zi/)	'doc.tor	'sul.fur
'skep.tic	'eth.nic	'haˆtred
mag'nol.ia (.jə/)	'or.cheˆstra	ˌin.flu'en.za
/'ɒk.sɪˆjən/	tech'nique	hyp'noˆsis
'syn.theˆsis	spas'moˆdic	lin'guiˆstics

6F FEEDBACK

(a) Sample words are given for the sequences which exist; a blank appears beside each non-occurring sequence.

/-aip/	pipe	/-ail/	file	/-aup/		/-aul/	howl
/-aib/	tribe	/-aič/		/-aub/		/-auč/	couch
/-aif/	wife	/-aiǰ/	oblige	/-auf/		/-auǰ/	gouge
/-aiv/	dive	/-aiʃ/		/-auv/		/-auʃ/	
/-aim/	time	/-aik/	like	/-aum/		/-auk/	
/-ait/	kite	/-aig/		/-aut/	out	/-aug/	
/-aid/	side	/-ais/	rice	/-aud/	loud	/-aus/	mouse
/-aiθ/		/-aiz/	rise	/-auθ/	south	/-auz/	rouse
/-aið/	blithe	/-ain/	dine	/-auð/	mouth	/-aun/	clown

Some of the words given, such as *oblige* and *blithe*, may be the only examples of the particular sequence.

(b) Only coronal consonants (apical and laminal) occur after /au/.

Notes

Gimson (1980) contains a similar account of the clusters of consonants which occur in word-initial, -medial, and -final positions. A different approach is that of Trnka (1966), which examines the sequences that exist for each phoneme in combination with every other phoneme that may follow it or precede it.

7

Consonant and Vowel Variation

As pointed out in chapter 1, speech is a dynamic process. It is a constant flowing of sound as the vocal organs keep changing positions and air is constantly modified as it passes through the vocal tract. However, the speaker and hearer are not aware of this dynamic process. For them speech represents elements of language – words and combinations of words – which are expressed as sequences of phonemes. Phonemes are abstract units which are realized as specific articulations, momentary gestures or positions of the vocal organs in the stream of speech. Since any phoneme occurs in different environments within the stream of speech, it has different pronunciations depending on what precedes or follows it. The actual pronunciations of a phoneme are called its **allophones**. All allophones of a phoneme have the same distinctive features but different non-distinctive features. Speakers of the language are aware of phonemes but generally have no awareness of the allophonic variants.

We are interested in two kinds of phenomena: the positions in which variations occur, and the kinds of variations that occur. Positions of occurrence can be stated in terms of:

1 phonemes that precede or follow – a feature of one phoneme may spread to a neighboring phoneme;
2 position in a word;
3 position in a syllable;
4 whether the syllable is stressed or unstressed.

We examine six kinds of variation here (sections 7.1 to 7.6), and then we consider the numerous variants of the most frequent consonant, /t/.

7.1   Variation in point of articulation

7.1a

The consonants /p b m f v/ together are classed as labials. More specifically, the fricatives /f v/ are labiodental: there is light contact between the lower lip and the upper front teeth, and air is squeezed out between lip and teeth. The stops and nasal /p b m/ are usually bilabial – the lower lip is in contact with the upper lip – but these consonants are likely to be labiodental when they precede /f/ or /v/. Compare:

comfort   symphony   obvious   cupful

with:

compass   sympathy   obnoxious   rupture

Consonants which are typically bilabial become labiodental when they are followed immediately by a labiodental consonant. We can express this in a formula:

labial ⟶ labiodental / _____ labiodental

The formula has three parts. Something with the feature [labial] (on the left side of the arrow) has a more specific or additional characteristic, labiodental (the term on the right side of the arrow) when it is in an environment, labiodental. The environment is indicated by the blank following the slant line and the term that goes with the blank. That may be a term following the blank, as here, or there may be one term before the blank and another term after it.

When two phonemes occurring in succession have the same place of articulation, as in *comfort, cupful,* and *obvious,* they are said to be **co-articulated**. (Instead of making /m/ labiodental before /f/, as in *comfort* and *symphony,* we may insert a transitional /p/ between the two consonants: /ˈkʌmpfərt, ˈsɪmpfəni/. This kind of insertion is discussed in section 6.8.)

7.1b

The consonants /t d θ ð s z n l/ are apical. More specifically, the flat fricatives /θ ð/ are apicodental, articulated with tongue-tip near or lightly touching the edge of the upper teeth. The other consonants are typically apicoalveolar; the tongue-tip touches or comes close to the alveolar ridge. However, this is not always the case.

7A   QUESTIONS ABOUT APICAL CONSONANTS

(a)   Examine your pronunciation of the words and phrases below to determine when you have apicodental articulation for the consonants indicated in italics

at bat   bi*d*   es*t*eem   i*s* it   ten   we*ll*
a*t* that   wi*d*th   es*t*hetic   i*s* this   te*n*th   wea*l*th

(b)   When there is apicodental articulation, what phoneme follows?
(c)   How would you complete this formula?

apical ⟶ apicodental / ____

7.1c

The same apical consonants may be articulated with tongue retracted, in a post-alveolar position, when they follow /r/ – in the speech of those who pronounce /r/ as a post-alveolar consonant. Compare the post-alveolar pronunciation of these consonants in

hur*t*   car*d*   hor*se*   tur*n*

with the apicoalveolar pronunciation in

hu*t*   co*d*   mo*ss*   to*n*
apical ⟶ postalveolar / r ____

7.1d

The nasal consonant /n/ is not apical but laminal when it precedes the laminoalveolar affricates /č/ and /ǰ/,

bra*n*ch   lu*n*ch   fla*n*ge   lu*n*ge

whereas it is apical in other positions, such as

te*n*t   le*n*d   *n*oo*n*

7.1e

The dorsal consonants /k g ŋ/ vary in articulation from a more fronted (palatal or prevelar) to a more back (velar) position.

7B   QUESTIONS ABOUT DORSAL CONSONANTS

(a)   In which of the following words is the more fronted articulation found?

    li*ck*   *c*ool di*g* *g*eese si*ng*
    loo*k* *k*ill   do*g* *g*oose so*ng*

(b)   What kind of vowel precedes or follows the more fronted articulation of these three consonants?

7.1f

The lateral consonant /l/ has various articulations, all with lateral curl so that air escapes over the sides of the tongue; there is usually contact between the centerline of the tongue and the roof of the mouth, but not necessarily. A so-called 'clear *l*' is produced with the front of the tongue high in the mouth and the back of the tongue low. A 'dark *l*' is made with the back of the tongue raised; the center is low; the front may be raised, so that the whole tongue has more or less the shape of a spoon, or the tongue-front may be down. However, the variation depends mostly on what position /l/ has in a syllable and only partly on what kind of phonemes follow.

7C   QUESTIONS ABOUT CLEAR AND DARK /l/

(a)   In the following words where do you pronounce a clear /l/ and where a dark /l/?

    *l*eaf   *l*et   p*l*ease   c*l*ean   a *l*ittle
    fee*l*   te*ll*   he*l*p   mi*l*k   a *l*ot
    fee*l*ing te*ll*ing me*l*on   ho*ll*ow   Pau*l*a
    simp*l*e simp*l*y probab*l*e probab*l*y

(b)   In what environments does each kind of /l/ occur? Consider two sorts of factors, position in syllable and the kind of phoneme that follows.

The first four of the paragraphs above, 7.1a to 7.1d, deal with assimilation in place of articulation; consonants are articulated in the position of phonemes which precede or which follow: labial becomes labiodental, apical becomes apicodental, apical becomes post-alveolar, dorsal becomes dorsopalatal. On the other hand, the alternation between clear and dark /l/, treated in 7.1e, depends more on position in syllable than on what kind of vowel (front or back) precedes or follows.

7.1g

Looking back at the material in paragraphs 7.1a to 7.1e, we see that two consonants in sequence within a word are likely to be coarticulated. Consider the
homorganic sequences of nasal + obstruent:

Bilabial:	temper timber compose combine
Labiodental:	comfort symphony
Apicodental:	month tenth
Apicoalveolar:	Santa sandal contain condemn
Laminoalveolar:	pinch sponge
Dorsopalatal:	tinker finger
Dorsovelar:	bunker hunger

There are exceptions to these homorganic clusters. Sequences of apicoalveolar
/n/ and labiodental /f v/ occur in *confident, infirm, convex, invent,* and the like.
Words such as *concrete, concur, income, inclose* may be pronounced with /-nk-/
or /-ŋk-/.

7.2   An example of mutual assimilation

The liquids /l/ and /r/ are usually frictionless; for their articulation the tongue
is not ordinarily close enough to the roof of the mouth for friction to occur.
After certain consonants, however, /r/ may be pronounced with friction between tongue and alveolar ridge when it follows /t/ or /d/, as in

train   strain   drain.

Compare the articulation of /r/ in these words with that in, for example,

rain   brain   praise   crane   grain

There is a groove in the tongue-tip for the articulation of /r/, and the
tongue-tip touches the alveolar ridge for /t d/. As the tongue is released, air
moves through the groove and friction results. Contact is generally farther
back for /t d/ than when these consonants precede vowels. So /t/ and /d/
are assimilated to /r/ in place of articulation (slightly farther back) and /r/ is
assimilated to /t d/ in becoming fricative. To be sure, the plosives /t d/ are
not fricative – do not have a feature [+ fricative] that can be spread to /r/.
But if we look at these manners of articulation on the vertical scale

plosives
fricatives
frictionless consonants
vowels and glides

we see that the change from frictionless /r/ to fricative /r/ is an approximation to the kind of articulation of /t d/. The change from frictionless to fricative is a movement towards the complete closure of /t d/.

The acoustic effect of /tr dr/ is close to that of /č ǰ/, as in *chain, Jane*. The essential difference between /tr dr/ and /č ǰ/ is that the groove is in the tip of the tongue for /tr dr/ and in the front of the tongue for /č ǰ/.

7.3   Variation in lip shape

A consonant preceding a rounded vowel or /w/ is most likely articulated with anticipatory lip-rounding. Compare

noose   goose   twin   too   doom

with

niece   geese   tin   tea   deem
consonant ⟶ [+ round] / ____ [+ round]

7.4   Variation in nasality

7D   QUESTIONS ABOUT NASALIZED VOWELS

In which of the following words is the vowel most likely to be nasalized? Why?

boot   boom   sick   sing   sink   camp   cap   late   lane   laid

7.5   Variation in onset and release

7.5a

In a very precise description of how a consonant is articulated it is usual to refer to the beginning, the middle, and the end of the articulation with the technical terms **onset, hold**, and **release**, respectively. When a consonant occurs between vowels, as in *habit, ready, eager*, it is easy to recognize the onset and the release, but when another consonant precedes or follows, the onset or release may be modified.

7E EXPLORING ONSET AND RELEASE OF STOPS

The following words and phrases show two stops (or a stop and an affricate) in sequence. Does each stop have a separate onset and release in such sequences?

captain	uptown	rubdown	jump down
actor	Magda	necktie	big turn
hot pad	what kind	nightgown	bad guy
hatcheck	meatball	red balloon	bad joke

7.5b

If an apical or dorsal stop is followed by /l/, the stop usually has lateral release. This is especially true for the apical stops: the tongue-tip touches the alveolar ridge shutting off the flow of air, then the sides of the tongue curl in while the tip remains in place. The same stops sometimes have nasal release: the velic opens to let air through the nasal cavity while the tongue-tip is still in contact with the alveolar ridge.

7F EXPLORING LATERAL AND NASAL RELEASE

Find examples of both lateral and nasal release in the following words and phrases.

widely fiddler hydrant handy kidney buddy
butter butler catnip atlas nightly mattress
Whitney good time good night good evening

7.5c

The onset of a voiced consonant may be voiceless when preceded by a voiceless consonant or when word-initial (preceded by zero in the word). Similarly, a voiced consonant may have a voiceless release when followed by a voiceless consonant or zero.

7G QUESTIONS ON THE ONSET OF SONORANT CONSONANTS

In which of the following words are /l r w/ most likely to have voiceless onset – that is, to begin with the vocal cords not yet vibrating?

blade play slow glass class
shrill crazy gravy dry try
twin dwindle Gwen queen swell

7H QUESTIONS ON THE ONSET AND RELEASE OF VOICED OBSTRUENTS

The voiced obstruents /b d ǰ g v ð z ʒ/ may be voiced throughout their articulation, or they may have voiceless onset, or they may have voiceless release. They are illustrated below in four positions of occurrence. Which variants are most likely to occur in which positions?

Initial:	buy die jade gate vast that zoom
Intervocalic:	rubber ready magic buggy liver bother easy measure
Final:	rob rod budge bug love smooth fizz rouge
Before voiceless consonants:	obtain bedtime is cold big smile

7.5d

Voiceless stops in English have a kind of release called **aspiration**. In some articulations of English /p t k/ the vocal cords are close together and not vibrating; as the lip, tongue-tip, or tongue-back is released, air is squeezed between vocal folds, producing a sort of *h*-sound, [pʰ tʰ kʰ]. This happens in some positions but not all.

71   EXPERIMENT WITH ASPIRATION

Hold a small strip of paper loosely in front of your mouth as you say the words below; if the stop is aspirated, the paper should flutter as air is expelled; an unaspirated stop does not cause such movement. (The fluttering is especially noticeable with an aspirated labial stop, [pʰ].) Seven positions of occurrence are illustrated below. In which positions does aspiration occur? In one of these positions there may be free variation.

Initially in a stressed syllable:

pill   present   pleasure   till   treasure   kill   quiver   clever

Initially in an unstressed syllable:

potato   platoon   today   tremendous   canoe   Quebec

After initial /s/:

spill   splint   still   street   skill   squint   stiletto

Word-medially in a stressed syllable:

appoint   apply   attend   attract   account   acquire

Word-medially in an unstressed syllable:

happy   temper   whisper   octopus
water   shelter   mister   sanity
lucky   anchor   whiskers   medical

Word-finally after /s/:

lisp   list   risk

Word-finally after a vowel or other consonant:

cup   camp   hat   heart   look   milk

Aspiration of a voiceless stop means that as the release of the lower lip, tongue-tip, or tongue-back is effected, the non-vibrating vocal cords are close enough together that air is squeezed between them. Another variation that affects the voiceless stops /p t k/ and /č/ as well is due to a different action of the vocal cords. These consonants may be glottalized: the vocal cords come together just before, or simultaneously with, the closure that occurs in the oral cavity. Glottalization is most frequent when stops are syllable-final before a following stop, fricative, or nasal.

Sleep [$^{?}$p] tight   quite [$^{?}$t] nice   take [$^{?}$k] sides

7.6   Variation in length

7.6a

When two instances of the same consonant come together, there is only one onset and one release; the hold lasts as long as two consonants. In English two instances of the same consonant can only happen at a morpheme boundary, when the first morpheme ends in a consonant and the second morpheme begins with the same consonant. Compare *bookcase* and *bookish*, *home-made* and *domain*.

misspent   ten nights   love Vickie
bad day   ripe peach   unknown

7J   QUESTION: TWO CONSONANTS IN SEQUENCE

What happens when two consonants which differ only in voice come together?

soup bowl   red tie   leg cramp   five fingers

7.6b

Sonorants (sonorant consonants and all vowels) vary in length according to what, if anything, follows.

7K QUESTION: LENGTH OF SONORANTS

Each set of three words below has one phoneme in three different positions of occurrence. Decide where the phoneme is short, where longer, where longest.

seed, seat, see   lute, lewd, Lou
bent, bend, Ben   belt, weld, bell
fierce, fears, fear   tempt, hemmed, hem

7.7 Multiple variation for /t/

So far we have been dealing with kinds of variation that apply to groups of phonemes – voiceless stops, apical consonants, all vowels, etc. In this section we take a look at a single consonant and note: (1) its various pronunciations, especially as they are determined by occurrence in tonic and atonic syllables; (2) how these variations affect its contrast with /d/ and other consonants. We have already seen, in section 7.5b, that /t/ and /d/ have nasal release before /n/ and lateral release before /l/. In 7.5d we noted that /t/, like /p/ and /k/, has aspirated release in some positions and not in others. We repeat some of these observations below and then consider two other variants, /t/ as a weak tap and as a glottal stop.

(a) /t/ is aspirated, [tʰ], before a stressed vowel.

   tie   retire   absentee   guitar   contain

In such minimal pairs as *time* and *dime*, *train* and *drain*, the difference is between a consonant which is voiceless and aspirated versus a consonant which is voiced and unaspirated. Phonologically we say that the distinctive difference is in voice – voiceless versus voiced – but the aspiration on /t/ and the lack of aspiration on /d/ may be the more helpful cue in determining what sounds we, as hearers, actually perceive.

(b) /t/ is typically aspirated in initial position before an unstressed vowel, though the aspiration is weaker here.

   today   Tibet   tenacious   tuberculosis

Note that there are no minimal pairs with /d/ in this position.

(c) In final position /t/ may or may not be released, as with other stop consonants. If there is release, there may or may not be aspiration. The more emphatic and energetic the speech, the greater the likelihood of aspiration. Without aspiration the most obvious perceptual difference in such pairs as the following is not in the consonants themselves but in the length of the vowel preceding.

    coat, code   wet, wed   seat, seed
    [koᵘt, koːᵘd wɛt, wɛːd   siˈt, siːˈd]

In such a pair as *tight*, *tide* the difference in vowel nuclei may be more than a matter of length; see the next paragraph.

(d) In North America especially, and to a lesser extent in other parts of the English-speaking world, speakers produce a voiced tap of the tongue tip, [ɾ], for /t/ and /d/ when these consonants occur between a stressed vowel and an unstressed vowel. The tongue-tip brushes quickly against the alveolar ridge; the tongue does not remain in place long enough for air pressure to build up behind it, as in the usual articulation of a stop.

    matter   city   water   ladder   wedding   medical
    [ˈmæɾɚ   ˈsiɾi ˈwɔɾɚ   ˈlæɾɚ   ˈwɛɾiŋ   ˈmɛɾi-k-il]

The tapped consonant may be preceded by /r/; the articulation of /-rt-/ is a forward flap of the tongue-tip against the alveolar ridge, [ɾ].

    party   mortar   artist   turtle   accordion
    [ˈpʰaɾi ˈmɔɾɚ   ˈaɾɨ-st ˈtʰɝɾəl əˈkʰɔɾiən]

Thus Canadians and Americans may not distinguish such pairs of words as the following:

    atom   shutter   petal   coated   conceited
    Adam   shudder   pedal/peddle   coded   conceded

If a distinction is made, the difference is not in the medial consonants themselves but in the vowels which precede. Generally this means that the vowel is longer before the tap which represents /d/ and shorter before the tap that stands for /t/.

(e) Some North Americans have a nasalized tap, [ɾ̃], as the articulation of the sequence /nt/ in the same position, between a stressed vowel and an unstressed vowel.

    Atlantic   county   dainty   twenty   winter
    [ætˈlæɾ̃ik ˈkaᵘɾ̃i   ˈdeˈɾ̃i   ˈtwɛɾ̃i   ˈwɪɾ̃ɚ]

Note that there is no tap, but a full stop, when /t/ and /d/ are preceded by any consonant other than /r/ or /n/ – and for /d/ when it is preceded by /n/.

actor shelter optical master building fender

And /t/ and /d/ are full stops when followed by /r/.

citrus hatred mattress patron Audrey

(f) In words like the following, where /t/ occurs between unstressed vowels, the consonant may be a tap or a stop.

cavity charity property
negative positive relative
diameter heritage janitor senator

Perhaps the more common the word and the more frequently it is used, the more likely that /t/ will be articulated as a tap, and, on the other hand, the more formal the speech the less likely is the tap pronunciation.

(g) The next words are different from those in group (f). In the words that follow, /t/ is always pronounced with aspiration in Canada and the United States, as in the rest of the English-speaking world.

agitate meditate appetite comatose
longitude gratitude vicissitude
hereditary secretary dormitory territory

In the words of group (f) /t/ occurs in a weak syllable and may be tapped or aspirated; in the words of group (g) /t/ occurs in a strong syllable and is aspirated.

(h) The realization of /t/ may be a glottal stop [ʔ] or a simultaneous – or nearly simultaneous – double closure, the vocal cords coming together while the tongue-tip makes contact with the alveolar ridge, [ʔt] or [tʔ]. It would take some space to tell the phonetic environments and the geographic dialects in which these realizations occur. It was noted in section 7.5 that /p t c k/ may be glottalized in syllable-final position before a following stop, fricative, or nasal. In Cockney, the speech of working-class Londoners, this glottalization goes further: /p t k/ are likely to be glottalized in absolute final position: *Stop, Wait, Look*; and in rapid speech they may be replaced by a glottal stop. In Cockney an intervocalic /t/ is realized as a glottal stop alone: *water* ['wɔʔə], *city* ['sɪʔi]. In other parts of England, in Scotland, in North America, and in the southern hemisphere the glottalized /t/ or the glottal stop alone are found, variably, in these environments:

(i) before syllabic /n/ [n̩] – *button   curtain   shirt 'n' tie* – especially when /t/ is preceded by non-syllabic /n/ as well as followed by syllabic /n/ – *mountain   maintenance   sentence*

(ii)   before syllabic /l/ [l̩] – *bottle   total   startle   that'll do*
(iii)   syllable-final before any consonant – *treatment   Scotland   brightness*

7.8   Some questions of perception

  pill   till   kill   bill   dill   gill

In the first three words the initial consonant is voiceless and aspirated, which means that the vocal cords are not vibrating when the consonant articulator is released and they do not begin to vibrate for several centiseconds after the release. The initial consonants of the second three words are voiced, probably with voiceless onset, and unaspirated; the vocal cords begin to vibrate when the release takes place. Considering these plosive consonants as part of the whole sound system of the language, we have viewed the voiceless/voiced contrast as the distinctive difference. But which feature is actually most important in enabling us to distinguish one stop from its counterpart? Probably the difference in voice onset time, aspirated versus unaspirated.

  cap   cat   luck   rich   safe   ice
  cab   cad   lug   ridge   save   eyes

In the words of the first line the final consonant is voiceless and follows a vowel which is phonetically short. In the words of the second line the final consonant is voiced, probably with voiceless release, and follows a vowel which is longer in articulation. What is the real cue in our hearing the words of each pair, the voicing of the final consonant or the duration of the vowel which precedes it?

7.9   Summary

Every language has a limited inventory of phonemes, the units of its sound system. Each phoneme is manifested, or articulated, in various ways in the stream of speech. The principal kinds of variation have been discussed under five headings: variation in place of articulation, in nasality, in lip-rounding, in onset and release, and in duration. Most of these variations may be seen as ways in which the phoneme is adjusted to its environment through assimilation. A feature spreads from one phoneme to a neighboring phoneme: the allophone is more fronted or more backed depending on the articulation of an adjacent phoneme; a vowel is nasalized before a nasal consonant; a consonant has lip-rounding before a rounded vowel; a stop has lateral release before /l/, and so on. These variations, we may say, are 'natural'. But not all variations can be called natural and not all can be explained as assimilation. English has a clear /l/ in the onset of syllables and a dark /l/ in the coda; this is a characteristic of English that has nothing to do with the nature of neighboring phonemes.

Then, consider these facts: voiceless stops have aspirated release at the onset of strong syllables and in word-initial position; the same voiceless stops may be pronounced with simultaneous closure of the glottis (that is, the vocal cords close and open at the same time closure is made with the lower lip, the apex, or the dorsum), and there may be a glottal stop alone as the realization of the phoneme /t/. These facts point to a sort of hierarchy among features. The larynx controls the flow of the breath stream and the way it controls the air affects the articulations made in the mouth. The vocal cords are often closed together when a voiceless stop is articulated in the mouth (glottalization) and they are released with a kind of friction (aspiration) when energy is needed for the next syllable. Features associated with the larynx affect oral articulations. The description of this hierarchy has been called Feature Geometry (see the Notes at the end of this chapter).

A system or structure is made up of elements, units, which have analogous relationships with one another. The contrast between two of the units is the same as the contrast between two other units. Among English consonant phonemes the analogous relations are fairly easy to recognize: /p/ is to /b/ as /t/ is to /d/ as /k/ is to /g/; /b/ is to /m/ as /d/ is to /n/ as /g/ is to /ŋ/, and so on. The distinctive features of a phoneme are the characteristics in which it differs from other phonemes of the system. When we say that /t/ is a voiceless apical stop, we are telling how it differs from /d/, from /p/ and /k/, and from /n/. In its different occurrences, its different allophones, /t/ or any phoneme has various non-distinctive features. From the point of view of a system these 'extra' features do nothing. In terms of human perception, however, the non-distinctive features may be all-important.

7A   FEEDBACK

(a)   at that, width, esthetic, is this, tenth
(b)   /θ/ or /ð/
(c)   apical ⟶ apicodental / ____ apicodental

7B   FEEDBACK

(a)   lick, kill, dig, geese, sing
(b)   The more forward articulation occurs when a dorsal consonant precedes or follows a front vowel.

   dorsal ⟶ dorsopalatal / front vowel

(When there is no blank to the right of the slant line, as in the rule above, the context is understood to mean either before or after the determining factor; here, the rule says that a dorsal consonant is dorsopalatal when it occurs either before or after a front vowel.)

7C   FEEDBACK

Answers may vary, but in general the darker /1/ occurs in post-vowel position (*feel, tell, help, milk*) and when syllabic (*simple, probable*). A clearer /1/ is heard in pre-vowel position (*leaf, let, please, clean, simply, probably*). Between vowels the articulation may vary somewhat, the clearer phone occurring in the neighborhood of front vowels (*feeling, telling, melon, a little*) and the darker one near back vowels (*hollow, Paula, a lot*). In Ireland and Scotland clear articulation is the rule in all positions.

7D   FEEDBACK

  boom   sing   sink   camp   lane

A vowel is nasalized before a nasal consonant.

  Vowel ⟶ [+ nasal] / ____ [+ nasal]

Note that it is possible to pronounce *camp, plant, tank*, for example, without the nasal consonants, /m n ŋ/, and still be understood so long as the vowels are nasalized. Exactly this sort of articulation seems to be common in rapid speech.

7E   FEEDBACK

The first stop does not have a release separate from the following stop. In *actor*, for instance, the tongue-tip is in place for the /t/ before the tongue-back is released from the position of /k/ articulation. This is, in a way, another instance of fuzzy transition between syllables. Compare French *acteur*, in which [k] is clearly released before the onset of [t].

   Note that when an affricate precedes another consonant the affricate is clearly released – that is, the stop has clear fricative release: *each boy, page ten, which card*.

7F   FEEDBACK

Lateral release: widely   fiddler   butler   atlas
Nasal release: kidney   Whitney   good   night

  t, d (k, g) ⟶ lateral release / ____ l
  t, d ⟶ nasal release / ____ n

7G   FEEDBACK

  play   slow   class;   shrill   crazy   try;   twin   queen   swell
    l, r, w ⟶ voiceless onset / voiceless consonant ____

7H   FEEDBACK

Voiceless onset is usual in initial position; voiceless release in final position and before a voiceless consonant; voiced throughout between voiced segments.

$$\text{voiced obstruent} \longrightarrow \begin{cases} \text{voiceless onset } / \text{ \#} \underline{\hspace{1cm}} \\ \text{voiceless release } / \underline{\hspace{1cm}} \text{ \#} \\ \text{voiceless release } / \underline{\hspace{1cm}} \text{ vl. C} \end{cases}$$

7I FEEDBACK

Aspirated   word-initially in a stressed syllable
             word-initially in an unstressed syllable
                  (though the aspiration is weaker)
             word-medially in a stressed syllable
             word-finally after /s/
Aspirated or unaspirated (free variation)
             word-finally except after /s/
Unaspirated in other positions

$$\text{p, t, k} \longrightarrow \text{aspiration} \quad / \quad \begin{bmatrix} \text{\# } \underline{\hspace{1cm}} \text{ (C) V} \\ \cdots \underline{\hspace{1cm}} \text{ (C) stressed V} \\ \text{s} \underline{\hspace{1cm}} \text{ \#} \\ \text{V (C)} \underline{\hspace{1cm}} \text{ \# [optional]} \end{bmatrix}$$

7J FEEDBACK

There is one onset, one release, and the duration of two consonants, with voice changing during the hold.

7K FEEDBACK

short	*longer*	*longest*
seat	seed	see
lute	lewd	Lou
bent	bend	Ben
fierce	fears	fear
belt	weld	bell
tempt	hemmed	hem

Sonorants are shortest before a voiceless consonant, longer before a voiced consonant, and longest in final position. The comparison could be carried further; sonorants are typically shorter before fricatives than before stops, for instance.

Notes

In detailing allophonic variation the following have been especially helpful: Jones (1976), Kurath (1967), Hubbell (1950).

   Useful introductions to the theory of Feature Geometry are Clements (1985) and Keyser and Stevens (1994).

8

Some Consequences of Phonotactics

In chapter 6 we discussed constraints on the occurrence of consonants, noting that some sequences of consonants are possible in English while other sequences do not occur and that certain clusters of consonants are possible within a word but not in word-final position. In this chapter we shall see that certain morphemes have different forms, depending on where they occur in a word and what consonants they follow.

8.1 Consonant clusters and some grammatical suffixes

The suffix which forms the past tense of regular verbs is written -*(e)d*, as in *looked* and *baked*. The pronunciation is /t/, /d/, or /ɪd/, depending on the last phoneme of the verb to which the suffix is added: for example, *kicked* /kɪkt/, *begged* /bɛgd/, *waited* /weitɪd/. Though these three are different forms, they express the same meaning, 'past tense'. The unit of meaning which we label Past Tense is a **morpheme**. Some morphemes are always expressed in the same way; other morphemes, such as the one we are discussing now, have two or more forms, called its **allomorphs**. /t/, /d/, and /ɪd/ are three allomorphs of the morpheme Past Tense – and there are other allomorphs seen in irregular verbs.

8A   EXPLORATION: REGULAR PAST TENSE

(1)   The verbs listed in the exhibit below illustrate all the consonants and some vowels in word-final position. Write /t/, /d/, or /ɪd/ after each verb according to the pronunciation of the suffix. Then figure out the rule which determines the pronunciation.

step	wait	reach	look
rub	need	budge	hug
laugh	race	finish	hum
love	breathe	raise	massage
fan	play	annoy	gnaw

Rule:
(a) The regular past tense suffix is pronounced /ɪd/ after verbs that end
     with _____ or _____ ;
(b) it is pronounced /t/ after _____ ;
(c) it is pronounced /d/ after all other phonemes.
(Note the importance of stating the rule in this order. First, the smallest group
is identified, then the next group in size, and finally the largest group can be
identified simply as 'all others'.)

(2) The suffix which forms the plural number of regular nouns, written *-(e)s*,
is pronounced /s/ or /z/ or /ɪz/, depending on the last phoneme of the noun
to which the suffix is added. Thus *cats* ends with /s/, *dogs* with /z/, and
horses with /ɪz/. These three forms are allomorphs of the morpheme Plural
Number (which also has irregular allomorphs).

8B   EXPLORATION: REGULAR PLURAL NUMBER

The nouns shown below illustrate all consonants and some vowels in word-
final position. Write /s/, /z/, or /ɪz/ after each noun according to the
pronunciation of the suffix, and then determine the rule which tells in what
positions each of the three variants occurs.

rib	bed	bridge	leg
cuff	smith	hive	lathe
kiss	wish	rose	garage
arm	pin	ring	bell
tree	day	law	car

Rule:
(a) The regular plural suffix is pronounced /ɪz/ after _____ ;
(b) it is pronounced /s/ after _____ ;
(c) it is pronounced /z/ after all other phonemes.

(3) The regular possessive suffix, as in *Tom's* and *Jerry's*, also has three
variant pronunciations, /s/, /z/, and /ɪz/. This is a different morpheme,
Possessive, which has the same three regular allomorphs as the Plural
Number morpheme. (Possessive has no irregular allomorphs.) Here are some
representative nouns, ending with most of the possible consonants and some
vowels.

Chris   Rose   Mr Fish   Ms Finch   the judge
Hope   Robert   Dick   Ralph   Beth
Bob   Ted   Peg   Steve   Tom   Ann   Sue   Joe   Mary

8C   QUESTION: POSSESSIVE

Is the form of the possessive suffix chosen by the same rule that applies to the regular plural suffix?

(4)   Another suffix is the so-called 'third person singular present' of verbs, as in (he) *likes*, (she) *loves*, (it) *misses*, with the same three variants, /s, z, ɪz/. Examine the verbs in the exhibit of paragraph (1), above, and determine the pronunciation of the suffix after each one.

8D   QUESTION: THIRD PERSON PRESENT

Is the variation in this suffix determined by the same rule as for plural number?

(5)   The verb form *is* is often contracted, as in *The milk's here, The coffee's boiling, The glass's broken.* The auxiliary verb *has* undergoes the same kind of contraction, as in *Steven's been working, Alice's told me*, and so on.

8E   QUESTIONS: REDUCED 'IS' AND 'HAS'

What are the variant pronunciations for the contracted forms of *is* and *has*? What are the determining factors?

8E   FEEDBACK AND DISCUSSION

The variants are the same, /s, z, ɪz/. The rule is the same as for the /s, z, ɪz/ suffixes.

Note that the contraction of *has* occurs only when *has* is an auxiliary verb. Most speakers of English don't make such a contraction when *has* is a main verb, as in *Sue has an appointment at two o'clock, The violin has a broken string.* Of course, contraction can take place in the equivalent *Sue has got an appointment at two o'clock, The violin has got a broken string.*

There is one difference between the suffixes (plural, possessive, third person verb forms) and the verbs *is* and *has*. The latter have the forms /s, z, ɪz/ if contraction occurs, but contraction is optional. There is no such option for the suffixes.

In discussing these variations, /d, t, ɪd/ and /z, s, ɪz/, we have so far only described what the variants are and in what environments they occur. But if we look a bit further, we can observe that the choice is partly determined by phonotactic constraints or, we may say, by what is 'natural' in the English sound system.

The variant /ɪd/ occurs after /t/ and /d/: *waited, needed*; /t/ occurs after voiceless obstruents except /t/: *slipped, kicked, kissed*, etc; /d/ occurs elsewhere – after voiced obstruents except /d/ – *rubbed, hugged, buzzed*, etc. – and after all sonorants – nasals, liquids, and vowels – for example, *fanned, called, played*.

Thus /d/ is the basic, or underlying, form of this morpheme, the suffix which indicates past tense for regular verbs. It occurs in more environments than the other two variants and, more importantly, the other two are the result of necessary adjustments. English words do not end with two identical consonants like /tt/ or /dd/ or with consonants that differ only in voice like /td/ or /dt/; the past tense of *wait* /weit/ and *need* /niid/ can't be */weitd/ and */niidd/. Such consonant sequences occur in some languages but not in English. English requires the insertion of a vowel between /t/ or /d/ and the suffix /d/.

Likewise, English words do not end with two obstruents which differ in voice: the past tense forms of *skip, kick, kiss* can't be */skɪpd, kɪkd, kɪsd/. An adjustment is made: /d/ becomes voiceless /t/ to match the preceding phoneme.

Finally, we note that /d/ occurs after voiced obstruents, where we would not expect /t/ to occur, but it also occurs after sonorants – e.g. *fanned, called, played* – where /t/ and /ɪd/ are theoretically possible: /fænt/ and /fænɪd/ are pronounceable. Clearly /d/ is the basic form of this morpheme.

To treat the matter within the framework of generative phonology we say that the suffix has a single underlying form occurring with all regular verbs. We represent the suffix as //#d//. The surface forms, or actual pronunciations, of the suffix are the results of two adjustments, or **rules**, which apply to the underlying form in order to make it pronounceable within the general sound system of English. The rules are:

Vowel insertion: after /t/ or /d/ insert /ɪ/ before //#d//.

Voice assimilation: after a voiceless consonant change //#d// to /t/.

We show these changes as derivations of surface forms from underlying forms. In the underlying forms the suffix is identical.

Underlying forms	//#pɛt#d#	#kɪk#d#	#bɛg#d#//
Vowel insertion	ɪ		
Voice assimilation		t	
Surface forms	/pɛtɪd	kɪkt	bɛgd /

8F   QUESTION: GENERATIVE TREATMENT OF PAST TENSE MORPHEME

Could the order of the two rules be changed so that the voice assimilation rule takes effect before the vowel insertion rule? Would the results be the same with either order for the rules?

The alternation of /s, z, ɪz/ is exactly parallel to the /t, d, ɪd/ alternation. /z/ is the basic form of the different suffixes which have this alternation – regular plural, possessive, third person singular. This /z/ can't occur immediately after a sibilant, /s z ʃ ʒ č ǰ/, so the insertion of a vowel is necessary. /z/ also can't occur after a voiceless obstruent, /p t k f θ/, so a different adjustment is required, a voice assimilation.

Vowel insertion: Between a final sibilant and the suffix //#z// insert /ɪ/.

Voice assimilation: After a final voiceless obstruent change //#z// to /s/.

Here are three sample derivations:

Underlying forms	//#h ɔrs#z#	kæt#z#	#dɒg#z#//
Vowel insertion	ɪ		
Voice assimilation		s	
	————	——	————
Surface forms	/h ɔrsɪz	kæts	dɒgz/

The vowel insertion rules for the two suffixes are very similar, so they can be put together as a single rule:

Between a final apical stop and //#d// and between a final sibilant and //#z// insert /ɪ/.

It is even easier to conflate the two voice assimilation rules:

When two obstruents occur together in word-final position, they must agree in voice; assimilation is progressive.

(We say that the 'basic' or underlying form of the plural suffix is //#z//; this is also the underlying form of the possessive suffix and the third person singular suffix in verbs. But we cannot say that *is* and *has* have this underlying form, even though they have the same possible pronunciations as the suffixes. The underlying forms are the full, uncontracted forms.)

8G   Exercise: final clusters

The preceding section has dealt with grammatical suffixes which may be single consonants, /z/, /s/, /d/, /t/, in the surface forms. Each of these may be added to a word which already ends in one or more consonants, producing a cluster of consonants. In some instances the consonant cluster may coincide with a cluster which can occur at the end of a word without a suffix; for example the words *lapse* and *laps* end with the same consonant cluster and in fact are homophonous, and the same is true of *chaste* and *chased*.

Another single-consonant suffix is -/θ/, which is actually two derivational morphemes, the Ordinal Number suffix which occurs in *fourth* and *tenth* and the Abstract Noun suffix of *warmth* and *growth*

All the following words end with a suffix pronounced /t/, /d/, /s/, /z/, or /θ/. In each case the suffix is added to a word which ends in one or more consonants. After each word write in phoneme symbols for the cluster of consonants. Then decide if that consonant cluster also occurs at the end of monomorphemic words and, if so, give an example. The first two are done for you.

packs	/ks/	Yes, *tax*	bridged
bags	/gz/	No	coughed
lacked			cuffs
lagged			loves
breathed			fourth
rapped			fifth
clips			sixth
rubs			width
rubbed			depth
beds			length
brushed			warmth
shoved			tenth

8.2 Morpheme variation

Some morphemes – indeed most morphemes – are always pronounced the same way; for example, *dog, dirt, duty*. Other morphemes have two or more forms, allomorphs, occurring in different environments. This is true of grammatical morphemes such as Past Tense and Plural Number, and it is also true of some lexical morphemes; for example, *thief* /θiif/ has an alternate form, or allomorph, *thiev-* /θiiv/ before the plural ending: *thieves* /θiivz/; it has another allomorph *thef-* /θɛf/ which occurs in *theft* /θɛft/; the auxiliary verb *have* /hæv/ has an alternate form *'ve* /v/ which occurs in contractions like *I've* and *we've*. Some allomorphic variations are due to phonotactic constraints, and we examine some of them below. Other allomorphic variations depend on style of speaking, like *have* and *'ve*; these are discussed in chapter 13. Other variations, like *thief, thiev-, thef-*, are due to neither phonotactic constraints nor style of speech, and we deal with them in chapter 14.

8.2a

Some morphemes end in clusters of consonants which are permitted in word-medial position, with a vowel following, but not in word-final position. The word *entrance*, for example, obviously has a suffix *-ance* added to a base *entr-*, which must be the same morpheme that occurs alone as the word *enter*. We see similar variation in *angry* and *anger*, *cylindrical* and *cylinder*. Each of the three base morphemes has two allomorphs.

Before a vowel	*Independent word*
/ɛntr-	ɛntər/
/æŋgr-	æŋgər/
/sɪlɪndr-	sɪlɪndər/

Instead of *entrance* speakers of English could say *enterance*, a sequence of phonemes that is pronounceable but which happens not to be the standard form. On the other hand, they could not say **entr* instead of *enter*, since that is contrary to phonotactic norms. To describe the facts of alternation we say that the basic or underlying form of the morpheme is //ɛntr// and that there is a rule which adds /ə/ where it must be added – between a consonant and /r/ in word-final position. Analogous statements can be made for the other two base morphemes: their underlying forms are //æŋgr// and //sɪlɪndr//, respectively, and the same schwa insertion rule applies to them.

The schwa insertion rule can be stated in prose or as a formula, but before stating it in any fashion we need to make another observation. Consider these words:

entering   angered   cylinders

Here the schwa is present even though /r/ is not final. We must reformulate our statement: a schwa is inserted between a consonant and /r/ in final position or before certain suffixes. Three suffixes are illustrated, *-ing*, *-d*, and *-z*. These are **neutral suffixes**, attached to independent words after any necessary adjustments, such as schwa insertion, are made to that word. If we use the symbol # to represent a word boundary and the symbol + for a word-internal boundary between a base and a non-neutral suffix, the essential information about some items we have discussed can be shown this way:

#enter#   #anger#   #cylinder#
#enter#ing#   #anger#ed#   #cylinder#s#
#entr+ance#   #angr+y#   #cylindr+ical#

And now we are ready to state the rule, in prose and as a formula:

Insert schwa between a consonant and //r// when a word boundary follows.

$$0 \longrightarrow ə \ / \ C\_\_\_\_r\#$$

We show the effects of this rule as a set of derivations:

Underlying forms	//#ɛntr#	#ɛntr#d#	#ɛntr+əns#//
Schwa insertion	ə	ə	
Surface forms	/ɛntər	ɛntərd	ɛntrəns/

8H   PRACTICE: BASES IN -CR

The words below are like *entrance*, with a suffix attached to a base. Strip off the suffix and show the underlying form in ordinary spelling (like *entr-*) and the surface form of the base word (like *enter*).

hungry   disastrous   theatrical
wintry   monstrous   central

8.2b

The words *fiddle*, /fɪdəl/, and *fiddler*, /fɪdlər/, must have the same underlying form, except for the suffix in the second word: //#fɪdl// and //#fɪdl+ər#//. The insertion rule that applies to the base word without a suffix is similar to the insertion rule introduced in section 8.2a.

$0 \longrightarrow ə \;/\; C\_\_\_\_l\#$

8I   PRACTICE: BASES IN -CL

The words below are like *fiddler*. Take away the suffix of each and give the base word, in its surface form, that corresponds to *fiddle*.

muffler   peddler   suckling
juggler   sampler   twinkling

8.2c

The words *rhythmic* and *rhythm* have the same relationship to each other as *entrance* and *enter*, the same relationship as *fiddler* and *fiddle*. There are not many such pairs of words with morpheme-final -Cm; two of them are *cataclysmic*, *cataclysm* and *prismatic*, *prism*. But there are somewhat more words like *chasm*, *plasm*, and those with the suffix *-ism*. The same rule applies to all of them:

$0 \longrightarrow ə \;/\; C\_\_\_\_m\#$

8.2d

A rule should be as general as possible. In sections 8.2a, 8.2b, and 8.2c three similar rules have been introduced. They are not three different rules but parts of a single rule, which should be stated as such:

$$0 \longrightarrow \partial \; / \; C \underline{\quad\quad} \begin{Bmatrix} r \\ l \\ m \end{Bmatrix} \#$$

or, since /r l m/ are sonorant consonants, in this form:

$$0 \longrightarrow \partial \; / \; C \underline{\quad\quad} [+ \text{cons}, + \text{son}] \#$$

8.2e

Now we turn to a different kind of adjustment rule. Consider these items:

autumn – autumnal   damn – damnable   hymn – hymnal
column – columnist   condemn – condemnation   solemn – solemnize

In each pair of words the first is a simple base and the second word has the same base plus a suffix. The underlying form of each base must be the same with or without the suffix, but the surface pronunciation of each base varies slightly because of English phonotactic constraints. Each morpheme ends with -*mn* but that cluster is not permitted in word-final position. Rather than the insertion of a vowel between the two consonants, we have instead the deletion of the second consonant in word-final position:

$$n \longrightarrow 0 \; / \; m \underline{\quad\quad} \#$$

A sample derivation:

Underlying forms	//#hɪmn#	#hɪmn+əl#//
N-deletion	0	
Surface forms	/hɪm/	hɪmnəl/

8J   QUESTIONS: BASES IN -MN

(a)   What is the pronunciation of *damning, condemned, hymns*? What are the underlying forms of these words?
(b)   Instead of a rule which deletes the //n// in final position, why not say instead that there is an insertion rule which operates here? The underlying form for *hymn*, for instance, would be //#hɪm#// and the rule would insert /n/ before a non-neutral suffix which begins with a vowel, such as the -*al* of *hymnal*. However, this would be the wrong analysis. Why?

The alternations we have observed above are **phonologically conditioned,** but only in part. The rules for schwa insertion and N-deletion are phonologically conditioned, in part, because /ɛntr/ and /dæmn/, for example, cannot occur as whole words or before suffixes which consist of a single consonant, like #*d* and #*z*. There must be a vowel inserted or a consonant deleted to make them conform to English pronunciation standards. However, there is no *phonological* reason for inserting a vowel or deleting /n/ in *entering* and *damning*. The suffix -*ing* begins with a vowel, just like the suffixes -*ance* and -*ation* of *entrance* and *damnation*. So if a schwa in inserted in *entering* but not in *entrance* and //n// is deleted in *damning* but not in *damnation*, these rules are **morphologically conditioned** in part. It is one particular morpheme that blocks the application of the rules.

Now that we have made this point, we have to admit that the facts are actually more complex. The deletion of //n// is consistent; *damning* and *condemning* are never pronounced with /n/ after the /m/. On the other hand, the insertion of a vowel in -C*r* and -C*l* clusters is variable. Such words as *entering*, *cent(e)ring*, *whistling*, *fiddling*, *simpler*, *simplest* may be pronounced in three syllables or in two – with a schwa inserted or without.

8.3   Differences in morpheme division

What kind of noise annoys an oyster?
A noisy noise annoys an oyster.

In the previous chapter we examined the possible sequences of consonants and possible sequences of vowels and consonants. We have looked at minute matters which the ordinary speaker of the language takes for granted. Does it really matter what sequences occur? Does this examination lead us to some better understanding of the English language, and of language in general?

Yes, knowledge of this sort is important for speech pathologists whose patients are learning to acquire or re-acquire the ability to produce the kinds of utterances that all speakers of the language produce. The pathologist or speech teacher needs to diagnose the patient's difficulties in a general way. To make a list of words which are troublesome for the patient is not a systematic approach. To recognize what sequences are troublesome can lead to questions about, and experimentation with, similar sequences. In a similar way, the teacher of English as a second or foreign language can acquire some sense of what difficulties face the student from a particular native language background. Since languages differ in their phonotactics, the learner of a new language does not merely have to acquire new sounds, new phonemes, but also new kinds of sequences. Again, the teacher is not well informed by knowing simply that this or that word is a source of trouble to the student; the teacher will profit from more general knowledge, from a grasp of the scope of the trouble.

Recognition of what can and what cannot occur in the utterances of English (or whatever language) helps us to appreciate somewhat the process of perception. What sort of information about a language do people have stored in the unconscious part of their brains that makes it possible for them to recognize what they have heard. We do not need to hear everything that is in the stream of speech of someone talking to us, and often we cannot – there are various disturbances in the environment, the speaker makes errors, and our attention may be less than 100 per cent. And yet we usually get the message because language has redundancy – or better, messages have redundancy. Part of the redundancy is in syntactic and semantic cues, but it must also be of use to us that we eliminate some potential sequences of sounds, quite unconsciously, because we have an awareness of what sequences do not occur in our language. In much the same way, a skillful reader does not need to perceive every possible visual cue because there is redundancy in the sequences of letters which occur in a written text.

Here is a specific example. The consonants /m/ and /p/ occur in word-initial, word-medial, and word-final position. The cluster /mp/ does not occur word-initially. It occurs finally and medially, as in *lamp* and *temper*, but only after a checked vowel. A free vowel, such as /ei/, occurs in final position (e.g. *play*) and before final /m/ (*tame*) and /p/ (*tape*) – among other possibilities – but not before /mp/. A checked vowel like /ɛ/ occurs before /m/, /p/, and /mp/ (e.g. *stem, step, hemp*) but not word-finally. These observations are true, in general, for all checked vowels like /ɛ/, for free vowels like /ei/, and for consonant clusters like /mp/.

To express these facts in formulas (where V = a checked vowel, V: = a free vowel, and # denotes a word boundary), here are the possible and impossible word endings:

V: #	V # (impossible)
V:m #	Vm #
V:p #	Vp #
V:mp # (impossible)	Vmp #

The possible and impossible sequences have an effect on what may occur when two words come together in an utterance – and therefore on what is involved in our processing and interpreting of what we hear. A sequence of

free vowel – /m/ – /p/ – vowel

must divide between /m/ and /p/, as in *tame panther, seem poor, home power*. A sequence of

checked vowel – /m/ – /p/ – vowel

may divide after /m/ or after /p/, as in *plum pie* or *dump out, trim parade* or *limp away*. To use formulas again,

$$\ldots \text{V: m p} \ldots = \ldots \text{V: m \# \# p} \ldots$$

but

...V m p...=...V m # # p... *or* ...V m p # #...

Some sequences of English phonemes are like the first of these (Vː m p); they occur only at the boundary of two morphemes, and there is only one way the sequence can be divided between the morphemes. For example, when two instances of the same consonant occur in sequence, they must belong to different morphemes,

night time   homemade   half fare

and the same is true for sequences of two consonants which differ only in voice,

bus zone   red tie   log cabin.

Usually when any consonant is followed by /h/, the morpheme division is before /h/,

pinch-hit   outhouse   childhood

(possible exceptions: *abhor, adhesive*).

And usually when /ŋ/ is followed by anything other than /k/ or /g/, the morpheme division is after /ŋ/,

singer   ring it   kingdom

(exceptions: *dinghy, gingham, hangar*, and names like *Langham*)

Other sequences are like the second, (V m p); they occur in single morphemes like *temper*, and they occur at morpheme boundaries, with two possible places for the boundary, as in *plum pie* versus *plump eye* and in *a noise* versus *an oyster*. Here are some more examples:

I scream	gray day	we dressed
ice cream	Grade A	we'd rest
a name	Lou skis	been selected
an aim	loose keys	since elected
see Mabel	like you	nitrate
seem able	my cue	night rate
		dye trade

(A pair like *ice cream* and *I scream* may differ in stress as well as in syllable division.)

How do speakers of English recognize such differences in syllable division? The first answer is that we don't – don't necessarily and don't always. It would be a rare occasion on which we might need to decide whether we had heard, for example, 'While they were waiting, we dressed' or 'While they were waiting, we'd rest.' Whichever of these was intended, we would no doubt interpret correctly through our knowledge of the situation – events, persons, and what had been said previously – without even recognizing the possibility of the other utterance.

But if our attention is directed to such potential distinctions (as your attention is directed by reading this section), can we unfailingly catch the distinctions? Not with 100 per cent accuracy. Experiments have been carried out in which subjects heard one utterance of such a pair, saw both sentences (or phrases) written on their test paper, and then matched what they thought they heard with one member of the written pair. The results indicate that, whatever audible clues there are for distinguishing the two or more utterances, performance in perceiving these clues is less than perfect – but then performance is always less than perfect. If people consistently perform with better than 50 per cent accuracy in such discrimination, we may be sure there is something 'there' which makes discrimination possible.

What makes discrimination possible is the presence of a number of phonetic features which are non-distinctive, redundant, on the level of phonological contrast but which perform a function in the structuring of syllables. In chapter 7 we dealt with such features as roundness of consonants, aspiration on voiceless stops, nasality in vowels, and the like. These features have no role in distinguishing one consonant from another, one voiceless stop from another, or one vowel from another, but they have a role in telling us to which syllable a vowel or consonant belongs or where it belongs in the syllable.

Note how the linguistic forms above are distinguished by presence or absence, or different position, of phonetic features like the following:

Aspiration: The /k/ of *I scream, Lou skis,* and *like you* is unaspirated, the /k/ of *ice cream, loose keys,* and *my cue* is aspirated. Similarly, the /t/ of *night rate* is not aspirated while that of *dye trade* is.

Vowel nasality: The /ə/ in *an aim* and in *an oyster* is likely to be nasalized, while the /ə/ of *a name* and *a noise* is not nasalized, or at least less likely to be. There is a corresponding difference of nasality in the first syllable of *seem able* versus that of *see Mabel*.

Sonorant length: When a vowel is syllable-final, as in the first syllable of *see Mabel, Lou skis, gray day, my cue, I scream, dye trade,* it is longer than when it is followed by a consonant in the same syllable (*seem able, loose keys, Grade A, like you, ice cream, night rate*), and, as we have seen, the phonetic nature of /ai/ especially may be quite different in final position from what it is before a voiceless consonant. Similarly, the syllable-final /n/ of *been selected* is longer than the non-final /n/ of *since elected*.

Fricative /r/: The /r/ of *nitrate, dye trade,* and *we dressed* is apt to be articulated with some friction after /t/ and /d/. In *night rate* and *we'd rest,* on the other hand, the articulation of /r/ is similar to that which is found in initial position.

Note that there is often a clustering of such feature differences. If we compare *night rate* versus *dye trade*, we find a difference in the length of the first vowel, the /t/ which follows is unaspirated in one item and aspirated in the other, and the /r/ is made without friction in *night rate* but with friction in *dye trade*.

8.4   Summary

Constraints on the clustering of consonants are responsible, in part, for the fact that certain **morphemes** have more than one phonological form. The suffix which expresses past tense, when attached to regular verbs, has three forms, or **allomorphs**, /ɪd, d, t/. Three other morphemes have the regular allomorphs /ɪz, z, s/: plural number and possessive, which are attached to nouns, and third person singular, attached to verbs. We see that /d/ and /z/ are the common expressions of their respective morphemes, whereas the other allomorphs are found only where /d/ and /z/ are impossible because of phonotactic constraints. We posit //#d// and //#z// as abstract, or **underlying forms**, and we derive **surface forms** from them through **rules**, specifically **vowel insertion** and **voice assimilation**.

Just as **grammatical morphemes** like past tense and plural number have variation, some **lexical morphemes** also have allomorphs. In this chapter we have examined morphemes that have final consonant clusters which are not permitted word-finally. Morphemes which end in a cluster of obstruent + sonorant consonant (-Cr, -Cl, -Cm) insert /ə/ between the obstruent and the sonorant before the boundary marker # – that is, in word-final position and before a **neutral suffix**; morphemes which end /mn/ delete the /n/ under the same conditions. The respective rules are labeled **schwa insertion** and **N-deletion**. The rules do not apply before non-neutral suffixes, which are indicated in the underlying form by the boundary marker +.

When the application of a rule depends entirely on sequences of phonemes (or stress), the rule is said to be **phonologically conditioned**; if a rule applies according to some sequence of morphemes, it is **morphologically conditioned**.

Certain sequences of phonemes can only occur across morpheme boundaries. Other sequences are ambivalent, occurring both within a morpheme and across a morpheme boundary. The phonological information by which speakers of English recognize the boundary differences is provided by such phonetic features as aspiration, sonorant length, vowel nasalization – in short, features which are redundant with respect to the system of segmental phonemes. Of course, syntactic and semantic information also facilitate interpretation.

8A   FEEDBACK

(a)   The regular past tense suffix is pronounced /ɪd/ after verbs that end with /t/ or /d/;

(b)   it is pronounced /t/ after other voiceless consonants – that is, /p č k f s θ/;

(c)   it is pronounced /d/ after all other phonemes.

8B   FEEDBACK

(a)   The regular plural suffix is pronounced /ɪz/ after sibilants – /s z ʃ ʒ č ǰ/;

(b)   it is pronounced /s/ after other voiceless consonants – that is, /p t k f θ/;

(c)   it is pronounced /z/ after all other phonemes.

8C   FEEDBACK

Yes.

8D   FEEDBACK

Yes.

8F   FEEDBACK

No, because the voice assimilation rule would change //#pɛt#d#// to /pɛtt/, and then the vowel insertion rule would make it /pɛtɪt/. Of course, this is not the actual pronunciation.

8G   FEEDBACK

packs	/ks/	Yes, *lax*	bridged	/ǰd/	No
bags	/gz/	No	coughed	/ft/	*soft*
lacked	/kt/	*act*	cuffs	/fs/	No
lagged	/gd/	No	loves	/vz/	No
breathed	/ðd/	No	fourth	/rθ/	*north*
rapped	/pt/	*apt*	fifth	/fθ/	No
clips	/ps/	*ellipse*	sixth	/ksθ/	No
rubs	/bz/	No	width	/dθ/, /tθ/	No
rubbed	/bd/	No	depth	/pθ/	No
beds	/dz/	Only *adze*	length	/ŋ(k)θ/	No
brushed	/ʃt/	No	warmth	/rm(p)θ/	No
shoved	/vd/	No	tenth	/nθ/	*month*

8H FEEDBACK

//#hʌŋgr#// hunger   //#dizæstr#// disaster   //#θiætr#// theater
//#wɪntr#// winter   //#mɒnstr#// monster   //#sɛntr#// center

8I FEEDBACK

muffle   peddle   suckle
juggle   sample   twinkle

8J FEEDBACK

(a) /ˈdæmɪŋ, kənˈdɛmd, hɪmz/
     //#dæmn#ɪŋ# #kəndɛmn#d# #hɪmn#z#//
(b) There are words which have a final /m/ but don't add /n/ before a
     suffix that begins with a vowel: *drummer, Vietnamese.* The /n/ pronounced
     in *condemnation, columnist, solemnize,* etc. must be derived from the under-
     lying form.

Notes

Descriptions of English pronunciation which avoided the recognition of syllables
as units of phonology, such as Trager and Smith (1951) and Hockett (1958), attempted
to account for such differences as *night rate* and *nitrate* as a difference in transition
between phonemes. Thus *night rate* was said to have open transition (or 'plus juncture')
between /t/ and /r/ while *nitrate* has close transition (or lack of 'plus juncture') between
the two phonemes.

9

The Rhythm of English Speech

An utterance consists of consonants and vowel phonemes but it also contains melodies: the voice rises and falls, some syllables are accented and others are not. Melodies are meaningful in a contrastive way. We can best understand these meanings by examining how two or more utterances which contain the same words in the same order can have different meanings because they are spoken with different melodies.

9.1 Prosody

Up to this point we have dealt mostly with 'segmental phonology,' the description of the segmental phonemes – consonants and vowels – and of the sequences in which they occur and the variations they have. We turn now to 'suprasegmental phonology,' or 'prosody,' which is concerned with three matters:

1   The ways in which an utterance is broken into 'chunks.' Compare the utterance 'We don't want any' spoken in a single breath and the same sequence of words said in four separate breaths, as perhaps by somebody who is irritated or insistent:

(1-a)   / We don't want any /
(1-b)   / We / don't / want / any /.

The technical name which we use for 'chunk' is **tone unit**. Sentences (1-a) and (1-b) obviously have the same verbal content but they differ in what Halliday (1967) calls **tonality**: Sentence (1-a) consists of one tone unit; sentence (1-b) consists of four tone units. (Other writers have used the terms 'tone group' or 'macrosegment' where we use 'tone unit.') From here on we show tone groups by putting a slant line before and after each one.

2   Within a tone unit the **position of accent** – the emphasis that makes one syllable more prominent than other syllables, and therefore makes one word more prominent than the other words in the tone unit. Each of the sentences below is one tone unit in length and therefore has one accented syllable, indicated by bold face. Notice how the meaning changes when the accent is moved.

(2-a)   / We don't want **those**. /
(2-b)   / We don't **want** those. /
(2-c)   / **We** don't want those. /
(2-d)   / We **don't** want those. /

In a sense each of these four utterances has the same meaning: the meaning of *we* (whoever 'we' may be), the meaning of *those* (whatever 'those' are), the meaning of *want*, and the meanings of Negative and Present Time. However, they differ in an important kind of meaning, **focus**, which we will study in greater detail in the following pages. In Halliday's terminology these four sentences differ in **tonicity**.

3   The **intonation** or melody – or simply what Halliday calls the **tone** – the patterned way in which the pitch of the voice changes in the utterance. Compare the two sentences:

(3-a)   / You don't **know**. /
(3-b)   / You don't **know**? /

The voice falls or the voice rises, and the hearer knows whether the speaker is telling or asking.

   This chapter deals with the first two of these matters. The next chapter deals with intonation. Before we get started, we should recognize a few important points:

(a)   Prosody is more subtle than word phonology (sometimes called segmental phonology). As a consequence, numerous languages have writing systems – alphabets or syllabaries – which represent their consonants and vowels adequately if not perfectly, but no language has an orthography which adequately represents the rhythms and melodies of its utterances. Punctuation marks, italics, underlines, and capital letters are crude and inadequate ways of representing prosodic elements.

(b)   It follows that one written utterance may correspond to two or more spoken utterances (or, if you prefer, one written utterance may be read aloud two or more ways). To take a simple example, compare the pronunciation of 'When?' in these two short dialogs:

1   A: We're going to have a picnic next huckaluxx.

```
                        n? /
                   e
               h
    B:   / W
```

(B understands enough of A's utterance to know that the time of an event was mentioned but doesn't understand completely and is asking for a repetition.)

2   A: We're going to have a picnic.
    B: / W

```
               h
                 e
                     n? /
```

(B is asking about something not yet said – new information.)

Or compare these two different utterances:

```
                    s       J
    / This is my       on, /   o
                                h
                            n.
```

```
                    s
    / This is my       o           n. /
                          n, / Joh
```

The first utterance suggests that 'John' is the speaker's son, the second, that John is the person addressed.

(c) Thus, although prosody deals with subtle matters, these matters are important. There are personal differences in the ways that people use speech, and there are dialect differences, but there are also ways of talking which are common to all speakers of the language. By using differences in the 'tone of voice' we convey different messages which, by and large, all speakers of the language recognize and react to.

The examples above and others that will follow show that prosodic elements can perform several kinds of functions:

Focus: Prosody can highlight one particular word in an utterance and thus make other words less significant by comparison (e.g. /**We** don't want those/ vs. /We don't want **those**/) or highlight different numbers of words in what are otherwise identical utterances (e.g. /**We**/ don't want **those**/).

Role in discourse: Prosodic elements can indicate the role of an utterance within a larger discourse (/**When**?/ as a request for repetition vs. /**When**?/ as a request for information not yet supplied; /The Blakes have a new **car**/, which conveys entirely new information, vs. /The Blakes **have** a new car/, which suggests that 'a new car' has previously been mentioned).

The speaker's intention: Prosody can make a difference in the way the elements of an utterance are to be interpreted, in the grammatical nature of the whole utterance (the question /You don't **know**?/ vs. the statement /You don't **know**/) or in the way the parts of an utterance are related to one another (/This is my **son**,/ **John**/ where the name 'John' is in apposition with 'my son' or is an address-form added to the sentence).

Still, it would be wrong to exaggerate the role of prosody in communication. We are all likely to feel that we can judge a person's mood by the 'tone of voice' – that we can tell whether he or she is angry, sad, tired, or elated by the way utterances are delivered. But there is no intonation which consistently indicates anger or elation or boredom or any other emotion. Our judgments are determined, in any instance, by the speaker's choice of vocabulary, gestures, and body language and by our knowledge of him or her and the attendant circumstances – not by tone of voice alone. Furthermore, although some grammatical differences may depend on how an utterance is pronounced – /You don't **know**?/ vs. /You don't **know**./, for an obvious sort of example – it would be a mistake to assume that there is a close tie between prosodic forms of utterances and their grammatical nature. It is not the case, for example, that questions always have rising intonation, nor that only questions have rising intonation. Finally, we should note that, just as the functions of prosody are not specific, neither are they exclusive. The focus that can be achieved by accent in /We didn't give **Ralph** the tickets/ can also be achieved by other devices with or without accent, for example, /It wasn't Ralph we gave the tickets to/.

9.2   Tone units

An utterance may be spoken as a single tone unit or it may be broken into several tone units, as indicated in sentences (1-a) and (1-b). The way the utterance is divided into tone units depends partly on the tempo of the speech. The faster a person speaks, the longer and fewer the tone units; the slower the speech, the shorter and more numerous the tone units. We say it depends *partly* on the tempo of speech because speakers can, to a large degree, control the 'chunking' the way they want to.

9A   PRACTICE: DIVIDING AN UTTERANCE INTO TONE UNITS

(a)   Each utterance below can be spoken as a single tone unit or can be divided into two or three, or even more, tone units. Where do you think the breaks are most likely to occur?

> We're going downtown this afternoon.
> On the way home we'll stop at the library if we have time.
> Cape Ann Lighthouse was erected in 1910.
> A lot of ships have reached harbor safely because of it.

(b)   Sometimes two sentences may have the same sequence of words but still have different meanings because the words go together in different syntactic groups. For instance, *I'd like bread and butter or cheese* can mean *I'd like (bread) AND (butter or cheese)*, or *I'd like (bread and butter) OR (cheese)*. The way an utterance is divided into tone units by the speaker does not necessarily remove ambiguity, but it may. Consider the sentences below. Can different ways of dividing the sentences determine two different meanings?

> She told everyone that she knew the answer.
> The tennis courts are to be used by club members only on Thursdays.

Obviously a tone unit must contain at least one syllable – you can't divide *Help!* or *Yes* into smaller chunks. So ordinarily a tone unit contains at least one word. It is possible to divide a polysyllabic word into tone units (e.g. / ab / so / lute / ly /), but that is not very common.

9.3   Stress timing

Notice the staccato rhythm of these unlikely sentences:

> Sue bought nice, fresh, warm, sweet rolls.
> Ten big white ducks swam home fast.

In each sentence every syllable has equal prominence – held for the same amount of time and given the same amount of stress – except that the final syllable is just a bit longer and louder. The sentences have staccato rhythm, or **syllable timing**, for two reasons: (1) each word is a monosyllable, and (2) each word is a 'content' word, a noun, verb, adjective, or adverb, each with a definite meaning of its own. We lose the staccato rhythm if we replace one-syllable words with polysyllabic ones:

> Susan purchased fancy, sugared cookies.

or if we insert 'function words' – articles, prepositions, conjunctions, or auxiliary verbs:

A group of black and white ducks were swimming in the pond.

In some languages – French is a good example – syllable timing is usual; every syllable has nearly the same prominence, no matter what function it has. In English **stress timing** is customary; the stressed syllable, which may be the only syllable, of each content word stands out, and other syllables are relatively weak – the function words and the unstressed syllables of the content words. We can represent the relative prominence of syllables in the four sentences this way:

/ 'Sue 'bought 'nice 'fresh 'warm 'sweet '**rolls**. /
/ 'Ten 'big 'white 'ducks 'swam 'home '**fast**. /
/ 'Susan 'purchased 'fancy 'sugared '**cook**ies. /
/ A 'group of 'black and 'white '**ducks** / were 'swimming in the '**pond**. /

In each tone unit the accented syllable is most prominent, other stressed syllables are less prominent, and unstressed syllables are least prominent. The vowel of a stressed syllable is long, the vowel of an unstressed syllable is short and it is often a schwa. Sometimes this pronunciation of unstressed syllables is spoken of as 'slurring.' In everyday usage the verb *slur* may be used with negative connotations, but that is unfortunate. In spoken English unstressed syllables are weak and occupy less time than stressed syllables; consequently unstressed syllables do not have the full vowels of stressed syllables. The pronunciations of some words may be different in stressed position and unstressed position; these differences are described in chapter 13.

In a language with syllable timing the amount of time required to produce an utterance depends on how many syllables it has. In English the time, and the rhythm, of an utterance are determined by the number of stressed syllables. Each of the following sentences has two beats – two tone units, two accents – even though the number of unstressed syllables varies. As you say each sentence, hit a table twice with a pencil, keeping the strokes at the same tempo.

The **box** / is **big.**
The **pack**age / is **big**.
The **pack**age / is **hea**vy.
The **pack**ages / are **hea**vy.
The **pack**ages / are **hea**vier.
The **pack**ages / are the **hea**viest.

However many unstressed syllables there are, they are more or less 'squeezed' into the same amount of time.

Sentences with the same number of syllables and the same arrangements of accented syllable, stressed syllables, strong syllables, and weak syllables have the same rhythm. Sentences with the same rhythm may have the same grammatical structure, as the first two groups of sentences below illustrate; but identical rhythm does not require identical grammar, as the remaining groups indicate. (Here we use 'w' to indicate a weak syllable, 's' for a strong syllable, and 'S' for the strongest syllable, the one that has the accent of the tone unit.)

I 'didn't under'**stand**.	w s w s w S
You 'shouldn't inter'**rupt**.	
They 'haven't misbe'**haved**.	

He's 'looking at the '**file**.	w s w s w S
She's 'waiting by the '**door**.	
We're 'sitting on the '**floor**.	

'What's the '**mat**ter?	s w S w
'Brown's a '**law**yer.	
'Raise the '**win**dow.	

They 'left for the '**sta**tion.	w s w w S w
Your 'taxi is '**wai**ting	
I 'didn't ex'**pect** it.	

'How do you 'know '**that**?	s w w s S
'This is a 'nice '**view**.	
'When do they 'serve '**lunch**?	

'Mister 'Harris 'gave us 'good ad'**vice**.	s w s w s w s w S
'Reser'vations 'should be 'sent to'**day**.	
'Our com'panions 'had to 'wait an '**hour**.	

9.4   Marked accent: paradigmatic focus

As the example sentences in the previous section show, the accented syllable of a tone unit is very often the stressed syllable of the last content word in the tone unit. To repeat one example,

/ A 'group of 'black and 'white '**ducks** / were 'swimming in the '**pond**. /

When the accent falls on the last word of a tone unit, we say that the tone unit has a neutral or unmarked accent. When accent falls on an earlier content word or on any function word, we have a marked occurrence of accent.

In the unmarked sentence (with one tone unit):

/ 'Mary 'told 'John 'all the '**secrets**. /,

it is hard to determine whether there is some special emphasis on the word *secrets* or not. But if accent is moved to an earlier word, the emphasis is obvious, and so is the purpose of this marked occurrence:

/ 'Mary 'told 'John **'all** the 'secrets. /
    [Not just a few secrets]
/ 'Mary told **'John** 'all the 'secrets. /
    [She didn't tell Harold or Richard or . . .]
/ 'Mary **'told** 'John 'all the 'secrets. /
    [She didn't hint, imply, or write them . . .]
/ **'Ma**ry 'told 'John 'all the 'secrets. /
    [It wasn't Angela or Beatrice or . . .]

This use of accent is contrastive. It is **paradigmatic focus**. By emphasizing one word the speaker is excluding any other word or term which might occur in the same position or with the same general function; emphasis on a noun makes that noun stand out in contrast to some other noun or nouns which might have been said, emphasis on a verb excludes other possible verbs, and so on. Just what is excluded depends on the context and what the speaker and hearer know about each other.

Sometimes, however, even a casual passer-by can tell what is excluded. Some words belong to very small sets; choosing one word of the set automatically excludes the other word or words of the set. Such sets include *in* and *out*; *up* and *down*; *on* and *off*; *all, some*, and *no* or *none*. Some compound words like *inside* and *outside*, *upstairs* and *downstairs*, and the numbers from *thirteen* to *nineteen* are stressed on the last syllable when used alone, but stress shifts to the initial syllable when contrast is intended, whether the contrast is obvious from the context or just 'in the speaker's mind.' Thus we say *up'stairs* in most contexts, as in 'My bedroom is up**'stairs**.' But when there is contrast, we would say, for instance, 'I've spent the whole morning running **up**stairs / and **down**stairs.' If you overheard somebody say 'Let's put this one **up**stairs,' you wouldn't necessarily know what was being put, but you would suspect that something else had been put downstairs.

In a similar way, neutral prefixes can contrast with their absence – contrast with zero. The verb *rewrite* typically is stressed on the second syllable, the base of the verb, but in a phrase like *write and rewrite* the most prominent syllable is *re-*. The contrast with zero is clear when two terms are used together, as in that phrase and in the following examples:

the president and the **ex**-president
occupied or **un**occupied
deeds and **mis**deeds

The contrast may be merely implied, as in the second sentence of this short dialog:

ˌIs your 'boss 'satis,fied with your '**work**?
'Well, he's 'not '**un**'happy.

One kind of contrast is conversational turn-about, involving the words *you*, *I*, and *we*. Compare:

A: / Hel'**lo**. / 'How '**are** you? /
B: / '**Fine**, 'thanks. / 'How are '**you**? /

Note that the *you* of B's utterance is in contrast with the *you* of A's question. Though it is obviously identical in form, it is different in its reference, its meaning. (A, speaking first, might pose the question as / 'How are '**you**? / instead of / 'How '**are** you? /. Either would be acceptable as the opener in this stereotypical exchange. The choice seems to depend on dialect or even on idiolect. But B's rejoinder must have the accent on the contrasting item. For B to reply / '**Fine**, 'thanks. / 'How '**are** you? / would be impossible.)

9B PRACTICE: SENTENCES ACCENTED DIFFERENTLY

(a) Comment on the difference of meaning of these sentences:

   1 Her 'new '**dress** / is 'light '**green**.
   2 Her 'new '**dress** / is '**light** 'green.
   3 Her '**new** 'dress / is 'light '**green**.
   4 Her 'new '**dress** is 'light 'green.

(b) In each of the pairs of sentences below the first sentence of the pair is unmarked and the second has marked focus. Tell in what way the second sentence of each pair is 'special' – how it differs from the first sentence.

   1 (i) Does 'this 'bus 'go ˌdown'**town**?
       (ii) Does 'this 'bus 'go '**down**'town?
   2 (i) Will 'this 'plant 'grow 'better in'**side**?
       (ii) Will 'this 'plant 'grow 'better '**in**'side?
   3 (i) I 'said fif'**teen**.
       (ii) I 'said '**fif**'teen.
   4 (i) I 'told you to ˌdiscon'**nect** it.
       (ii) I 'told you to '**dis**con'nect it.

9.5 Marked accent: syntagmatic focus

Marked occurrence of accent is not always for contrast. Sometimes the words which are at the end of a sentence are de-accented because they provide little or no information.

The 'telephone's 'ringing.
The '**news**paper's just come.
'**Din**ner is 'ready.

Each of these sentences has a noun phrase followed by a short verb phrase. The speaker of the first sentence, for instance, is not talking about the telephone as opposed to something else (the doorbell, for instance), that might be ringing, though that is one possible interpretation of the sentence. Just as likely, the speaker calls attention to the telephone because it is doing what one expects telephones to do, and that is the reason for calling attention. The other two sentences are similar. Here we may say that *telephone* and *newspaper* and *dinner* have **syntagmatic focus**: they are not emphasized for contrast with some other words which might stand in their place; they are highlighted because what follows is played down.

Part of a sentence may be played down – de-accented – because it represents something that has been said before; it is old information. Compare these sentences:

We 'spent our va'cation in '**Flo**rida.
We 'spent our va'**ca**tion in 'Florida.

In the first sentence all the information is 'new.' The second sentence, however, would only be possible if *Florida* had recently been mentioned. The information about spending the vacation is 'new,' but the rest essentially repeats something which has already been said. The speaker could just as well have communicated this by saying 'We spent our vacation there.'

9C   EXPLORATION: PLACING ACCENT IN A DIALOG

In the following dialog each sentence consists of one or two tone units, as marked. Each tone unit should have one accent. In some cases the tone unit consists of a single word so that the position of the accent is obvious. In longer tone units the accent is on the last *informative* word. Read the dialog aloud and mark the accent.

A: / Have you taken your family to the zoo yet, / John? /
B: / No, / but my kids have been asking me to. /
      / I've heard this city has a pretty big one. /
A: / Yes, / it doesn't have a lot of animals, / but it has quite a variety of animals. / I think your kids / would enjoy seeing the pandas. /
B: / I'm sure they would. / I'd like to see them, / too. /
A: / Also, / the tigers are worth looking at. /
B: / Is it okay to feed them? /
A: / No, / they're not used to being fed. /
B: / What bus do you take / to get there? /

A: / Number Twenty-eight. / But don't you have a car? /
B: / We used to have one, / but we had to sell it. /

9C   FEEDBACK AND DISCUSSION

There is no guarantee that any two people will place the accents as we have marked them below, but some placements are more likely than others, and the following are quite probable.

A: / Have you taken your family to the '**zoo** yet, / '**John**? /

(The word *yet* is almost never accented, perhaps because it adds nothing much to a sentence. Notice that the meaning of the question would be much the same without this word.)

B: / '**No**, / but my kids have been '**ask**ing me to. /

(The word *to* stands for old information 'to take the family to the zoo'; it is not accented. In a two-person conversation the pronouns *I-my-me* and *you-your* can generally be taken for granted, therefore are not accented. *Asking* is the last informative word.)

/ I've heard this city has a pretty '**big** one. /

(The word *one* is a substitute here for *zoo*, which is old information.)

A: / '**Yes**, / it doesn't have a '**lot** of animals, / but it has quite a va'**ri**ety of animals. /

(The words *lot* and *variety* are in contrast, paradigmatic focus.)

/ I think your '**kids** / would enjoy seeing the '**pan**das. /

(In the first tone unit *think* might be accented instead of *kids* since the word *kids* has appeared before. In the second tone unit *pandas* is new.)

B: / I'm '**sure** they would. / '**I'd** like to see them, / '**too**. /

(*They would* is likely to be de-accented because it stands for the old information, *the kids would enjoy seeing the pandas*. However, accenting *would* – /I'm sure they '**would**./ – is also possible, suggesting strong agreement with A's remark. In the next tone unit *I* is accented for two reasons: it contrasts with *your kids* in the previous remark (paradigmatic focus), and the following words *like to see them* are de-accented because they repeat the meaning of *enjoy seeing the pandas*, so that *I* also has syntagmatic focus. The word *too* usually forms a separate tone unit and is discussed in section 9.6, below.)

A: / 'Also, / the 'tigers are worth looking at. /

(Focus is on another kind of animal. In this context *to be worth looking at* is another way of talking about seeing.)

B: / Is it okay to 'feed them? /

(*Them* represents old information.)

A: / 'No, / they're not 'used to being fed. /

(*Being fed* is grammatically different from *to feed them* but semantically equivalent – old information.)

B: / What 'bus do you take / to 'get there? /

(The verb *take* has little meaning of its own in such expressions as *take a nap, take a bath, take a ride, take a walk, take a bus, take pictures*, so that it is not accented even when it follows its object, as it does in this kind of question. In the second tone unit *there* stands for the previously mentioned zoo.)

A: / Number Twenty-'eight. / But don't you have a 'car? /

(New topics.)

B: / We 'used to have one, / but we had to 'sell it. /

(*To have one* repeats the meaning of *to have a car*. *One* is equivalent, in this context, to *a car*, and *it* in the second tone unit is equivalent to *the car*.)

9.6   A note on 'too' and 'either'

Compare these sentences:

/ Harry studied painting in 'Paris, / 'too. /
/ Harry studied 'painting in Paris, / 'too. /
/ Harry 'studied painting in Paris, / 'too. /
/ 'Harry studied painting in Paris, / 'too. /

What is the meaning of *too* (or *also*)? Its 'meaning' is to indicate that what has been said previously with the use of one word or term applies as well with the use of another word of the same part of speech, the accented word in the tone unit which *too* follows. The first sentence, then, emphasizes that Harry studied painting in Paris as well as in some other place; the second sentence says that Harry studied painting as well as some other, previously mentioned subject; the third tells us that Harry studied painting in addition to some other activity connected with painting; and the fourth that Harry, as well as some other person or persons, studied painting in Paris.

The word *either* is exactly analogous to *too*, except that it occurs in negative sentences. Consider the following:

/ The maintenance men didn't wash the windows on '**Tues**day / 'either. /
/ The maintenance men didn't wash the '**win**dows on Tuesday / 'either. /
/ The maintenance men didn't '**wash** the windows on Tuesday / 'either. /
/ The '**main**tenance men didn't wash the windows on Tuesday / 'either. /

9.7 De-accenting: anaphoric words

It is possible to say, 'I know Archibald but I don't like Archibald,' but it is far more usual to say, 'I know Archibald but I don't like him.' English has certain **anaphoric words** whose function is to refer to what has previously (and recently) been communicated in a different way. The pronoun *he-his-him* refers to 'Archibald' in one context, to 'Paul' in another context, 'the old man selling newspapers on the corner' in another context. The pronoun *he-his-him* is equivalent to the last masculine singular noun or noun phrase that has been expressed. Since anaphoric words contain no new information – in fact, are intended to repeat old information – they are typically not accented. Anaphoric words include:

(1)   the pronouns *he, she, it,* and *they*, which replace definite nouns and noun phrases:

Everybody likes **Archibald**.   Everybody **likes** him.
I was sitting behind **Lisa**.   I was sitting be**hind** her.
She ordered the **cake**.   She **ord**ered it.
We waited for our **friends**.   We **wait**ed for them.

(2)   the pronouns *one* and *some*, which replace indefinite noun phrases:

She ordered a **cake**.   She **ord**ered one.
I'll lend you some **money**.   I'll **lend** you some.

(3)   the pronoun *one, ones*, which replaces nouns after certain modifiers:

Are you wearing your **brown** suit / or the **blue** one?
Are you wearing the **brown** shoes / or the **black** ones?

(In these examples note that paradigmatic focus – contrast – and syntagmatic focus – the result of de-accenting old information – create a sort of pull-and-push effect. The color words *brown, blue, black* are highlighted because they are in contrast as modifiers of a following noun. The following noun is replaced by the anaphoric *one(s)*, which is de-accented.)

(4)   the words *so* and *not*, which replace clauses after certain verbs and adjectives:

> Did your horse come in **last** / in the **race**?
> I **hope** not, / but I'm a**fraid** so.

(5)   the adverbs *there* and *then*, which replace place phrases and time phrases, respectively:

> Ever been in **Wee**hawken?   I used to **live** there.
> Next Monday's a **ho**liday.   I think I'll stay home and **rest** then.

(6)   the auxiliary *do*, which replaces a whole verb phrase:

> Who tracked in all this mud and got the whole house so **dir**ty?
> **I** did.

(Here again there is a pull-and-push effect. *I* is accented, highlighted, because it contrasts with all other possible answers to the question word *who*. At the same time, *did* is de-accented because it stands for the previous verb phrase *tracked in all this mud and got the whole house so dirty*.)

(7)   Finally, there is an anaphoric 'word' which is not a word – zero, nothing at all. Just as a verb phrase in predicate position is replaced by *do*, as in the example above, so a verb phrase after the infinitive marker *to* or after an auxiliary verb, like *be, have, can, will, would, may, should*, and others, is replaced by 'zero.'

> Are you going to **fin**ish soon?   I ex**pect** to.
> Is the committee **mee**ting today?   It **is**.
> Has your horse come **in** yet?   I **hope** it has.
> Are you going to get a **raise**?   I **should**.

While it sounds silly to talk of de-accenting 'zero,' it is important to notice that an anaphoric sentence with 'zero' shows the same sort of accent advancement as any other anaphoric item.

> I expect to **fin**ish soon.   It is meeting to**day**.
> I ex**pect** to.   It **is**.

I hope it has come **in**.   I should get a **raise**.
I **hope** it has.   I **should**.

When an anaphoric word is accented, the accent signals contrast or something special.

You won't catch '**him** doing work like that, / not '**him**.
Do you know Mr and Mrs '**Brown**? / I know '**her**.

Accented pronouns can tell us to shift the usual references. Consider this:

Pat and *Lou* are names which can belong to either men or women.

Pat shook hands with '**Lou**, / and then he '**kissed** her.
Pat shook hands with '**Lou**, / and then '**he** / kissed '**her**.

Which is the woman in the first sentence? In the second?

9.8   Lexical anaphora

In addition to the anaphoric words listed above, whose only function is to refer back to something already said, we can recall old information by using words which, in a different context, would present new information. Such lexical items are de-accented, and the de-accenting is what tells us that the lexical items are being used anaphorically. There are several kinds of lexical anaphora:

Repetition

I've got a **job** / but I don't **like** the job.

[The same meaning can be conveyed by saying . . . *but I don't* **like** *it*. Repetition of the same lexical item, this time de-accented and with the definite article *the*, tells us that the object of *I don't like* is the same as the object of *I've got*.]

Synonyms

Maybe this man can give us di**rec**tions.
I'll **ask** the fellow.

[*the fellow = the man*.]

Superordinate terms

Did you enjoy *Blue Highways*?   I haven't **read** the book.
This wrench is no **good**.   I need a **bigger** tool.

(These sentences would be incomprehensible unless one knows, or can deduce, that *Blue Highways* is the name of a book and that a wrench is a kind of tool, and that is precisely the purpose of de-accenting – to relate the more general term (*book* and *tool*, in these examples) to the more specific term of the preceding sentence.)

The de-accented word or term does not necessarily refer directly to a previous term.

> That's a nice looking **cake**.
> **Have** a piece.

But it must be de-accented. That is usually the meaning of de-accenting: the reference for this term is to be found in the previous discourse.

Of course, a word or term does not necessarily refer to something previously said; it may refer to something that is obviously in the physical environment. Suppose one person picks up an object and asks another person

> Is this **your** recorder?

De-accenting the word *recorder* expresses the presupposition, or assumption, that both speaker and hearer use this word to refer to this object. Here the speaker takes the name of the object for granted and asks about the ownership of the object (which might also be expressed 'Is this recorder **yours**?'). If the speaker said, 'Is this your re**cor**der?' it would be a question about the identity as well as the ownership of the object.

It is also true that de-accenting occurs when a word is repeated, even though it has a different referent the second time. We say, for instance,

> between one man and a**no**ther man
> a room with a view or with**out** a view

just as we say *deeds and **mis**deeds, written or **un**written*. Note that we do a similar thing even with sequences of numbers and letters. A telephone number, for instance, is usually accented on the name of the last digit, but not necessarily if the last digit repeats an earlier digit.

369–4578	is	three six **nine** / four five seven **eight**.
369–4575	may be	three six **nine** / four five seven **five** or
		three six **nine** / four five **seven** five.

Likewise with acronyms:

FBI	is	/ɛf bii **ai**/
USA	is	/juu ɛs **ei**/
USIS	may be	/juu ɛs ai **ɛs**/ or /juu ɛs **ai** ɛs/.

9.9   De-accenting to embed an additional message

De-accenting can be used for a very subtle form of communication:

> What did you say to **Roger?**
> I didn't **speak** to the idiot.

The last sentence actually conveys two messages, one embedded in the other: 'I didn't speak to Roger' and 'I call Roger an idiot.' De-accenting the noun phrase *the idiot* is equivalent to saying: the referent for this phrase is the same as the last noun or noun phrase that fits. Just as, in the example above with the word *recorder*, de-accenting means that the name of the item is taken for granted, here the speaker expects the hearer to take for granted that *the idiot* refers to 'Roger.'

A clause is often de-accented because it repeats old information:

> I think your kids would enjoy seeing the **pan**das.
> I'm **sure** they would.

In this context, *they would* stands for 'the kids would enjoy seeing the pandas.'

9D   EXPLORATION: DIFFERENCES IN DE-ACCENTING

It is possible to present a new message (somewhat like 'I call Roger an idiot') while actually saying something else. Imagine that you are in the interior of a room at the end of the afternoon and someone else is standing at the window, looking out. Suppose the person at the window says one of the following. What different meanings would you get from the two utterances?

(a) I thought it would **rain** today.
(b) I **thought** it would rain today.

Compare these two short dialogs:

(a) Does Harry want an adding machine or a **cal**culator?
     I don't know **what** he wants.
(b) What does Harry **want?**
     I don't **know** what he wants.

The second sentence of dialog (a) has both paradigmatic and syntagmatic focus on *what*. It has syntagmatic focus because *he wants* repeats something from the preceding question. More important, it has paradigmatic focus because the word *what* matches inanimate noun phrases like *an adding machine* and *a calculator*. The focus is on part of the preceding question. The second sentence of dialog (b) has only syntagmatic focus on *know*. The part that follows, *what he wants*, is de-accented because it repeats, in an indirect way, the whole question that preceded.

9E   PRACTICE: CREATING DIFFERENT DIALOGS

(a)   Make up two short dialogs similar to those above. Have the first one begin with a question that will bring the answer

I'm not sure **when** she left.

Have the second dialog begin with a question for which the answer is

I'm not **sure** when she left.

(b)   What is a possible question that will get this answer?

I can't remember **where** they met.

What is a possible question that leads to this answer?

I can't re**mem**ber where they met.

9.10   Accent on operators

Consider the short dialogs below as three separate conversations which happen to end with the same sentence:

1   / John seemed very **busy** this morning. /
     / He **was** busy. /
2   / Is John **bu**sy now? /
     / I don't **know**. / He **was** busy. /
3   / John wasn't **busy** / this **mor**ning, / **was** he? /
     / Oh **yes**, / he **was** busy. /

Marked accent always has some special function, but what that function is depends on the total context in which it occurs. In these three rather artificial dialogs the word *was* has paradigmatic focus each time, denoting a contrast, but the contrast is different in each instance. These different contrasts are possible because of the different meanings or functions of the word *be*.

In the first dialog the form *was* shows **lexical contrast**: forms of *be* may occur in contrast with *seem*, as here, or with other verbs that occur before an adjective phrase, such as *look, feel, appear, taste, act*. Some other examples of lexical contrast with *be*:

/ This soup tastes **sal**ty. / – / It **is** salty. /
/ You look **tired**. / – / I **am** tired. /

In the second dialog *was* shows **modality contrast**. More specifically here, the past tense form is contrasted with the present tense form *is*. We will have more to say about modality contrast as we consider the auxiliary verbs, *have, do, can, will, may*, and others.

The ending of the third dialog is intended to illustrate **polarity contrast**, the contrast of affirmative and negative. The dialog contrasts an affirmative sentence with a previous negative one, but the reverse also occurs:

/ It seems John was very **bu**sy. /
/ Oh **no**, / he **was**n't busy. /

These three kinds of contrast are possible with forms of *be* because of three semantic-syntactic properties that this verb has:

1 It is a verb in its own right, contrasting with a limited number of other verbs like *look, appear, seem, feel, taste*.
2 Its forms contain the kind of modality we call tense, either present (*am, is, are*) or past (*was, were*), which are of course in contrast with each other.
3 It is the locus of the word *not*, commonly reduced to the clitic *n't*. Whether in the full form or the reduced form, *not* is in contrast with its absence – every statement is either affirmative or negative. The clitic *n't* is never accented; the accent is on the form of *be*, or other verb, to which it is attached.

When we consider the many other lexical verbs of English – *walk, swim, choose, describe, imagine, understand*, etc. etc. – we note these facts:

1 Any lexical verb can be accented for lexical focus, as can any lexeme of English.

/ We don't need the **car**. / We're going to **walk** to the meeting. /
/ Did you hear about the **ac**cident? / – / I **saw** it. /

2 Every lexical verb is either present or past in form (*walk, walked; choose, chose*, etc.), but focus on tense is achieved by use of the auxiliary verb *do*, either present (*do, does*) or past (*did*) preceding the simple form of the verb.

/ Alice works at Commercial **Bank**, / **does**n't she? /
/ I'm not **sure**. / She **did** work there. /
/ Peter used to direct the **glee** club, / I **think**. /
/ He still **does** (direct it). /

(/He '**still** 'does./ is also possible.)

3   Similarly, to make a lexical verb negative we use the word *do* with *not* or *n't* following. Accordingly, to emphasize that the sentence is negative we accent *do* in the negative form (*doesn't, don't*) and to emphasize that the sentence is affirmative we use accented *do* without the negative particle following.

/ Why don't you like this **picture**? / – / I **do** like it. /

9.11   Summary

An utterance consists of at least one **tone unit**, which has a describable **intonation** and in which one syllable, the **accented syllable**, is more prominent than any other. Two utterances which contain the same words in the same sequence may differ from each other in their intonations; in the number of tone units into which they are divided; and in the position of the accented syllable within a tone unit, which determines the **focus** of what is said. The **rhythm** of an utterance depends on the number of stressed syllables it contains. English has **stress timing**, so that stressed syllables are relatively long and prominent, unstressed syllables are short and 'slurred.' In contrast, languages in which all syllables are nearly equal in intensity and timing have **syllable timing.**

We consider the occurrence of accent on the last content word of a tone unit to be neutral, or an **unmarked** occurrence of accent; accent occurring on an earlier word is a **marked** occurrence, giving a marked focus. Two kinds of focus are recognized, **paradigmatic** and **syntagmatic**. These terms do not refer to a difference in what is said and what is heard, but to a difference in how an utterance is related to its context. In paradigmatic focus the speaker is contrasting, explicitly or implicitly, one word or term with other possible words or terms of the same grammatical and semantic set. The word or term is highlighted with respect to other items of the language that might occupy the same position in the utterance. In syntagmatic focus, on the other hand, one word or term is highlighted with respect to other items of the same utterance. These non-highlighted items are **de-accented** because they contribute little or nothing to the information conveyed in the utterance. Most often, de-accented words are **anaphoric**, referring to some previously used linguistic form and thus carrying information which is already 'given,' not 'new.' Like any language, English has certain words whose sole function is anaphoric; in addition, it uses **lexical anaphora**; that is, it exploits semantic relationships such as synonymy to refer to something previously said. De-accenting is also used to embed one message in another one, to present what is actually new as if it could be taken for granted.

Paradigmatic focus is **lexical contrast**, which ordinarily means the contrast of verbs with other verbs, nouns with other nouns, and so on. Forms of *be* may occur in lexical contrast with other verbs that occur before an adjective phrase. But *be* and the auxiliary verbs – sometimes called 'anomalous finites' – can be the focus of two other kinds of contrast, **polarity contrast** and **modality contrast**. Polarity contrast is the simple opposition of affirmative and negative. Consider:

/Today's not **Tues**day./
/It **is** Tuesday./

Modality contrast is the opposition of any items that express modality in English: present vs. past tense, perfective vs. non-perfective aspect, and anything which is expressed by a modal auxiliary. The example below shows the contrast of tense.

/Is **Cyn**thia here?/
/She **was** here./

9A   FEEDBACK

(a)   If the first utterance is spoken as two tone units, the most likely division is:

/ We're going downtown / this afternoon. /

If the number of tone units increases, these are possible ways in which the utterance might be divided:

/ We're going / downtown / this afternoon. /
/ We're going / downtown / this / afternoon. /

The second utterance might be:

/ On the way home / we'll stop at the library / if we have time. /

The third and fourth may be divided this way:

/ Cape Ann Lighthouse / was erected in 1910. /
/ A lot of ships / have reached harbor safely / because of it. /

(b)   The possible meanings of these ambiguous sentences become more obvious if the 'cuts' are made in different places:

/ She told everyone / that she knew the answer. /
/ She told everyone that she knew / the answer. /
/ The tennis courts are to be used by members only / on Thursdays. /
/ The tennis courts are to be used by members / only on Thursdays. /

9B   FEEDBACK

(a)   Sentence (1) may be considered neutral, unmarked. Sentence (2) seems to emphasize that the dress is not dark green. Sentence (3) tells the color of a new dress, as contrasted with other dresses which are not new. Sentence (4) suggests that the speaker has felt a need to clarify which new garment is of this particular color; it is the dress, not the hat or the sweater or . . . .

(b)   1(ii) suggests that the conversation may already have included information as to whether or not the bus goes uptown. 2(ii) might be spoken, for instance, after someone has commented that the plant is outside but not growing well. 3(ii) is very likely when the speaker has been misinterpreted; the speaker wants to clarify that the number is 15, not 16. 4(ii) might suggest that the person to whom the sentence is spoken has mistakenly connected some object because he or she thought the speaker said *connect* rather than the opposite word, *disconnect*.

9D   FEEDBACK

Sentence (a) is 'normal' or unmarked. One may assume, since the speaker says 'I thought . . . ,' that it has not rained. Sentence (b), on the other hand, has syntagmatic focus: by de-accenting *it would rain today* the speaker presents the notion of 'rain today' as a fact. The speaker seems to be telling someone that rain is falling.

9E   FEEDBACK

A sentence such as / I'm not 'sure when she left. / is likely to follow a question such as 'When did Mary leave?' The utterance / I'm not sure 'when she left. /, with a focus on time, would more likely be a response to a question such as 'Did Mary leave at noon?'

Notes

The word *accent* has several different meanings in ordinary usage and, unfortunately, also in the usage of language scientists. The term may refer to the way different groups of people speak ('an Australian accent,' 'a foreign accent') or to one of several marks placed over vowel letters in some language orthographies to indicate particular pronunciations ('an acute accent,' 'a grave accent'). I follow Bolinger (1958, 1961b) in using this term to designate the most prominent syllable (and therefore the most prominent word) in a tone unit.

   The terms *tone unit, tonality, tone,* and *tonicity*, as used here, were introduced by Halliday (1967 and 1970), as well as the concept of marked and unmarked focus. Halliday uses the term *tonic syllable* for what I call the accented syllable. Brown, Currie, and Kenworthy (1980), and Currie (1980 and 1981) have questioned the assumption that a tone unit contains only one accented syllable.

I use the term *paradigmatic focus* for what other authors, for example Bolinger (1961a) and Bing (1983), call 'contrastive' focus. My reason for preferring 'paradigmatic' can best be explained through examples like the following:

Did 'John 'leave at '**noon**?
I 'don't 'know '**when** he 'left.

Does '**Mary** 'know about 'this?
'Everybody's been told?

When is not in contrast with *at noon* nor *everybody* with *Mary*. The two words have special functions with regard to their syntacto-semantic classes, the first as interrogative-relative, the second to express totality with respect to the class of humans.

The examples 'I thought it would **rain** today' and 'I **thought** it would rain today' are taken from Crystal (1969: 265).

The description of de-accenting and its role in discourse cohesion owes much to Halliday and Hasan (1976) and to Ladd (1980). These are highly recommended to the reader, as is Couper-Kuhlen (1986) for a general survey of prosodic elements in English. Coulthard (1977) contains a chapter which deals with the uses of prosody in discourse structure.

In any discourse what is 'old (or given) information' versus 'new information' is indicated by syntactic and lexical devices as well as prosodic ones. Allerton (1978), Chafe (1976), Daneš (1960), and Gunter (1974) treat this topic from various points of view.

10

Intonation

Intonation is part of the language system. We produce melodies by changing the frequency of vibration of the vocal cords, mostly at the accented syllable. We recognize falling and rising tunes of different length – long fall and short fall, long rise and short rise – and combinations of these tunes.

10.1   Intonation and perception

English utterances are seldom spoken in a monotone. Speakers produce melodies of different kinds, with the voice rising and falling, and hearers perceive different melodies. Strangely, though, the tunes which the speaker produces are not exactly what the listener hears. Recent research has shown that in English (and probably in other languages, possibly in all languages) a speaker begins an utterance at a high pitch. From this beginning the pitch generally falls until the end, except that the downward trend – the line of declination – is interrupted by one or more shifts upward or downward from the basic line.

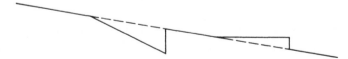

The hearer, however, perceives the shifts more than the basic line. What most listeners would consider a 'rising intonation' seems to be higher at the end than at the beginning of the utterance. In reality, the final pitch may not be as high as the initial one; it is the upward shift from the line of declination that gives the impression of a high ending. For example, the way a listener perceives the question *Are you going*? (a single tone unit) can be represented as on the left below. On the right below is a way of showing what the actual physical facts are more likely to be.

'Pitch' refers to the relative frequency of vibration of the vocal cords: 'high pitch' is rapid vibration, 'low pitch' is slow vibration; 'rising' and 'falling' indicate increasing and decreasing speed, respectively. Frequency of vibration depends partly on the force with which air comes up from the lungs and partly on the tension of the vocal cords (due to the positioning of the arytenoid cartilages). Since heavy pressure of air and rapid vibration of the vocal cords often go together, loud stress and high pitch often coincide in English utterances, but not always.

If an utterance consists of a single syllable – for instance, *Yes* or *No* or *Good* – all the change of pitch takes place in the voiced elements of that syllable, and especially in the vowel.

If an utterance, or one tone unit of an utterance, consists of several syllables, the change of pitch may coincide with just one of the syllables

or it may be spread over a sequence of syllables so that part of the change, up or down, occurs with each stressed syllable in the sequence.

There have been two basic ways of describing the melodies of English, the 'levels' approach and the 'contour' approach. The levels approach uses a sort of scale, similar to the scale used in music but simpler. This approach is based on the assumption that English has an inventory of distinctive pitch levels, just as it has an inventory of distinctive vowel and consonant phonemes. Further, just as any utterance is a sequence of vowels and consonants, it is also a sequence of the distinctive pitch phonemes which accompany the segmental phonemes. This has, at least until recently, been the approach of American linguists, who have maintained that there are four such levels. The levels may be numbered, say, 1 to 4 from lowest to highest pitch, or given names, such as Low, Mid, High, and Extra High. Of course, these levels are relative, not based on any given numbers of vibrations. In absolute terms a child's lowest pitch may be physically identical to an adult's highest pitch since chilren have shorter vocal cords than adults and thus have higher-pitched voices.

For graphic presentation the intonation of an utterance can be shown with lines at four levels with respect to the line of print – just under the line of print, a little below that, just above the print, and a little higher. Less dramatic-ally, the intonation can be shown with letters or numbers interspersed in the line of print. Thus, the utterance *I'm 'going 'home* might appear in one of these forms:

I'm 'going ˈ**home**.
[2] *I'm 'going* [3] '**home** [1]
[m] *I'm 'going* [h] '**home** [1]

These alternative exhibits all indicate an utterance which is perceived as begin-ning at the speaker's middle range, rising to a high note at the beginning of the word *home*, and dropping to low during the pronunciation of that word.

The contour approach to describing intonation assumes that the relevant elements in a tune are not so much levels as *movements*, changes of pitch – rises and falls. This seems to be more in line with the way people actually perceive intonation patterns. As we listen to someone talk, we may recognize a high point or a low point in the utterance, but are probably more aware of the rises and falls of the voice.

If contours are the relevant parts of intonation melodies, how many con-tours are there? Some phonologists have said that there are basically only two tunes or contours, Fall and Rise. It seems essential, however, to divide each of these by two, so that we recognize a long fall, a short fall, a long rise, and a short rise. The word 'long' is appropriate, since *long* can refer to distance or to time. The word 'short' may not be so appropriate; perhaps 'abrupt fall' and 'abrupt rise' would be better terms, for it is not the amount of change that is being discussed; it is the time allotted to the change. Though we represent intonation as changes in spatial dimensions, we need to keep in mind that intonation, like other parts of speech, refers to activities, temporal events.

Other linguists have added a third tune, 'fall–rise' and a fourth tune 'rise–fall.' Whatever the number of contours recognized, there must be some semantic contrasts, or ranges of semantic functions, associated with the differ-ent contours.

Contrary to popular belief, all analysts of English intonation have insisted that there is no melody which is exclusively associated with one type of sen-tence: statements do not necessarily have a falling tune, questions do not necessarily rise. The tunes do not correlate with any specific kinds of gram-matical structure, and yet there is an element of truth in the popular belief.

In discussing accent (chapter 9) our procedure was to assume that occur-rence of accent on the last lexical item of a tone unit is neutral, unmarked, essentially meaningless, and that other occurrences of accent have meanings which can only be understood in the way they relate to other parts of the discourse and to the expectations of the hearer. In a similar fashion we assume that a falling intonation is 'normal' or neutral because vibration of the vocal cords naturally decreases as the voice moves to the end of an utterance – to silence. With this assumption a long fall is unmarked, and other tunes – long or short rise, short fall, rise–fall, fall–rise – are marked and thus meaningful in special ways.

10.2   The falling tunes

The long fall generally indicates finality: the speaker has delivered a message and that is all. Nothing else is communicated by this tune; the speaker does not indicate an intention to continue speaking and any response expected will fit within a framework of anticipations. Thus the long fall is common in statements; in replies to questions; in Wh-questions (questions that begin with a question word – *who, what, when, where, why, how*) since such questions presuppose the possibility of an answer ('Who told you that?' presupposes that somebody told the hearer something; 'When will the concert be held?' presupposes that a concert will be held at some time.) The long fall may be used in commands if the speaker expects that the hearer will carry out the command.

> [F] **Yes.**   [F] **No.**   [F] **Here.**   [F] **Why?**

When the contour consists of a single syllable, as in these examples, the basic falling contour is a 'glide' down: all the change of pitch occurs in the voiced elements of the syllable.

> [F] '**May**be.   [F] '**Sure**ly.   [F] '**Yes** sir.   [F] '**Cer**tainly.

When the contour consists of an accented syllable followed by one or more other syllables, as in these examples, the falling tune is a 'step' down: the accented syllable has a high pitch and the following syllable(s) low pitch.

> 'Very [F] '**much**.   'Yes, in[F]'**deed**.   ,I ,under[F]'**stand**.
> 'How do you [F] '**do**.   To[F]'**mor**row.   Ex[F]'**cuse** me.
> 'Where are you [F] '**go**ing?   'How 'much [F] '**is** it?

Syllables before the accented syllable are perceived as being on a lower pitch than the accented syllable, though they probably are not.

> [F] '**Yes**terday.   'This [F] '**morn**ing.
> 'Right a[F]'**way**.   'Not 'very [F] '**of**ten.
> They're [F] '**lea**ving.   I'm 'rather [F] '**bu**sy.

'Stay ^F '**here**.   'Please 'close the ^F '**win**dow.
'What 'time is your ap^F'**point**ment?
'Where can we 'get a ^F '**ta**xi?

The meaning of the short fall can be expressed as 'almost finality.' This tune differs from the long fall in suggesting that more is to follow. Thus, if the speaker says nothing more, the hearer will probably have an impression of abrupt termination. 'Certainly,' spoken with a long fall, denotes deliberateness and carefulness on the part of the speaker; the same with a short fall may give the impression of brusqueness, impatience, lack of concern.

The rise–fall adds emphasis to what would be communicated by the long fall alone. What we indicate as a rise at the beginning of a tone unit means simply that the speaker maintains the initial high pitch for a longer time than in the long fall.

^rI ^F'**like** it.   ^rShe's ^F'**won**derful.

It has been suggested that questions which begin 'Why don't you . . . ,' are true questions if they are spoken with a long fall but are meant to be suggestions when uttered with a rise–fall.

'Why 'don't you 'look for a ^F'**job**?   (a question)
^r'Why 'don't you 'look for a ^F'**job**?   (a suggestion)

When the rise is not initial in the tone unit, the pitch goes up on one syllable and down on a following syllable. For at least some speakers such a rise is common on words like *actually, really, very*.

They're ^r'actually ^F'**go**ing.
'That's ^r'awfully ^F'**kind** of you.

10.3 The rising tunes

The long rise is the opposite of the long fall: it is non-final, not conclusive. In a statement it suggests that the message is uncommon, even absurd, or it contradicts what was said previously. It is used to ask for a repetition of what was said, and it is frequent in yes–no questions, the sort of question that does not begin with a question word, since such questions do not carry the presuppositions of information questions. 'Did Alex tell you that?' and 'Will there be a concert?,' for example, presuppose nothing.

If the accented syllable is initial in its tone unit, the 'rise' is simply the maintenance of high pitch. Any unaccented syllables which follow are intoned at approximately the same pitch.

^R**Yes?**   ^Rı**Ready?**   ^Rı**Maybe.**

When the accented syllable is non-initial, that syllable begins a rise from the line of declination. Any following syllables continue the rise.

ı**Are you** ^Rı**ready?**   ı**Won't you** ı**come a**^Rı**long with us?**

A short rise can be a call for attention or a signal that the speaker is listening and expects the conversation to go on. The word 'Really?,' spoken with a long rise in response to some statement, may suggest doubt or surprise at what was said; the same word with a short rise would be taken only as a show of interest.

The fall–rise can be just a variation on the long rise, another way of asking a yes–no question or of signaling that the statement is somehow unusual. If the fall–rise has a meaning of its own, it somewhat combines the meanings of the fall and the rise; it expresses but does not conclude. It states something but implies that more can be said on the subject; what is said is not untrue but it is not necessarily the whole truth; or what has been said is open to various interpretations.

(Ellen's rather pretty, don't you think?)   ı**Not** ^Fı**bad**^r.
(Can you help us out?)   I ^Fı**might**^r.

Rising tunes are common in various kinds of phatic communion. The circumstances differ dialectally and perhaps idiosyncratically, but it is common to hear a rise or fall–rise in greetings, leave-takings, expressions of thanks and other social formulas.

Good^fı**bye**^r   ı**See you to**^fı**morrow**^r

10.4   Comparisons

The different tunes contrast with one another semantically. It would be a mistake to assume that each tune has some specific, clearcut meaning, but, for that matter, it would be a mistake to think that lexical items like *table* or *love* or *democracy* have simple, clearcut meanings. The different tunes occurring with the same sequence of words signal differences of meaning, but what the meaning is depends on the context in which the utterance occurs, just as the meanings of words vary with context.

Compare these utterances of the single word *Yes*.

(1)   ^F ı**Yes**
       (An affirmative answer to some question; the speaker leaves no doubt about his or her feelings or beliefs and seems to regard the matter, whatever it may be, as important.)

(2) ^{f} 'Yes

(Also an affirmative answer, of course, but the speaker seems to indicate diffidence or to regard the matter as obvious or unimportant.)

(3) ^{R} 'Yes

(A question which, according to the context, may mean 'Did you say "Yes"?' or 'Can we count on this?' or 'Is that the way it's going to be?' – in short, a question for which the speaker expects an affirmative answer.)

(4) ^{r} 'Yes

(Nothing more than a signal of attention; the speaker's name has been called, perhaps, and he or she is ready to listen.)

(5) ^{f} 'Yes^r

(Expresses partial agreement mixed with doubt or reservations; the message, in effect, is 'Yes, that's true but . . .'.)

(6) ^{r} 'Yes^F

(By maintaining high pitch for an instant longer than in the long fall, no. (1), the speaker indicates that this message is somehow special – the utterance contains an expression of something extra, which may be enthusiasm or exasperation or some other emotion.)

If you replace the word *Yes* with *No* and repeat these six tunes, you will produce utterances with the opposite lexical meaning, but the general effects – the meanings of the tunes – are practically the same as above.

Here are more examples, first with a name, *Pat*, and then with the sentence *I'm sorry*.

(7)	^{F} 'Pat	Possibly an answer to a question, such as 'Who's playing the piano?'
(8)	^{R} 'Pat	A very brief question, equivalent to, for instance, 'Was it Pat?'
(9)	^{r} 'Pat	A call to Pat, a short distance away.
(10)	^{f} 'Pat^r	Possibly the same, at a greater distance.
(11)	I'm ^{F} 'sorry	An emotionless, matter-of-fact statement.
(12)	I'm ^{R} 'sorry	Equivalent to 'What did you say?' or 'Would you repeat that?'
(13)	I'm ^{f} 'sorry^r	An apology, quite likely for something foreseen, as when the speaker needs to interrupt.
(14)	^{f} I'm 'sorry^r	An apology, perhaps when the speaker has just become aware of his/her mistake.

The next utterances have the form of ordinary statements.

(15)	They're ^{F} 'going	A flat statement.
(16)	They're ^{f} 'going	Incomplete; we have the impression that the speaker has not finished.

(17) They're ^{F} **'going**^{r} The speaker implies more than he says; some special meaning has to be derived from the circumstances.

(18) They're ^{R} **'going**   A kind of question – a request for repetition or clarification.

The next utterances have the inverted word order which is usually associated with yes-no questions. We describe them all together.

(19) Are they ^{R} **'going**
(20) ^{f} Are they ^{R} **'going**
(21) Are they ^{F} **'going**
(22) Are they ^{R} **'go**^{f}**ing**

No. (19) is the most common way of asking a question in North America, fairly flat until near the end, while no. (20) seems the usual way in the rest of the English-speaking world, with a high beginning, a dip down, and then a rise. No. (21) is a different way of asking a yes–no question, used by those whose work requires them to ask numerous such questions, for example, customs inspectors. This falling tune might be used by anyone who has asked a number of similar questions with rising intonation – something like this:

Is it ^{R} **'pink?**
^{r} **'No?** / Is it ^{R} **'orange?**
^{r} **'No?** / Is it ^{R} **'brown?**
^{r} **'No?** / 'Well, is it ^{F} **'tan?**

The last of the utterances above, no. (22), is exclamatory: 'How can you ask such a question?'

Note these melodies in questions which begin with a question word:

(23) 'When are they ^{F} **'going**
(24) 'When are they ^{F} **'going**^{r}
(25) ^{R} **'When** are they going
(26) 'When are they ^{R} **'going**

No. (23) should be considered neutral, the usual way of asking a Wh-question. With a slight rise at the end, no. (24) asks the same question but is milder, more deferential. No. (25) is a request for clarification; the speaker knows that he/she has been told the time when 'they' are going but is not sure or needs a repetition. No. (26) is quite different; the speaker is repeating someone else's question and asking for verification. It is roughly equivalent to 'Is this what you asked me?'

The difference between the fall, as in (23) and the rise, as in (26), is especially obvious when the Wh-word is used alone. Compare these two short dialogs:

I'll 'meet you in 'front of the '**Went**worth 'Building.
^R '**Where?**

I'll 'meet you at 'half 'past '**two**.
'That's ^F '**fine**. / ^F '**Where?**

Consider these sentences which have the form of commands.

(27)   'Stay ^F '**here**
(28)   'Stay ^F '**here**^r
(29)   'Stay ^R '**here**^f
(30)   ^f '**You** / 'just ^f '**stay** / 'right ^F '**here**

No. (27) is a brusque command; no. (28) softens it, turning it into a plea or entreaty. No. (29) is not a command at all; it might be the answer to a question such as 'Should I go now or stay here?'; the speaker intends to be helpful. No. (30), on the contrary, with its cascade of short falls, can only be said by someone in control of the person to whom this is addressed.

10.5   Compound tunes

A long utterance is almost necessarily a sequence of several tone units, each of which has its own tune. Some combinations of tunes are typical of certain kinds of sentences. In general, it can be said that when two (or more) tone units in sequence have the same kind of tune – both falling or both rising – they fit together; they make a longer unit than either one alone, the whole sequence falling or rising. When two tone units in sequence differ in their tunes, rising and then falling, or falling and then rising, they present an anti-thesis; the message of the tune is special.

Compound statements with two or more clauses may have a short fall on each clause except the last, with a long fall on the last clause.

(31)   Mc'Carthy 'plays the 'old bas^f'**soon** / and 'Hennesey 'tootles the ^F'**flute**.

Of course, a clause is not necessarily a tone unit, nor a tone unit a clause.

(32)   We're 'going ₁down^f'**town** / 'this ₁after^F'**noon**.

Any long utterance is broken into tone units, as we saw in the previous chapter. The longer the utterance and/or the more slowly and deliberately the style of speaking, the greater the number of 'chunks' in the utterance. Thus, adding to the previous sentence might give us:

(33)   We're 'going ˌdownᶠ'**town** / 'this ˌafterᶠ'**noon** / to 'do some ᶠ'**shopping** / 'while the 'big ᶠ'**sales** are 'on.

A subordinate clause is likely to have a short rise or a fall–rise:

(34)   'While we were ⁽ᶠ⁾'**waiting**ʳ / ᶠ'**Jane** 'wandered 'in.
(35)   ᶠ'**Jane** 'wandered 'in / 'while we were ᶠ'**waiting**ʳ.

Shorter subordinate elements with rise or fall–rise are common:

(36)   Ordiᶠ'**narily** / I 'wouldn't have ᶠ'**been** 'here.
(37)   In ᶠ'**that** 'case\`ʳ / I 'wouldn't have ᶠ'**been** 'here.
(38)   I 'wouldn't have ᶠ'**been** 'here / in ᶠ'**that** 'case\`ʳ.

The following, though they have the same verbal content, are different questions:

(39)   'Would you 'like ᴿ'**coffee** or 'tea?
(40)   'Would you 'like ᴿ'**coffee** / or ᴿ'**tea**?
(41)   'Would you 'like ᴿ'**coffee** / or ᶠ'**tea**?

The first of these is a simple yes–no question. No. (40) is actually two questions. Perhaps while offering coffee to someone, the questioner happens to think of suggesting tea, also. No. (41) is an alternative question, or choice question; the speaker offers two possibilities only and asks the listener to choose between them.

Tag questions are common in English. They consist of an operator – a form of the verb *be* or an auxiliary (*do, have, can, could, will, would, should, may, might, must*) – followed by a personal pronoun (or the word *there*). A negative tag is common after an affirmative clause (*Robert played goalie, didn't he?*) and an affirmative tag after a negative clause (*There aren't any cookies left, are there?*), but an affirmative tag after an affirmative clause is possible (*You like that kind of music, do you?*). With regard to intonation, there are two kinds of tag questions:

(42)   The 'Campbells are ᶠ'**coming** / ᶠ'**aren't** 'they?
(43)   The 'Campbells are ᶠ'**coming** / ʳ'**aren't** ˌthey?
                              (or ᴿ'**aren't** they?)

In the first instance the questioner is not so much seeking information as asking for confirmation of what he/she is asserting. The questioner feels sure of the fact presented and expects agreement. In the second question, no. (43), the speaker is less assured, or not at all sure, and is truly asking for information.

Another kind of tag is an appended name, used as a term of address, a vocative. Attached to a tone unit with a long rise, the tag simply continues the rise – the voice remains relatively high.

(44) ,Are you ^R'**com**fortable, / Mrs '**Grun**dy?

A similar high continuing tag occurs when a yes–no question is framed within another yes–no question:

(45) 'Will they ,be 'here ^R'**long** / ,do you '**think**?

and even when a yes–no question is framed within a statement:

(46) 'Will they ,be 'here ^R'**long** / ,she '**asked**.
      ('Will they be here long?,' she asked.)

A low continuation tag occurs after a long fall.

(47) ,We 'won't be 'here 'very ^F'**long**, / '**Har**old.
(48) 'This is a 'very 'bad ^F'**law**, / it 'seems to '**me**.
(49) 'I can 'help with the ar^F'**range**ments, / ,if you '**want** me 'to.

This low continuation tag may produce, for the hearer, the effect of indifference on the part of the speaker, especially if the tag contains a name, as in no. (47). Any of these utterances can be 'brightened' by the use of a low rise in the tag:

(50) ,We 'won't be 'here 'very ^F'**long**, / ^r'**Har**old.
(51) 'This is a 'very 'bad ^F'**law**, / it 'seems to ^r'**me**.
(52) 'I can 'help with the ar^F'**range**ments, / ,if you ^r'**want** me 'to.

Finally, in our summary of common tunes, consider the serial intonations, those which are used for naming a series of words, phrases, or clauses joined together, often with *and* or *or*. Three familiar patterns are:

(53) ^F'**Jack** / ^F'**Jon**athan / ^F'**Jer**emy / and Je^F'**rome**
(54) ^R'**Jack** / ^R'**Jon**athan / ^R'**Jer**emy / and Je^F'**rome**
(55) ^r'**Jack** / ^r'**Jon**athan / ^r'**Jer**emy / and Je^F'**rome**

The first is a slow, deliberate listing; perhaps the speaker, as each item or individual is named, does not know what will be named next in the list. No. 54 is a highly dramatized enunciation, favored especially by some adults in talking to small children. No. 55 is a normal listing intonation. There is a slight rise on every expression except the last, which has a long fall.

10A Practice: utterances that differ in intonation

Read the following sets of sentences and decide what tune is appropriate for each sentence. The material in parentheses is intended to explain the meaning of the sentence and/or the context in which it is spoken.

1   (a)   They're leaving.   (a statement)
    (b)   They're leaving?   (a request for confirmation)
    (c)   They're leaving . . .   (. . . but they'll be back.)
2   (a)   Are you sure?   (The speaker is questioning.)
    (b)   Are you sure?   (The speaker is challenging.)
3   (a)   (I just found something.)   What?
    (b)   (I said I just found something.)   What?
          (A little gold pin that was lying on the floor.)
4   (a)   When are they leaving?   (an ordinary question)
    (b)   'When are they leaving?'   (a repeated question: 'Is that what
                                                        you asked me?')
5   (a)   This is my son, Henry.   (Henry is the speaker's son.)
    (b)   This is my son, Henry.   (Henry is the person spoken to.)
6   (a)   Is this your son, Henry?   (same difference as above)
    (b)   Is this your son, Henry?
7   (a)   (Is today Tuesday?)   Yes, it is.
    (b)   (Oh, today's not Tuesday.)   Yes, it is.
8   (a)   I'll see you tomorrow,   (a statement)
    (b)   (I'll) see you tomorrow.   (a way of saying goodbye)
9   (a)   (Is Pat speaking at the meeting   Speaking.
          or just attending?)
    (b)   (Voice on telephone: Speaking.
          Is Pat there? Pat replies)
10 (a)   Good morning, Jack.   (brusque, businesslike)
    (b)   Good morning, Jack.   (polite, friendly)
11 (a)   Roses are red, and violets are blue.
    (b)   Although some roses are red, not all of them are.
12 (a)   Give your ticket to the lady who's sitting by the door.
    (b)   Give your ticket to Ann, who's sitting by the door.
13 (a)   In *Winter's End* Lisa Lamarr played the leading role, naturally.
    (b)   In *Winter's End* Lisa Lamarr played the leading role, naturally.
14 (a)   Do you have a pencil or a pen?   (Do you have something to write
                                            with?)
    (b)   Do you have a pencil or a pen?   (I know you have one of them.
                                            Which is it?)
15 (a)   One. Two. Three. Four. Five.   (The speaker is counting slowly,
                                            perhaps sighting objects one by
                                            one.)
    (b)   One. Two. Three. Four. Five.   (The speaker is counting
                                            dramatically, perhaps handling
                                            the objects one by one.)
    (c)   One, two, three, four, five.   (normal, fairly rapid counting)

10.6 Summary

There have been two approaches to the description of English intonation, a levels approach and a contour approach. The levels approach is based on the assumption that the tune of any utterance can be described as a sequence of contrasting levels of pitch; almost universally, those who follow this approach consider that there are four such levels. The contour approach is based on the notion that speakers of the language react to the changes of pitch. In this chapter we have used the contour approach and have recognized these contours: long fall, short fall, long rise, short rise, rise–fall, and fall–rise.

No utterance or type of utterance occurs exclusively with one particular tune. In general, a falling contour often suggests finality; a short fall suggests more abrupt termination than a long fall; a rise–fall is more intense than a simple long fall. A rising contour may indicate the speaker's expectation of some response from the listener, or it may suggest a contradiction of what has been said previously; a short rise is a signal to begin a conversation or a vocal gesture indicating willingness to participate in a conversation. A falling–rising contour is likely to be used to denote that something more will be said, or can be said, or that a larger interpretation is possible. Thus, the fall is likely to occur in statements and often in 'Wh'-questions, and a rise in yes–no questions.

Combinations of simple contours produce **compound contours**. These make fairly obvious distinctions between an alternative question and a simple yes–no question; between apposition and attached vocative; between two clauses which are coordinate and two clauses when one clause introduces or modifies the other; between tag questions that ask for confirmation and those which ask for information; between a common kind of serial enunciation and more dramatic ways of counting.

10B   ADDITIONAL PRACTICE: THREE DIALOGS

Dialog one
A: /'Did you en'joy the ᴿ'**mee**ting 'last 'night?/
B: /ᶠ'**Yes**. /ˌIt was an 'interesting ᶠ'**session**./ ˌThere were a 'lot of 'different oᶠ'**pinions** exꝛ'**pressed**./
A: /ᶠ'**Yes**,/ it's ᶠ'**usually** 'that 'way./ 'Someˌtimes we 'have some ter'rific ᶠ'**arguments**, / but it 'never 'quite 'comes to ᶠ'**blood**ˌshed./
     /'How 'many 'people were ᶠ'**there**?/
B: /A'bout ᶠ'**thir**ty, / I'd 'say./

Variations
(a)   /'Did you en'joy the 'meeting 'last ᴿ'**night**?/
(b)   /'Did you en'joy the ᴿ'**mee**ting 'last 'night?/
(c)   /'Did you enᴿ'**joy** the 'meeting 'last 'night?/
(d)   /'Did ᴿ'**you** en'joy the 'meeting 'last 'night?/

(e)   /^{F}'**Yes**. / ,It was ^{F}'**interesting**./
(f)   /^{f}'**Yes**, / ,it was ^{F}'**interesting**./
(g)   /^{f}'**Yes**^{r}, /,it was ^{F}'**interesting**./

(There is nothing different in what is communicated by the three sentences (e–g). Some people may find differences in the mood or personality of the speaker, but it is not likely that we could find general agreement about what the differences are.)

(h)   /'How 'many 'people were ^{F}'**there**?/
(i)   /'How 'many 'people ^{F}'**were** ,there?/

(These questions are very different. In (h) *there* means 'in that place'; in (i) *there* is the 'existential there.' A grammatically appropriate answer to (h) would be 'Thirty people were there'; for (i) a grammatically appropriate answer is 'There were thirty people.' Pragmatically, of course, 'Thirty people' is appropriate for either.)

(j)   /A'bout ^{F}'**thirty**, / I'd 'say./
(k)   /A'bout ^{R}'**thirty**, / you 'think?/
(l)   /,It was ^{F}'**interesting**./
(m)   /,Was it ^{R}'**interesting**?/
(n)   /It 'must have 'been ^{F}'**interesting**^{r}./

Dialog two
A: /'How do you 'like 'this ^{F}'**weather**?/
B: /It's ^{r}'not ^{F}'**bad**. / I en^{f}'**joy** / the ^{F}'**snow**^{r}./ /But the ^{f}'**wind** / has ,been 'blowing 'hard 'all ^{F}'**day** / and ,I 'don't 'like ^{F}'**that**^{r}./
A: /The ^{f}'**weather** re'port / 'says we'll 'have ^{f}'**warm**er 'weather/ to^{F}'**morrow**./
B: /I 'hope they're ^{F}'**right**^{r}./

Variations
(a)   /I 'hope they're ^{F}'**right**^{r}./
(b)   /I ^{F}'**hope** they're 'right^{r}./
(c)   /I ^{F}'**hope** so^{r}./
(d)   /O^{F}'**kay**^{r}./
(e)   /^{r}'O^{F}'**kay**./
(f)   /Good^{F}'**bye**^{r}./
(g)   /^{r}'Good^{F}'**bye**./
(h)   /^{F}'**Maybe**^{r}./
(i)   /^{r}'**Here** it ^{F}'is./
(j)   /^{r}'**There** they ^{F}'are./
(k)   /Hel^{f}'lo, /^{r}'**Sally**./
(l)   /^{f}'**Hi**, /^{r}'**Tom**./
(m)   /^{r}'**Not** ^{F}'**bad**./

(n) /^{r}'Very ^{F}'**nice**./
(o) /^{r}'That's ^{F}'**good**./
(p) /^{r}'That's ^{F}'**true**./
(q) /I ^{F}'**like** it./
(r) /^{r}'I ^{F}'**like** it./

Dialog three

A: /'How 'long have you 'been in ^{F}'**Wa**shington?/
B: /ˌJust a'bout 'two ^{F}'**months** 'now. / 'We 'came 'here in ^{F}'**March**./
A: /'Have you 'seen 'all the ^{R}'**sights**?/
B: /'Well, I've 'seen a ^{F}'**lot**. / The ^{r}'**Ca**pitol, / the ^{r}'**White** 'House, / the 'Washington ^{r}'**Mo**nument, / the 'Lincoln Me^{r}'**mo**rial . . . /
A: /'Have you 'seen the 'National ^{R}'**Gal**lery?/
B: /Oh ^{F}'**yes**, / I've ^{F}'**been** 'there./
A: /'How a'bout the ^{F}'**Zoo**?/
B: /^{f}'**No**, / I 'haven't 'been ^{F}'**there**^{r}./

Variations

(a) /We 'came 'here in ^{F}'**March**./
(b) /We 'came 'here 'two ^{F}'**months** a'go./
(c) /'Have you 'seen 'all the ^{R}'**sights**?/
(d) /^{R}'**Have** you 'seen 'all the 'sights?/

(The question in (c) is neutral; (d), with its focus on the auxiliary verb, suggests a request for clarification of something said previously.)

(e) /I've 'seen 'everything you're sup^{F}'**posed** to see^{r}./
(f) /I've 'seen 'everything you're sup^{F}'**posed** to^{r}./
(g) /I've 'been to the ^{r}'**Zoo** . . . /
(h) /'Have you 'been to the ^{R}'**Zoo**?/
(i) /'How a'bout the ^{F}'**Zoo**?/
(j) /'Have you ^{R}'**been** 'there?/
(k) /'Have you 'been ^{R}'**there**?/
(l) /I 'haven't ^{F}'**been** 'there./
(m) /I 'haven't 'been ^{F}'**there**^{r}./

10A Feedback

These are possible answers, though not the only possible ones.

1 (a) They're ^{F} leaving.
  (b) They're ^{R} leaving?
  (c) They're ^{f} leaving ^{r} . . .
2 (a) Are you ^{R} sure?
  (b) Are you ^{F} sure?

3   (a) ^{R} What?
   (b) ^{F} What?
4   (a)   When are they ^{F} leaving?
   (b)   When are they ^{R} leaving?
5   (a)   This is my ^{f} son / ^{F} Henry.
   (b)   This is my ^{F} son / ^{r} Henry.
6   (a)   Is this your son ^{R} Henry?
   (b)   Is this your ^{R} son / Henry?
7   (a) ^{f} Yes / it ^{F} is.
   (b) ^{R} Yes it is.
8   (a)   I'll see you to^{F}morrow.
   (b)   (I'll) see you to^{f}morrow^{r}.
9   (a) ^{F} Speaking.
   (b) ^{f} Speaking^{r}.
10 (a)   Good ^{F} morning / Jack.
   (b)   Good ^{F} morning / ^{r} Jack.
11 (a)   Roses are ^{f} red / and violets are ^{F} blue.
   (b)   Although some roses are ^{f} red ^{r} / not ^{F} all of them are.
or: Although ^{F} some roses are red ^{r} / not ^{F} all of them are ^{r}.
12 (a)   Give your ticket to the ^{f} lady / who's sitting by the ^{F} door.
   (b)   Give your ticket to ^{f} Ann ^{r} / who's sitting by the ^{F} door.
13 (a)   In *Winter's* ^{f} *End* / Lisa Lamarr played the leading role ^{F} naturally.
   (b)   In *Winter's* ^{f} *End* / Lisa Lamarr played the leading ^{F} role / ^{r} naturally.
14 (a)   Do you have a pencil or a ^{R} pen?
   (b)   Do you have a ^{R} pencil or a ^{F} pen?
15 (a) ^{F} One / ^{F} Two / ^{F} Three / ^{F} Four / ^{F} Five.
   (b) ^{R} One / ^{R} Two / ^{R} Three / ^{R} Four / ^{F} Five.
   (c) ^{r} One / ^{r} two / ^{r} three / ^{r} four / ^{F} five.

Notes

Descriptions of English intonation contours differ considerably from one another in the mode of description and in details of what is described, and yet there is a commonality in what is described. The following must be cited: Bing (1980), Bolinger (1983, 1986), Brown, Currie, and Kenworthy (1980), Couper-Kuhlen (1986), Crystal (1969), Glenn (1976), Halliday (1967), Kingdon (1958b), Ladd (1980), Leben (1976), Lehiste (1970), O'Connor and Arnold (1973), Pierrehumbert (1987), Pike (1945). Cruttenden (1986), especially chapter 5, is the best statement of intonational differences in English dialects.

For the work of the 'Dutch School' see Willems (1982) and the bibliography cited there.

On the perception and acquisition of tone see Gandour (1978) and Li and Thompson (1978).

11

Predicting Word Stress

Phonology describes the sound structure of a language; morphology describes the structure of words; and syntax describes the uses of words in phrases and sentences. To explain the place of stressed syllables in different words we need to consider facts about sounds, word forms, and syntactic classes.

11.1   Is stress predictable?

In some languages the position of stress in a word is invariable. In Czech and Finnish it is always the first syllable of a word which is most prominent; in Polish the next-to-last syllable is stressed; in French, insofar as there is any stress difference at all, the last syllable is generally the most prominent. In languages like these, where stress is fixed on a particular syllable and therefore predictable, stress cannot differentiate meanings. In contrast, Spanish and Russian have sets of words which differ only in the position of stress. How about English?

   English is not like Czech, Finnish, Polish, or French. We have already seen that the stress of a polysyllabic word may be on the first syllable ('cannibal), the second (a'rena), the third (after'noon), or some later syllable. In a general sense stress is variable in English. To be sure, stress is invariable for any specific word. Although there are dialect differences in stress (garage is stressed on the second syllable in North America, on the first syllable everywhere else) just as there are dialect differences in vowels (either, half, roof, for example), we are not free to put stress on whatever syllable we want. If a person still learning English as a new language says 'beginner instead of be'ginner, those who already know the language consider it a mispronunciation, even though the meaning is probably clear enough. In English words stress is not fixed – but does that mean that it is not predictable?

   On the other hand stress does not play a large role in differentiating words. Billow and below, reefer and refer are sometimes cited as pairs of words which differ mostly in position of stress, but there are not many such pairs. There are somewhat more pairs like the noun 'insult and the verb in'sult, noun 'abstract, verb and adjective ab'stract, a type which we examine later, sets of words which are semantically related but grammatically different.

Every English dictionary uses some kind of key to pronunciation. Following the orthographic form of every word that is listed there is some kind of respelling in the special key to indicate the pronunciation of the word. Such a respelling implies that the usual orthography is not sufficiently regular for us to deduce the pronunciation from the ordinary spelling, and of course there is considerable truth in the implication; the irregularities and inconsistencies of English spelling are well known (though sometimes they are exaggerated).

One part of the respelling, for polysyllabic words, is an indication of stress. For every word of more than one syllable the dictionary's respelling indicates which is the stressed syllable; for example *maintain* (mān.tān'). Here again there is an obvious implication: that stress is completely unpredictable, that a reader cannot look at a written word and correctly figure out where the stress is. The implication is not entirely accurate; while it is not possible to predict the stress in all English words, there are many which follow general principles.

There are general rules which account for the place of stress in numerous words, though not in all the words of the language. Many of these rules you know already, though not in a completely conscious way. Words which end in *-tion*, such as *constitution, composition, interruption, proclamation, simplification* – literally hundreds of words – are stressed on the vowel before this ending. Similarly, words with a final *-ity* have stress on the vowel before the ending (*asininity, humidity, mediocrity, relativity, sentimentality*). These are two small generalizations that can be made about stress placement. There are other, more subtle ones which, by and large, are known to speakers of the language. For example, the following words may be new to you (or half-new), but you can probably stress each one of them correctly:

comatula   lobatic   metrify   polyphase   spiriferous

11.2   Stress rules

In the remainder of this chapter we explore the rules – that is, general statements – regarding the place of stress in different groups of words. We will see that there are limits to the rules. Each rule has its particular domain; not everything is predictable.

Stress rules are based on three kinds of information: syntactic, morphological, and phonological.

Syntactic information   The place of stress in a word depends partly on what part of speech it is. The noun 'insult is stressed differently from the verb in'sult. Similarly, compare the adjective con'tent and the noun 'contents, the noun 'present ('gift') and the adjective 'present ('not absent') with the verb *pre'sent*. The words we examine here are nouns, verbs, and adjectives, and somewhat different rules apply to each of these parts of speech.

Morphological information　We have seen that the suffixes *+tion* and *+ity* have a role in the location of stress. Every word has a morphological composition. A word may be **simple**, consisting of a single base: for example, *arm, baby, circle, fat, manage*. Some words, like *armchair, babysit, ice-cold, square dance* are **compounds**, consisting of two bases together (whether our orthographic conventions prefer them written as a single word, or with a hyphen, or with a space between the parts). Finally, some words are **complex**, consisting of a **prefix** plus a base (*disarm, encircle, mismanage, renew*) or a base plus a **suffix** (*babyish, fatten, happiness, management*). A word may contain prefix + base + suffix (*mismanagement, unhappiness*), base + base + suffix (*babysitting, square dancer*), base + suffix + suffix (*fattening, sharpener*), and so forth. The morphological composition has a role in determining stress. We will see that different kinds of suffixes, especially, are important in determining the place of stress. Strictly speaking, a prefix or a suffix must have a meaning or a function, as in the examples above. For the purpose of locating the stressed syllable in a word we consider certain elements which occur at the beginning of numerous words, 'prefixes,' and elements which often occur in final place, 'suffixes.'

Phonological information　The place of stress in particular words depends in part on the nature of the last two syllables, the ult and penult. We need to consider whether a syllable has a free vowel or not and the number of consonants, if any, which close the syllable. Since phonological facts interact with syntactic and morphological facts, we shall see that rules about vowels and consonants are different for nouns, verbs, and adjectives.

To review, a free vowel is one which can occur at the end of a one-syllable word. Free vowels are illustrated in these words:

see, seat	sue, suit	spa, calm
bay, bait	go, goat	law, laud
by, bite	cow, scout	toy, void

Notice that in each of the following words the last syllable, the ult, has a free vowel:

agree　remain　rely　destroy　cellophane　anecdote

And in each of the next words the next-to-last syllable, the penult, has a free vowel:

arena　aroma　diploma　hiatus　horizon

In the next group of words the penult ends with a consonant – the syllable division is between two consonants:

enigma   veranda   parental   detergent   amalgam

But in the following words the penult does not end with a consonant and does not have a free vowel:

abacus   cinema   generous   melody   evident

In the rest of this chapter we will be weaving in and out among the three kinds of phenomena, syntactic, morphological, and phonological.

11.3   Neutral suffixes

It was noted in chapter 5 that when a suffix of Old English origin is added to a word, stress does not change; e.g. *'neighbor, 'neighborly, 'neighborliness, 'neighborhood.* We say that suffixes of Old English origin (and a few others) are **neutral**: they are added to independent words and have no effect on the stress. For example, the words *ab'sorbing, 'interesting, pre'vailing,* and *'terrifying* have the same stressed syllables as *ab'sorb, 'interest, pre'vail,* and *'terrify,* respectively. This *#ing* is a neutral suffix, and so are *#hood, #ly,* and *#ness,* illustrated above. (A neutral suffix will be marked with the boundary symbol # before it.) A long list of neutral suffixes (and other kinds of suffixes) can be found in the Appendix.

Although most neutral suffixes are of Old English origin, this does not mean that the words to which they are added are necessarily of Old English origin.

11.4   Tonic endings

Nouns which end in *-oon* typically have stress on the ending: *balloon, raccoon, macaroon, saloon,* etc. An ending like this is a **tonic ending**. Most words that have tonic endings have been borrowed from Modern French, but not all. Some, like *absentee,* have been formed in English with a suffix of French origin. The following are some more examples of words with tonic endings (and more are to be found in the Appendix):

debonaire, millionaire
refugee, internee
Congolese, Vietnamese
brunette, kitchenette
antique, technique

11.5   The basic stress rule for verbs

Once we have recognized the neutral suffixes and the tonic endings we are ready for more general statements about stress. Let's consider the following sets of verbs:

1a	2a	3
agree	diagnose	abolish
delay	exercise	consider
exclude	intimidate	develop
cajole	monopolize	imagine
invite	persecute	remember
pronounce	ridicule	solicit

1b	2b
attract	compliment
consist	gallivant
depend	manifest
exempt	
involve	
reverse	

Note that in groups 1a and 1b the last syllable, the **ult**, is stressed; in 2a and 2b the third syllable from the end, the **antepenult**, is stressed; and in group 3 the **penult**, the next-to-last syllable, is the stressed syllable. Why?

The verbs in group 1 have what we may call a stressable ult: either the ult has a free vowel (1a) or it ends with at least two consonants (1b). Furthermore, each verb in the group consists of just two syllables. The ult is stressed.

In group 2 also each verb has a heavy ult, because of the free vowel (2a) or because of the cluster of consonants at the end (2b). These verbs have three or more syllables. The antepenult is stressed. (In centuries past they were stressed on the ult. Even today, in Scotland and in the Caribbean, one may hear *diagnose* or *dominate* stressed on the ult.)

Each word in group 3 has an unstressable ult: the ult contains a checked vowel followed by not more than one consonant. The penult is stressed.

This general statement, or rule, for what we have observed for verbs can be put into the form of a decision tree:

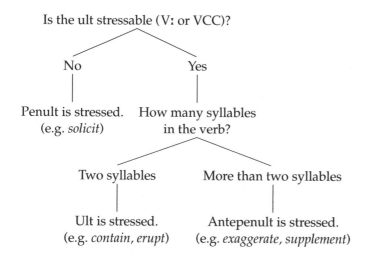

11A   EXERCISE WITH VERBS

All of the verbs below follow this basic rule. Note which syllable is stressed in each one and mark it 1a, 1b, 2a, 2b, or 3, according to the scheme above. (There aren't many examples of group 2b here because there aren't many such verbs in the language.)

adopt	exonerate	produce
answer	furnish	remark
covet	inhabit	substitute
dehumidify	mechanize	supplement
exhaust	offend	transcribe

11.6   The basic stress rule for nouns

The first question to ask about verbs when determining the position of stress is: 'Is the ult stressable or not?' Nouns are different. The first question to ask about a noun is: 'How many syllables does the noun have?' The next question is: 'Does the ult have a free vowel or not?' It doesn't matter how many consonants occur in final position. Examine these sets of nouns.

1a	2	3a
alcove	appetite	affidavit
membrane	hypotenuse	aroma
statute	institute	horizon
termite	porcupine	hypnosis
textile	vicissitude	papyrus

1b		3b
cavern		appendix
focus		intestine
menace		memorandum
premise		synopsis
ticket		veranda

3c
camera
citizen
deficit
gelatin
pelican

Note, first, that each noun of groups 1a and 1b has just two syllables. The penult is stressed whether the ult vowel is free (1a) or not (1b) – but see the note at the end of this chapter. If there are more than two syllables in the noun, it makes a difference whether the ult has a free vowel or not. If the ult vowel is free, as in group 2, the antepenult is stressed. If the ult vowel is not a free vowel, as in group 3, we ask if the penult is stressable. The penult is stressable if it has a free vowel (3a) or ends with a consonant (3b). If the penult is not stressable, the antepenult is stressed (3c).

The basic noun rule can be summarized in this decision tree:

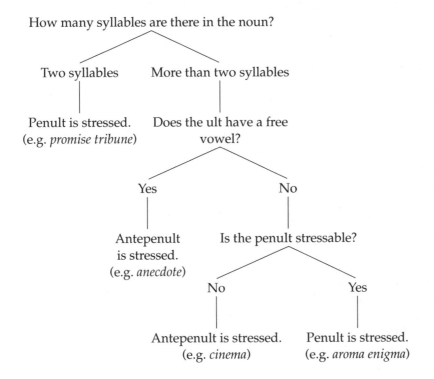

11B   EXERCISE WITH NOUNS

Note the stress in the following nouns and mark each one as 1a, 1b, 2, 3a, 3b, or 3c, according to how it fits the classification above.

javelin	closet	diploma
idea	satellite	veteran
bonanza	opera	platinum
harmonica	hypothesis	neuritis
tabloid	formaldehyde	vestibule

11.7   Rules for adjectives

We do not need a new rule for the stress of adjectives. There are essentially two types of adjectives, so far as the place of stress is concerned: one type follows the stress rule for verbs, the other the stress rule for nouns.

Type I   Observe these sets of adjectives:

(1a)		(2a)		(3)	
	contrite		asinine		academic
	inane		bellicose		decrepit
	obscene		erudite		intrepid
	serene		grandiose		periodic

(1b)		(2b)	
	absurd		difficult
	correct		manifest
	distinct		moribund

Note that these are exactly parallel to the grouping of verbs in section 11.5. Group 1 adjectives have two syllables and the ult is stressable, either because of the free vowel (1a) or the final cluster of consonants (1b); the ult is stressed. Group 2 adjectives have more than two syllables and a stressable ult, because of the free vowel (2a) or the final consonant cluster (2b); the antepenult is stressed. Group 3 contains adjectives with an unstressable ult (almost always -*ic* or -*id* or -*it*); the penult is stressed.

Type II   adjectives end with one of these suffixes: +*al*, +*ar*, +*ant/ent*, or +*ous*. Note that these suffixes are all monosyllabic, do not have a free vowel, and the vowel is initial in the suffix. We refer to these as weak suffixes. In adjectives with these suffixes either the penult or the antepenult is stressed, depending on the nature of the penult. The following exercise will help you to determine the general rule.

11C   EXERCISE WITH ADJECTIVES

(a)   Mark the stress in each of these words:

> fatal   global   polar   stellar   cogent   decent   dormant   nervous

> General statement: If an adjective has a weak suffix preceded by a base of just one syllable, stress is on the _____.

(b)   Each of the words below has a base of more than one syllable. Do three things:

> 1   If the vowel of the penult is a free vowel, put a macron over the vowel letter, e.g. *complācent*;

2 If the vowel of the penult is followed by two consonants (a consonant cluster which cannot occur in word-initial position), draw a line between the two consonant letters, e.g. *abun | dant*;

3 Use the tick to show whether the penult or the antepenult is stressed, e.g. *com'placent, re'luctant, 'adamant*.

ac	ci	den	tal	re	luc	tant	pe	ri	phe	ral
e	ter	nal	mag	ni	fi	cent	a	na	lo	gous
vi	gi	lant		bar	ba	rous	a	bun	dant	
ma	lig	nant		ge	ne	rous	a	nec	do	tal

We note that the penult is stressed if it meets either of these conditions:

(1)
(2)

If the penult meets neither of these conditions, the antepenult is stressed.

Adjectives of this type are just like nouns which have a checked vowel in the ult. In fact, the weak suffix +*ant*/*ent* appears in nouns as well as adjectives; compare *detergent, occupant, participant*.

To go a bit farther, we may consider the following noun endings also weak suffixes:

+*a*	mica, aroma, enigma, cinema
+*ance/ence*	hindrance, reluctance, evidence
+*is*	thesis, neurosis, synopsis, emphasis
+*on*	nylon, skeleton
+*um*	fulcrum, platinum
+*us*	circus, hiatus

11D QUESTION

Consider these words, all of which have a weak suffix:

algebra   citrus   discipline   eloquent   integral

In each word the ult is not streasable. The penult vowel is followed by two consonants (-br-, -tr-, -pl-, -kw-, -gr-), and yet stress is on the antepenult. Are these words exceptions to the rule just formulated?

11.8 Extending the basic stress rules

Consider these verbs and adjectives:

> copy envy marry worry easy happy ugly
> argue continue issue rescue
> borrow follow swallow hollow narrow yellow

The words in the three lines end with vowels that we have written, respectively, as /i/, /u/, and /o/. Are these free vowels? We have seen in section 5.7 that different speakers give different answers to this question. In final position there is no contrast between a free vowel /ii/ and a checked /ɪ/, a free /uu/ and a checked /ʊ/, nor between /ou/ and /o/. For the stress rules these three vowels in final position act like checked vowels. The ult is not stressable and therefore stress falls on the penult, just as it does in such verbs and adjectives as *consider, deposit, comic, valid*.

Similarly, in nouns the ult is light if it contains one of these three vowels without a consonant following, as in the following examples:

> albino macaroni commando jujitsu avenue revenue

In the first four of these words the penult is stressable, because it has a free vowel or is a closed syllable, and so receives the stress. If the ult were strong, the antepenult would be stressed. In the last two words neither ult nor penult is stressable; the antepenult is stressed.

> *Rule*: Final /i u o/ count as checked vowels, making the ult unstressable. A word with one of these vowels in final position has stress on the penult or antepenult according to the usual rules.

Next we consider certain vowels which are not final.

11E DISCOVERY EXERCISE

(a) Which syllable is stressed in the following words – the ult, penult, or antepenult?

> continuous manual casual contiguous

(b) What vowel occurs in the penult?
(c) Is the penult closed with a consonant?
(d) Which syllable is stressed in the following words?

> ceremonial remedial obedient radiant
> phobia   myopia   calcium   radius

(e)   What vowel occurs in the penult?

(f)   Is the penult closed or open?

When /i/ and /u/ occur immediately before another vowel, they appear to be free. But as we have seen before (section 5.7), there is no contrast between free /ii/ and checked /ɪ/, nor between free /uu/ and checked /ʊ/, in this position. For stress assignment, /i/ or /u/ in an open penult acts like a checked vowel.

> *Rule*: When /i/ or /u/ occurs in an open penult, the penult is unstress-able and stress is on the antepenult. In this case /i/ must be followed immediately by another vowel; /u/ may be followed by an ambisyllabic consonant.

11F   PRACTICE

Here is a list of type II adjectives, with unstressable ult. Determine for each one whether the penult or the antepenult is stressed, and why.

annual	corporal	feminine
innocuous	internal	luminous
masculine	nocturnal	oriental
ridiculous	significant	similar
superior	tedious	vigilant

11.9   Some variations in stress

Ever since the eleventh century English has been borrowing words from other languages, chiefly French, with stress on the last syllable. Often the stress has been moved forward; *beauty, companion, element,* and *ticket* are a small sample of the words which were once stressed on the last syllable but no longer are. This process of stress-advancement is still going on.

11G   QUESTIONS

All of the following words were originally stressed on the ult, and they may still be pronounced that way. But each of them has an alternative pronunciation in which stress falls, instead, on the penult or the antepenult.

(a)   Which are possibly stressed on the penult and which on the antepenult?

(b)   What determines whether stress advances to the penult or to the antepenult?

chimpanzee	employee	mezzanine
cigarette	lemonade	Portuguese
divorcee	macramé	referee

11H WHAT DO YOU SAY?

A number of three-syllable words which end in /iin/, like *magazine* and *mezzanine*, vary in pronunciation in this way: they may be stressed on the ult or on the antepenult. Examine the next group of words and decide which you stress on the ult, which on the antepenult, and which, if any, do you vary?

figurine gabardine gasoline guillotine kerosene
libertine limousine nicotine quarantine submarine tambourine
tangerine trampoline

All of these variable words which may be stressed on the ult or on the antepenult are nouns and of course more than two syllables long. Among two-syllable nouns there is also some variation; *routine*, for example, may be stressed on either syllable. For all such variable nouns our 'rule' is necessarily weak. In fact, our rule is generally weak for two-syllable nouns with a free vowel in the ult. As presented above (section 11.6), the rule says that all two-syllable nouns are stressed on the penult. This is fairly accurate for nouns which do not have a free vowel in the ult, such as *cavern, focus, ticket*. It is partly accurate for nouns with a free vowel in the ult: *alcove, statute, termite*. However, there are numerous two-syllable nouns with a free vowel in the ult which have final stress: *canoe, machine, police*. For more examples of all these kinds of nouns, see the Appendix.

11.10 Mixed endings

Neutral suffixes are mostly of Old English origin. Other suffixes have generally entered English from French, Latin, or Greek, originally as parts of words borrowed from those languages. But often these suffixes have come to have a life of their own in English and are used to form new English words. So it happens that some suffixes behave like heavy endings in words of foreign origin but act like neutral suffixes in words which have been created in English. Notice the following sets of words:

(a) agreement   (b) compliment
     encouragement   implement
     confinement   document
     development   impediment
     punishment   monument

In set (a) *-ment* is a neutral suffix. It is added to words which stand alone; stress in each suffixed word is on the same syllable as in the independent word to which the suffix is added. The words in set (b) are regularly stressed, but by a different principle: stress is on the antepenult of each word. In effect, these are two different suffixes, and they should be labeled differently. We might refer to them as -*ment₁* and -*ment₂*, but these labels do not tell what the suffixes have to do with the position of stress. A better way is to use different symbols for different kinds of suffixes. So we write #*ment* and +*ment*, where '#' indicates that what follows is a neutral suffix and '+' marks a suffix (or a special ending) which is not neutral.

The following groups of words illustrate three apparent suffixes which, like -*ment*, turn out to be three pairs of suffixes. In each pair one suffix is neutral and the other is a strong ult.

(a) materialize   (b) apologize
     naturalize   antagonize
     characterize   mechanize
     Americanize   monopolize
     popularize   hypothesize

(a) federalist   (b) anarchist
     industrialist   botanist
     modernist   ornithologist
     revolutionist   protagonist
     violinist   scientist

(a) nationalism   (b) ostracism
     imperialism   recidivism
     parallelism   somnambulism
     radicalism   syllogism
     secularism   ventriloquism

11.11 Some 'special' endings

Words written with final -*y* are quite numerous. There are two neutral suffixes written with #*ly* (as in *friendly* and *clearly*), and there are three other neutral suffixes with just #*y* (as in *dirty*, *smithy*, and *doggy*). See the Appendix for further details. There are some non-neutral endings which have a written *y*. They are illustrated in these words:

   delicacy   decency   geography   harmony   literary   territory

This section deals with stress-placement in such words.

11.11a

Certain nouns have an ending +*acy*, and certain other nouns have an ending +*ancy* or +*ency* (just a difference of spelling, so far as stress placement is concerned). These endings are like weak suffixes, differing only in having two syllables instead of one. If the syllable before the suffix is stressable or the initial syllable of the word, that syllable is stressed. If the syllable before the suffix is not stressable and not initial, stress is on the second syllable before the suffix. Study these examples:

fallacy	diplomacy	adequacy
legacy		celibacy
piracy		delicacy
privacy		literacy

decency	complacency	competency
frequency	consistency	exigency
pregnancy	dependency	hesitancy
tendency	emergency	presidency

The words in the last columns, on the right, are among the few English words which are stressed on the preantepenult. You have probably noticed that some of these nouns are related to adjectives or other nouns which end in /t/:

piracy – pirate   adequacy – adequate
decency – decent   hesitancy – hesitant

In chapter 14 we study this relationship further.

11I   QUESTION

What is irregular about the stress of the noun *discrepancy*?

Here is a decision tree for nouns which have the endings *-acy/-ancy/-ency*:

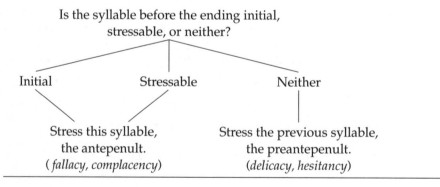

Is the syllable before the ending initial,
stressable, or neither?

Initial   Stressable   Neither

Stress this syllable,   Stress the previous syllable,
the antepenult.   the preantepenult.
(*fallacy, complacency*)   (*delicacy, hesitancy*)

11.11b

Nouns and adjectives which end in +*ary* have three different stress patterns, as in:

compli'ment+ary   con'tempor+ary   'veterin+ary

The last of these is uncommon; probably *'disciplinary* is the only other example of a word with two weak syllables between the stressed syllable and the suffix *+ary*. In *contemporary* there is one syllable between the stressed syllable and the suffix; in *complimentary* there is no syllable between.

The stress rule for these words is similar to the rule for weak suffixes. If the syllable before *+ary* is stressable or initial, it is stressed: *compli'mentary*. Otherwise, the preceding syllable is stressed and, in North American English, the first syllable of the suffix *+ary* is strong (and pronounced /eri/): *con'temporary*. In the British Isles and the southern hemisphere the suffix is /əri/ or just /ri/ in both the *complimentary*-type and the *contemporary*-type.

11J **PRACTICE**

(a) Use the tick to mark the stressed syllable in each of these words:

anniversary	elementary	exemplary	arbitrary
commissary	coronary	dictionary	imaginary
incendiary	literary	mercenary	monetary
necessary	proprietary	reactionary	sanguinary
sanitary	secretary	visionary	vocabulary
tadversary	sedentary	voluntary	

(b) According to our rule, three of the words are stressed irregularly: *adversary, sedentary, voluntary*. What is irregular about them?

11.11c

Nouns and adjectives which end in *+ory* likewise have three different stress patterns:

di'rect+ory   ob'servat+ory   'ambulat+ory

Here, as with the *+ary* suffix, stress falls on the syllable before the suffix if that syllable is stressable (*di'rectory*) or the only syllable (*'memory*). If the syllable before the suffix is neither stressable nor word-initial, stress is on the preceding syllable (*ob'servatory*). In a few words there are two weak syllables between the stressed syllable and the suffix (*'ambulatory*). When the stressed syllable is right before the suffix (*di'rectory*, *'memory*), the penult is light and the vowel may disappear; when this is not the case, as in *ob'servatory* and *'ambulatory*, the first syllable of *+ory* is strong in North American English; in the British Isles and the southern hemisphere the pronunciation is /əri/ or /ri/.

11K EXERCISE

(a) Decide which of the following words are like *directory* (or *memory*) and which are like *observatory*.

(b) There are three words in the group which are irregularly stressed by our rule. Which are they?

advisory	dormitory	migratory
amatory	explanatory	offertory
armory	illusory	perfunctory
compensatory	inflammatory	repertory
compulsory	interrogatory	inventory
derogatory	mandatory	trajectory

Several words have two possible stressings:

'obligatory   o'bligatory
'laboratory   la'boratory
'preparatory pre'paratory

Here is a decision tree for the regular words which end in *-ary* or *-ory*. Note that it is identical with the decision tree for words which end in *-acy, -ancy/-ency*.

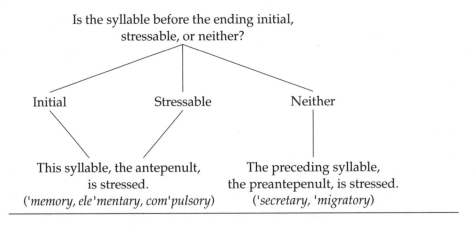

Is the syllable before the ending initial, stressable, or neither?

Initial   Stressable   Neither

This syllable, the antepenult,   The preceding syllable,
is stressed.   the preantepenult, is stressed.
('*memory, ele'mentary, com'pulsory*)   ('*secretary, 'migratory*)

11.11d

There are numerous abstract nouns of Latin and Greek origin which end in +*y* (other than *-ary* and *-ory*). All three-syllable nouns with this suffix are stressed on the initial syllable, like these examples:

colony energy galaxy harmony lethargy liturgy malady

For words of more than three syllables there are two patterns:

Pattern 1 ... 'x x x +y
'matriarchy 'taxidermy 'apoplexy
'ceremony 'testimony 'miscellany

The penult is strong and the preantepenult is stressed. (There may or may not be syllables before the stressed syllable, as indicated by the three dots.)

Pattern 2 ... 'x x +y
a'natomy bi'ology e'conomy ge'ometry phi'losophy

(and all the words that end in *-ology, -ometry, -ography, -opathy*). The antepenult is stressed.

11L   FORMULATE THE RULE

(a)   In nouns of three syllables with ending *-y* the stressed syllable is always the _____ .
(b)   In nouns of more than three syllables with ending *-y* the preantepenult is the stressed syllable if _____ ; the antepenult is stressed if _____ .

Here is a decision tree for this group of nouns:

apostrophe   catastrophe   epitome   facsimile

How many syllables in the noun (including the *-y*)?

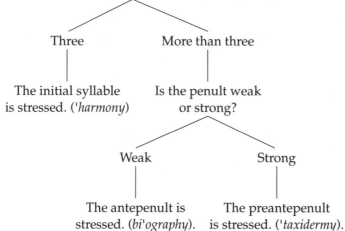

Words like those above, though spelled with a final *-e*, actually belong to the group just studied. If we wrote, for example, 'apostrophy,' the pronunciation and stress would be no different from what they are.

11.12   Summary

There is a certain degree of regularity in the occurrence of stress in English words. Factors in the determination of stress are syntactic (part of speech), morphological (recognition of different kinds of prefixes, suffixes, and bases), and phonological (recognition of free and checked vowels, open and closed syllables). First of all, it is necessary to recognize certain **neutral suffixes**, which are never stressed, and **tonic endings**, which are always stressed. Rules for stress assignment do not apply to the second group, and they apply to the first group only after the neutral suffix is removed. Different stress rules have been presented for verbs and for nouns. Adjectives are of two kinds: those which end in *-ic, -id, -it* follow the verb rule, and those which end in *-al, -ar, -an, -ant/-ent, -ous* follow the noun rule.

In applying the rules final /i, u, o/ count as checked vowels; so does /i/ in the penult when immediately followed by a vowel; so does /u/ in the penult if immediately followed by no more than one consonant.

In verbs, nouns, and adjectives which consist of three or more syllables and have heavy ults the antepenult is the stressed syllable. Some nouns of this type, however, show variation between stress on the antepenult and stress on the ult. Among two-syllable nouns with a free vowel in the ult some have an initial stressed syllable, some a final stressed syllable, and some vary.

Words with certain endings require more extended discussion. Some endings (*-ment, -ize, -ism, -ist*) may be attached to free bases – independent words – in which case they are neutral suffixes; attached to bound bases the words are stressed on the antepenult. Words with the endings *-acy, -ancy/-ency, -ary, -ory* are stressed on the syllable preceding the ending if that syllable is initial or stressable, otherwise one syllable earlier. For other abstract nouns with final *-y* the rule is: the antepenult is stressed in a three-syllable word and in a longer word with a weak penult; the preantepenult is stressed in a longer word with a strong penult.

11A   FEEDBACK

1b	adopt	2a	exonerate	1a	produce
3	answer	3	furnish	1b	remark
3	cover	3	inhabit	2a	substitute
2a	dehumidify	2a	mechanize	2b	supplement
1b	exhaust	1b	offend	1a	transcribe

11B   FEEDBACK

3c	javelin	1b	closet	3a	diploma
3a	idea	2	satellite	3c	veteran
3b	bonanza	3c	opera	3c	platinum
3c	harmonica	3c	hypothesis	3a	neuritis
la	tabloid	2	formaldehyde	2	vestibule

11C FEEDBACK

(a) 'fatal 'global 'polar 'stellar 'cogent 'decent 'dormant 'nervous

General statement: If an adjective has a weak suffix preceded by a base of just one syllable, stress is on the base.

(b) ac ci 'den tal   re 'luc tant   pe 'ri phe ral
     e 'ter nal   mag 'ni fi cent   a 'na lo gous
     'vi gi lant   'bar ba rous   a 'bun dant
     ma 'lig nant   'ge ne rous   tre 'men dous

The penult is strong if it meets either of these conditions:

1 it has a free vowel;
2 it ends with a consonant.

11D FEEDBACK

No, because the consonant clusters are the type of clusters which occur word-initially. The first consonant is ambisyllabic; it is not the coda of a syllable.

11E FEEDBACK

(a) the antepenult
(b) /u/
(c) open
(d) the antepenult
(e) /i/
(f) open

11F FEEDBACK

Three of these adjectives have heavy penults which are stressed:

in 'ter nal   noc 'tur nal   o ri 'en tal

Each of the others has an unstressable penult and therefore stress on the antepenult.

11G FEEDBACK

(a) These are likely to be stressed on the penult: chimpanzee, divorcee, employee; the others are more probably stressed on the antepenult.
(b) These three words have stressable penults; the others do not.

11H FEEDBACK

The stressings indicated by one dictionary (*Webster's New World Dictionary*) are these:

- in *figurine* and *tambourine* the ult is stressed;
- *guillotine, libertine, nicotine, quarantine,* and *trampoline* are stressed on the antepenult, the initial syllable;
- in *gabardine, kerosene,* and *limousine* either the antepenult or the ult may be stressed but initial stress is given first; for *gasoline* and *tangerine* the same two possibilities are indicated, but final stress is listed first;
- *Submarine* has final stress when the word is an adjective but intial stress when it is a noun or a verb.

These are stress possibilities for words in isolation. As we will see later, stress can vary in different sentence positions.

11I   FEEDBACK

Stress is on the syllable preceding +*ancy* even though that syllable is light, with a lax /ɛ/.

11J   FEEDBACK

(a)

anni'versary	ele'mentary	e'xemplary	'arbitrary
'commissary	'coronary	'dictionary	i'maginary
in'cendiary	'literary	'mercenary	'monetary
'necessary	pro'prietary	re'actionary	'sanguinary
'sanitary	'secretary	'voluntary	'vocabulary
'adversary	'sedentary		

Among these 22 words only *anniversary, elementary,* and *exemplary* have stress on the syllable before +*ary,* and an unstressed suffix. All the others have the more common pattern . . . 'x x ary.

(b) In *'adversary, 'sedentary,* and *'voluntary* the syllable before the suffix is stressable since it ends in a consonant, and yet the preceding syllable is stressed.

11K   FEEDBACK

(a) These words have stress on the syllable before +*ory,* like *directory* and *memory*:

  advisory   armory   illusory   perfunctory   trajectory

(b) The words *offertory, repertory,* and *inventory,* should, by the rule, be stressed on the syllable before the suffix, but they are not: *'offertory, 'repertory, 'inventory.* For the last word there is, in Britain, an alternative pronunciation *in'ventory.*

11L FEEDBACK

(a) In abstract nouns of three syllables with the ending +*y* the stressed syllable is always the antepenult (the initial syllable).

(b) In nouns of more than three syllables with ending +*y* the preantepenult is stressed if the penult is strong; the antepenult is stressed if the penult is weak.

Notes

The fact that stress is regular in certain groups of English words was stated as early as Walker (1791). The rules presented here are essentially those of Chomsky and Halle (1968). Halle has continued his analysis of stress placement in several works, Halle and Keyser (1971), Halle (1973), Halle and Vergnaud (1987), and a number of scholars have contributed to this investigation. Earlier discussions of stress are Arnold (1957) and Newman (1946). Pedagogical treatments of stress placement are Dickerson (1975) and Guierre (1984).

The perception of stress is sometimes explained as the motor theory of speech perception; see Lane (1965) for discussion.

Metrical Phonology originated in Liberman and Prince (1977). The only textbook treatment of the topic is Hogg and McCully (1987). Hayes (1995) investigates the relation between rhythm and word stress in a number of languages.

12

Prefixes, Compound Words, and Phrases

This chapter deals with stress in two kinds of constructions, compound words and phrases. A compound word can be part of a phrase and a compound word can be part of a bigger compound word (which can be part of a phrase). Compound words can be nouns, adjectives, adverbs, or verbs. A special kind of construction, which we call a Greek-type compound, such as *astronaut* and *thermometer*, consists of morphemes that do not occur as independent words but recur in numerous combinations.

12.1 Compounds

In the simple word *tennis* the first syllable is strong and stressed and the second syllable is weak and unstressed: S w. The simple word *racket* has the same pattern of strong and weak, S w. When the two words are put together to form a compound, *tennis racket*, the stress pattern is something like S w s w: the first syllable of *tennis* is strong and stressed; the first syllable of *racket* remains strong but is unstressed. If *tennis racket* is in accent position, the first syllable is the accented syllable, as in:

'Do you 'have your '**ten**nis racket?

Only if *racket* is contrasted with something else can it acquire stress and accent:

'tennis '**balls** / and a 'tennis '**rac**ket

12A   PRACTICE: COMPOUND NOUNS

In the following groups of compound nouns the stress pattern is the same in each group. Indicate the pattern with S for the stressed syllable, s for a strong unstressed syllable, and w for a weak syllable, as was done above for *tennis racket*, S w s w.

> airplane   football   keyhole   Main Street
> apple tree   basketball   movie star   waterfall
> fire engine   grandfather   post office   wastebasket
> filling station   physics teacher   office worker
> department store   discussion group   collection box
> farm equipment   tax collector   fire department

Most compound nouns have stress on the first word of the compound, like those above. However, some compound nouns are stressed on the second word.

> kitchen sink   Lake Louise   Mount Everest
> s   w S   s   w S   s   S ww

12B   PRACTICE: COMPOUND VERBS, NOUNS, AND ADVERBS

(a)   The words in the left-hand column below are compound verbs (sometimes called 'phrasal verbs' or 'two-word verbs'), consisting of a verb plus a particle. The nouns in the right-hand column have a similar composition. How do the verbs, as a group, differ in pronunciation from the nouns, as a group?

> to stand up   a look-out
> to sit down   a stand-in
> to look out   some throw-aways
> to go away   a cave-in
> to come back   a rip-off
> to fall in   a comeback

(b)   The following are adverbial (locative) compounds, composed of a particle plus a noun. Which part of each compound is stressed?

> up north   downtown   up front   indoors
> down south   backstage   out back   offstage
> out west   overhead   underfoot   outside

(c)   The following noun compounds also consist of a particle plus a noun. Which part is stressed?

an afterthought   backlash   downfall
an inroad   offshoot   upkeep
the overhead   outlook   underwear

Sometimes we have a compound within a compound; for example:

a football team

The study and description of compounds within compounds and within phrases is called **metrical phonology**. The way in which the parts of a compound are organized is shown in a structure tree like the one below. The tree shows that *foot* and *ball* go together to make a compound, *football*, with greater stress on the first word. *Football* and *team* together make a compound. Note that *foot* is the stressed syllable of the full compound, indicated here with S. The syllables *ball* and *team* are no longer stressed but they remain strong, indicated with s. However, when a strong syllable is between two strong syllables, as *ball* is, it may seem weaker than the syllable on each side. This potential weakening is indicated here with an italic s.

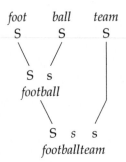

Here is another example, *fingernail polish*:

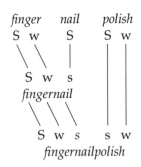

12C   **PRACTICE: STRUCTURE TREES**

Make structure trees like those above for these compounds:

goldfish bowl   typewriter ribbon

12.2   Compounds and phrases

As noted above, most compound nouns are stressed on the first word of the compound. As we will explore later, when a compound noun is part of a larger compound, the stress may be on either part. Syntactic groups – phrases – which consist of words of equal semantic weight typically have a stress on each of these words and, as we have seen, the unmarked accent falls on the last word of the group. Syntactic groups include the following:

Noun phrases	a nice day	w s S
	some interesting discussions	w s w w w S w
Verb phrases	found a ticket	s w S w
	work slowly	s S w
Adjective phrases	very lucky	s w S w
	quite ridiculous	s w S w w
Coordinate phrases	Tom, Dick, or Harry	s s w S w
	hopped, skipped, and jumped	s s w S
	tired but happy	s w S w
Subject and verb	Jean smiled.	s S
	The bus is leaving.	w s w S w

All the major words of a phrase (roughly, the nouns, verbs, adjectives, and adverbs) are stressed, and the last of these major words is a bit more prominent, having the accent. As we know, the accent may be moved to some earlier word for a particular purpose. Examples:

a **nice** day	w S s	(emphatically nice)
very lucky	S w s w	(extremely lucky)
Jean smiled.	S s	(emphasizing the name)

Compare these compounds and phrases:

a greenhouse   w S s
   (a glass structure with artificially controlled heat, for growing plants)
a green house   w s S
   (a house which is green)
playing-cards   S w s
   (pieces of cardboard, typically 52 to a deck, etc.)
Playing **cards**.   s w S
   (possible answer to a question 'What are those people doing?')

12D   PRACTICE: COMPOUNDS AND PHRASES

(a)   The following noun compounds and phrases have greater stress either on the first element, like *greenhouse*, or on the second element, like *green house*. Tell which part is stressed in the usual pronunciation (that is, without special contrast or emphasis).

a living room   a living wage
a brickyard   a brick house
a darkroom   a dark room
bus-driver   drives a bus

(b)   What is the difference between a 'Spanish teacher (S w s w) and a Spanish 'teacher (s w S w)?

It has been customary to call such expressions as *armchair, Fifth Street, information desk*, all with main stress on the first word, noun compounds and to use the term noun phrases for expressions with greater stress on the second word, such as *kitchen sink, Fifth Avenue, Brooklyn Bridge*. This is not a very helpful kind of labeling since there isn't always a clear criterion for deciding what is a compound and what is a phrase, except for knowing what the stress pattern is. We cannot say that compounds have one kind of meaning and phrases have another. In fact, there are dialect differences in stress as in other kinds of pronunciation; *ice cream* and *weekend* are two items which are stressed differently by different speakers of English.

12E   WHAT DO YOU SAY?

(a)   Read the following noun expressions and, for each expression, decide whether the first word is stressed or the second word. Native speakers of English do not agree in all cases.

It was _____.

the box office   a dividing line
a bay window   no laughing matter
a dollar bill   Swiss cheese
a toy soldier   hay fever
the front door   life insurance
waste paper   yellow fever
a snowman   self-control
a light-year   the ruling class
a fur coat   an X-ray
plate glass   a cure-all
an evening dress   a know-nothing
a fellow citizen   a good-for-nothing
a money order   a white lie

(b) Adjective expressions have similar variation: stress may be on the first word or on the second, and different speakers may not agree. How do you pronounce the following?

They're _____ .

handmade	thoroughbred
home grown	knock-kneed
hard boiled	homesick
middle-aged	trustworthy
old-fashioned	fireproof
broken-hearted	color blind
egg-shaped	dead drunk
bare-headed	worldly wise
near-sighted	blood red
well-mannered	jet black
henpecked	Kelly green
good-looking	air-conditioned
easy-going	tax-free

One kind of verb phrase consists of a verb and an adjective, for example: (It) *is good*, (She) *looks nice*, (They) *taste sweet*. A compound adjective may occur in such a verb phrase: (He) *seems 'near-sighted*, (She) is *'homesick*, (The building) *is 'fireproof* (It) looks *home'made*, (They) *are middle'aged*, (The egg) *is hard'boiled*. As these examples show, stress may be on the first part of the compound or the last; initial stress or final stress is a characteristic of each compound adjective.

Adjectives, including compound adjectives, can also be part of noun phrases, modifying the noun: *a good book, sweet cakes, a homemade present, middle-aged people, a fireproof building, a hard-boiled egg*. Usually the noun is more prominent than the adjective and a compound adjective as modifier has equal stress on both parts of the compound, no matter how it is stressed in a phrase. A strong syllable between two strong syllables may become weaker, indicated here with *s* in italics.

Compare:

1	'This 'egg is 'hard-'**boiled**.	s s w *s* S
	'This is a 'hard-'boiled '**egg**.	s w w *s s* S
2	The 'building is '**fire**proof.	w s w w S *s*
	'It's a 'fire'proof '**buil**ding.	s w *s s* S w

More examples:

'cross-eyed	cross-eyed '**looks**
home'grown	homegrown to'**ma**toes
'homesick	homesick '**stu**dents
'egg-shaped	an egg-shaped '**jew**el

Adverb (locative) compounds are similar to compound adjectives. Compare the stress pattern of the adverb as part of a phrase (first column, below), with a pattern of even stress and therefore accent on the noun in a compound that consists of modifier (adverb) plus head (noun).

It's downtown.   a downtown location
  w   s   S   w s   s   w S w

They looked overhead.   overhead projectors
    w s   s w S   s   w s   w S w

The head of a noun phrase may be a compound noun: *a green necktie, a large department store, an interesting discussion group*. The modifier may be a compound noun: *a weekend trip, crossword puzzles, a five-mile hike, department store employees*. So a noun phrase may consist of two compounds in which the first compound is the modifier and the second is head of the phrase: a department store office worker, a weekend bus trip, a newspaper staff meeting, the train station coffee shop. As these examples show, the second compound has the most prominent syllable.

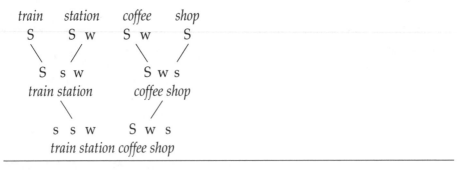

12.3   Compound verbs

English has several kinds of composite verbs, sometimes called two-word verbs or phrasal verbs. ('Two-word verbs' is not a good name since a three-word sequence like *look out for* behaves much the same as a two-word sequence such as *look for*. 'Phrasal verb' is equally poor since it implies that the verb *look out*, for example, is a phrase whereas the noun *lookout* is a compound.) One kind of compound verb is made up of a verb + a particle; another kind is made up of a verb + a preposition. Particles and prepositions are closed classes of words, few enough in number that they can be listed (which is easier than giving a definition of the classes). Particles are:

across,   away,   back,   through
down,   up
in,   out
on,   off
over,   under

All of the above words except *away* and *back* are also prepositions. The words *at, for, of, to, with,* and *without,* are only prepositions. The difference between particles and prepositions is quite subtle.

A compound verb which is intransitive consists of verb + particle:

stand up   start out   sit down   come back

Some transitive compound verbs consist of verb + particle. If the object of the verb is a noun phrase, it can occur in either of two possible positions. If it is a pronoun, only one position is possible.

look up a word   look a word up   look it up
put on the gloves   put the gloves on   put them on
hand in the paper   hand the paper in   hand it in

Notice how this differs from verb + preposition with an object, noun phrase or pronoun:

look at the pictures   look at them
listen to the record   listen to it
wait for Eddy   wait for him

Compare *look up* as verb + particle with *look up* as verb + preposition:

I looked up the article.   I looked it up.
I looked up the chimney.   I looked up it.

In addition, note that a verb and a preposition may occur side by side without forming a compound verb. *She waited for a friend* has a compound verb; *She waited for an hour* simply has a verb followed by a prepositional phrase indicating time.

A few compound verbs consist of verb + particle + preposition:

put up with this nuisance   put up with it
do away with the old papers   do away with them
look up to his father   look up to him

In a sequence of verb + particle + noun phrase, the noun typically has the accent, and verb and particle may be stressed equally:

She took back the **pres**ents.   w s s w S w
I crossed off your **name**.   w s s w S
We put away our **tools**.   w s w s w S
Did you turn in your as**sign**ment?   s w s s w w S w

Any construction like this can be converted to an equivalent sequence, verb + noun phrase + particle. In that sequence either the noun or the particle may have the accent, without any appreciable difference of meaning.

She took the **presents** back.   She took the presents **back**.
  w s w S w s   w s w s w S

We put our **tools** away.   We put our tools **away**.
  w s w S w s   w s w s w S

If the noun phrase is replaced by a pronoun, the pronoun goes between verb and particle and the particle is accented.

She took them **back**.   w s w S
I'll try it **on**.   w s w S
We turned it **in**.   w s w S
Did you call him **up**?   s w s w S

Likewise, when verb and particle are at the end of a tone unit, the particle has the accent.

What did you turn **in**?   s w w s S
When did they pass **by**?   s w w s S
Is this the paper you're throwing **out**?   w s w s w w s w S
Is this the sweater she tried **on**?   w s w s w w s S

On the other hand, in a sequence of verb + preposition + noun phrase the preposition is usually unstressed.

I was looking at the poster.   s w s w w w S w
We listened to some records.   w s w w w w S w
He asked for a **raise**.   w s w w S
Why don't you laugh at my jokes?   s s w s w w S

If the noun phrase is replaced by a pronoun, the verb is accented and either the preposition or the pronoun is strong.

I was **look**ing at them.   I was **look**ing at them.
s w S w s w   s w S w w s

What do you think of it?   What do you think of it?
  s w w S s w   s w w S w s

But if the noun phrase is replaced by an indefinite pronoun (*one* or *some*), the pronoun, not the preposition, is stressed.

We listened to some.	w S w w s
He asked for one.	w S w s

If verb + preposition come last, the verb is accented and the preposition is stressed.

What did you ask for?	s w w S s
What did they listen to?	s w w S w s
What are you **look**ing at?	s w w S w s
What was he sitting on?	s w w S w s
Is this the article you referred to?	w s w s w w s w S s

12.4 Prefixes

To classify the pieces of a language is not a simple job. We have called words like *down* and *up* particles or prepositions depending upon how they act in compound verbs. Consider the following sentences:

The boat floated down the stream.
The boat floated downstream.

It is usual to say that the first sentence contains a phrase *down the stream*, consisting of a preposition *down* and a noun phrase *the stream*, and that the second sentence has a compound adverb *downstream*, composed of a prefix *down-* and a base *stream*. However, there is little difference in meaning.

In chapter 11 a distinction was made between neutral suffixes, which are added to independent words (e.g. *arriv#al, build#ing, develop#ment*), and other suffixes which are attached to bases that typically have no independent existence (e.g. *nomin+al, delinqu+ent, monu+ment*). Similarly, there are prefixes which can be called neutral and others which are non-neutral. The distinction is seen, for example, in:

re-cover   s S w 'to cover again'
recover   w S w   'to get over an illness; to regain possession of'

The first, which we represent as *re#cover*, has a neutral prefix; the second, designated *re=cover*, does not. Generally, neutral prefixes are strong (and sometimes stressed) while non-neutral prefixes are not.

Four non-neutral prefixes, *a=, be=, for=, with=*, occur in various types of words – nouns, verbs, adjectives, adverbs – always unstressed.

arise   award   asleep   ahead
behold   belief   beneath   beside
forbear   forget   forgive   forsake
withdraw   withhold   withstand

In contrast, such neutral prefixes as *after#, by#, down#, fore#, in#, off#, on#, out#, over#, under#,* and *up#* are, as we have seen, typically stressed on the prefix in nouns; verbs with these prefixes generally have stress on the base.

Nouns: afterthought bylaw downfall forearm infield onset
          outbreak overcoat underbrush upkeep
Verbs: foreclose infringe offload outgrow overcome undergo
          uphold

There are several noun–verb pairs, written alike, which differ in speech because the nouns are stressed on the first syllable, the verbs on the second:

offset overflow overlap overthrow overlook upset upturn

Compare also these verb–noun pairs:

fore'see   'foresight
out'grow   'outgrowth
over'draw   'overdraft

In a few cases, such as *'bypass, 'outline,* the verb has been derived from the noun and so is identical in stress. On the other hand, nouns formed from verbs by addition of a neutral suffix, such as *under'standing, with'drawal,* have the same stressed syllable as the base verb.

Adverbs with these prefixes have stress on the second element, the base, as in *down'stairs, off'stage, over'head.* Since some of these prefixes exist in contrastive pairs, *down* and *up, on* and *off, in* and *out,* the prefix may become stressed and accented, a form of paradigmatic focus (chapter 9):

'onstage and '**off**stage
'inside or '**out**side

The neutral prefix *mis#* is regular so far as verbs are concerned:

mis'judge mis'lead mispro'nounce mis'spell etc.

Nouns are less regular: *'misfit* and *'misprint* are stressed on the prefix, but others are stressed on the base, e.g. *mis'deed, mis'fortune;* thus there are some verb-noun pairs which are homophonous: *mis'rule, mis'trust.*

The prefix *un#* occurs in verbs, nouns, adjectives, and derived adverbs. Some examples:

Verbs   unbutton undo unfurl unpack
Nouns   unbelief unconcern unrest untruth
Adjectives   uncertain unclean unfair unreal
Adverbs   unmercifully unquestionably unsuitably

In all of these the base is stressed. However, *un#*, like *mis#*, is often in contrast with zero (the absence of a prefix) and therefore takes on contrastive stress and accent:

'deeds and '**mis**deeds
'locked or '**un**locked

All the prefixes discussed so far are of Germanic (Old English or Scandinavian) origin. In words which have come from Latin, directly or through French, the number of prefixes is larger (about two dozen), the bases to which they are attached are numerous, and of course the number of words formed this way is large. Some prefixes vary in form according to the first phoneme of the base to which they are attached, but the variations are mainly in spelling:

abs=tract   ab=solve
ad=apt   ac=quire   af=fect   al=ly   an=nex   ap=pend   as=sume
    at=tract
con=tract   com=bine   co=here   col=lect   cor=rect
contra=dict
de=tract
dis=tract   di=vide   dif=fuse
ex=tract   e=vict   ef=fect
in=tend   im=pose   il=lude   ir=rupt
inter=rupt
intro=duce
ob=struct   oc=cur   of=fend   op=press   o=mit
per=fect
post=pone
pro=vide
re=sume
se=lect
super=sede
sub=tract   suc=ceed   suf=fuse   sug=gest   sup=press

In all these verbs we can observe a morphological rule for stress:

A verb which consists of a prefix plus a one-syllable base is stressed on the base. We can further observe that:

1   Most of the bases are strong syllables, with a free vowel (*post=pone, re=sume, suc=ceed*) or a cluster of consonants (*de=tract, in=tend, sug=gest*) so that the base, the ult of the word, is properly stressed by the phonological rule as well as the morphological rule.
2   Some bases are not heavy syllables, e.g. *o=mit, pro=pel, sup=press*; the basic verb rule would put stress on the penult, that is, the prefix; stress follows the morphological rule, not the phonological rule.

3   Some verbs have two-syllable prefixes, e.g. *contra=dict, inter=rupt, super=sede*. The basic verb rule would put stress on the antepenult, but they are stressed on the ult because the morphological structure is prefix + one-syllable base. The morphological rule takes precedence.
4   A few verbs contain two prefixes and a base. Stress is on the base:

  com=pre=hend cor=re=spond re=pre=sent re=col=lect
  re=sur=rect

12F   QUESTIONS: STRESS IN VERBS

(a)   Study the following verbs and determine whether the stress is determined by the morphological rule, or the phonological rule, or both, or neither.

  ca'jole com'pel con'sole ex'pect 'govern in'ter per'mit
  con'cern

(b)   The following verbs all have the same base but different prefixes. What irregularities do you find in the stress of these verbs?

  con'fer de'fer 'differ in'fer 'offer pre'fer 'proffer re'fer
  'suffer trans'fer (or 'transfer)

(c)   Here is a list of common bases, all monosyllabic. Using the list of prefixes above, think of at least one verb for each base. (There are no answers in the Feedback. You will probably be able to think of more than one verb containing each of the bases.)

=ceed/cede	=gest	=plete	=solve
=ceive	=gress	=pose	=spect
=cide	=here	=quire	=suade
=clude	=ject	=ride	=sume
=cur	=lect	=rode	=tect
=dict	=lide	=rupt	=tend
=duct	=lude	=scribe	=tract
=fect	=mit	=sede	=trude
=fend	=pand	=sent	=vade
=fess	=pel	=sert	=vene
=fine	=pend	=serve	=vide
=flect	=pete	=sist	=vert

Some verbs with these prefixes have a base which is two syllables long. The second syllable of the base is weak, and stress is on the first syllable of the base.

con=sider con=tinue de=liver de=termine de=velop ex=hibit
pro=hibit re=member sur=render

Other verbs with prefixes also have suffixes. The suffix determines the position of stress.

'com=plic+ate in'ter=rog+ate in='demn+ify 're=cogn+ize

Some adjectives, like verbs, consist of a prefix and one-syllable base of Latin-French origin. The following words are all adjectives, and a few of them are also verbs. Note that the base is stressed in each one.

ab=surd ad=ept com=plete con=trite cor=rect dis=tinct ex=empt
in=ane ob=scene oc=cult pre=cise re=mote

As with verbs, there are adjectives which contain both prefix and suffix, and the latter determines stress, e.g. *im=migr+ant, super=lat+ive*.

With some exceptions, then, verbs which consist of a prefix and a one-syllable base are stressed on the base. For adjectives which consist of a prefix and a one-syllable base there are more exceptions. Examples: *concave* and *convex* may be stressed on either syllable; *oblong, extrovert, introvert*, which are nouns as well as adjectives, are stressed on the first syllable.

There are numerous verb–noun pairs of this composition, which are either identical or identical except for stress. Note these three patterns of correspondence:

(a) *de'mand re'lease* – verb and noun both stressed on the base;
(b) *'contact 'preview* – verb and noun both stressed on the prefix;
(c) verbs *in'sult pro'ject*; nouns *'insult 'project* – verb stressed on the base, noun stressed on the prefix.

Of these three patterns, (b) is least common. However, there are variations among speakers.

12G Exploration: stress in related verbs and nouns

(a) The following words are all nouns and verbs, identical at least on paper. Indicate for each whether the noun and the verb follow pattern (a), (b), or (c). We will probably not all agree.

abstract	control	advance	decay
account	convert	affix	decrease*
addict	convict	annex	detail
address	converse	appeal	digest

approach	discard	overthrow	report
arrest	discharge	pervert	request
assent	discount	prefix	research
attack	disguise	preview	resort
collapse	excerpt	produce	respect
combat	exchange	progress	reverse
combine	export*	protest	review
command	express	rebound	revolt
comment	extract	rebuke	subject
console	import*	recall	supply
contract	incense	recoil	support
contrast	increase*	record	surprise
insert	refrain	recount	survey
interview	refuse	recruit	suspect
object	relay	refill	transfer
overflow	reply	reform	transform

*Words like these may acquire accent on the first syllable for paradigmatic focus. Here we want to observe the neutral occurrence of stress, not the contrastive use.

(b) In the following pairs the verb and noun differ in their final consonants, though the orthography doesn't necessarily show this fact. Do they also differ in stress?

abuse – abuse	descend – descent	pretend – pretense
ascend – ascent	exceed – excess	receive – receipt
believe – belief	excuse – excuse	relieve – relief
conceive – concept	offend – offense	respond – response
deceive – deceit	proceed – process	succeed – success
defend – defense	transcribe – transcript	

(c) In the following words each group has the same base, at least from an etymological point of view, but different prefixes. Each group includes nouns and verbs, and there are two adjectives here. Does difference in part of speech correlate with stress differences?

aspect inspect prospect respect
allude interlude prelude
district restrict
bisect dissect insect
distinct instinct
impulse repulse
precinct succinct

12.5   Greek-type compounds

An earlier part of this chapter dealt with compound nouns like *armchair, bus-driver*, and *lookout*, nouns composed of smaller, independent words but functioning just like a simple noun such as *chair, chauffeur*, or *guard*. There is another type of noun which is made up of two bases (and sometimes a suffix) which are ordinarily not independent words. Some examples: *monograph, telegram, telephone, phonograph*. The elements in these words are largely, but not entirely, of Greek origin, and so were called 'Greek-type compounds' by Roger Kingdon (1957). The first part typically ends with a vowel, *cata=log, tele=phone, epi=taph, auto=graph, poly=gon*, unless the second element begins with a vowel; compare *mono=log* and *mon=arch, homo=phone* and *hom=onym*. However, some first elements do not have a vowel at the end, e.g. *syn=drome, syn=onym*. If there is such a vowel, we call it the connecting vowel. The most common connecting vowel, at least as far as spelling is concerned, is *o*.

We recognize Greek-type compounds through familiarity with the elements that compose them, especially the first element. The following are among the most common first elements. Some of them are illustrated in the words above, and others will be seen in words that appear below.

acro=	ecto=	kilo=	philo=
amphi=	electro=	macro=	phono=
ana=	endo=	mega=	poly=
anti=	epi=	meso=	proto=
apo=	ethno=	meta=	pseudo=
archi=	exo=	micro=	psycho=
auto=	geo=	mono=	stereo=
bathy=	hemi=	neo=	syn=
bio=	hetero=	neuro=	techno=
brachy=	hexa=	ophthalmo=	tele=
cardio=	hippo=	ortho=	theo=
cata=	homo=	osteo=	thermo=
chrono=	hyper=	paleo=	xeno=
deca=	hypo=	para=	xylo=
demo=	ideo=	penta=	zoo=
dia=	iso=	peri=	

If the second element consists of just one syllable, the stress of the word is somewhere in the first element, and the second element has a strong syllable. Study these examples:

archi=tect	dino=saur	dia=log
thermo=stat	pachy=derm	epi=gram
tele=phone	alpha=bet	cata=pult

The first word is *'architect* (S w s), and all the other words have the same stress pattern. Main stress does not fall on the connecting vowel, so it must occur on the only syllable preceding. Note that these words have the same stress pattern as compounds like *motor boat* and *waterfall* – compounds with a two-syllable word followed by a one-syllable word.

Now consider this smaller group of Greek-type compounds. The first element has three syllables and the second element has just one syllable. Again, the stress of the word is in the first element, but where?

electro=lyte	cephalo=pod
kaleido=scope	hetero=dox
ophthalmo=scope	biblio=phile

The words on the left have the same stress pattern as *de'partment store* and *col'lection box* (w S w s). The words on the right have the same pattern as *'platinum mine* or *'radio wave* (S w w s). Thus the rule for stress in these Greek compounds follows a rule you already know.

12H   QUESTION

If the second element of the Greek compound has one syllable and the first element has three syllables, main stress is on the penult or the antepenult *of the first element*. What determines whether the stress is on the penult of the first element or the antepenult?

If the second element has more than one syllable, main stress falls on the penult or antepenult *of the whole compound*, according to a rule which is quite familiar to you. Consider these compound words:

bronto=saurus	archi=pelago
dia=betes	biblio=mania
poly=hedron	hippo=potamus
rhodo=dendron	hydro=phobia

Those on the left have a heavy penult, which is stressed (s w S w). Those on the right have a light penult, so the antepenult is stressed (s w (w) S w w). In both cases the main stress falls in the second element of the compound word. In the words below the penult is light and so stress is on the antepenult, but the antepenult happens to be the connecting vowel of the compound:

meta=thesis   metro=polis   thermo=meter   w S w w

Now consider this set of words:

cata=clysm   cate=chism   micro=cosm   proto=plasm

The stress pattern is, for instance, '*protoplasm* (S w s w) – which is entirely regular if the second element is analyzed as a monosyllable, even though it is pronounced as two syllables. The same is true for the following sets of words, which are Greek-type compounds but not strictly of Greek origin.

    agri=culture horti=culture archi=tecture super=structure
    melo=drama   S w s w

Then note the irregular stress in the following words which have appeared rather often in this text:

    'monosyllable 'polysyllable   S w s w w

Finally, there is a word *intersection* which has two pronunciations – two stress patterns – depending on its meaning. If it is an abstract noun meaning 'the fact of intersecting,' as in *the intersection of two lines*, the pattern is *inter'section* (s w S w). If the word has a more concrete meaning, referring to a place where two streets cross, the usual stress pattern is '*intersection* (S w s w). There is a similar difference between *subdi'vision*, the act of subdividing, and '*subdivision*, an area containing houses all built at approximately the same time by the same real estate company.

12.6 A rhythm rule

Up to this point we have been concerned with the position of stress in different kinds of English words. We have also noted the occurrence of a strong syllable *after* the main stress in certain kinds of words:

* words with a strong ult, like *interrogate, formaldehyde*
* compound words, like *blackbird, toothpaste*
* abstract nouns ending in +y with a heavy penult, like *apoplexy, patriarchy*
* in North America, certain words ending in +ary, +ory, like *ordinary, category*.

Long words usually also have a strong syllable *before* the main stress. As we saw in section 5.3, if stress falls on the third (or a later) syllable of the word, one of the pretonic syllables is more prominent than the other(s). An English word does not have two light syllables in word-initial position.

    ban'danna No'vember   ba'nana co'median
      s   S w   s S   w   w S w   w S ww

When there is just one pretonic syllable, that syllable is strong if it ends with a consonant (*ban-da-na*) or has a free vowel (*No-vem-ber*); otherwise, the syllable is weak (*ba-na-na, co-me-di-an*). Thus whether the syllable is heavy or light depends on the nature of its peak or its coda.

Unfortunately, there are exceptions to the rule just elaborated. Here are some of them:

compare　concern　pertain　surpass

When the initial syllable (immediately before the tonic syllable) ends with a nasal or /r/, the syllable is light and the vowel is /ə/. This may be the case when the initial syllable ends in other consonants, notably /b/ and /d/; compare: *obtain, submit, advance, adventure*.

As we have seen before (chapter 5), there are dialect differences with regard to what vowel is pronounced in an initial pretonic syllable. For example, *direct* may be pronounced with /ai/, making the first syllable strong, or with schwa, creating a weak syllable. Similarly, if *va'cation* has /ei/ in the initial syllable and *pro'motion* has /ou/, these initial syllables are strong; if the words are pronounced with schwa in the first syllable, that syllable is weak.

effer'vescent　memo'randum　Japa'nese　invi'tation
s w　S w　　　s w S　w　　　s w　S　　s　w S w

When the stressed syllable is preceded by two syllables, the initial syllable is strong. Note that it makes no difference whether that syllable has a free vowel or consonantal coda, it is strong by position. Note also that the second syllable may end with a consonant, as in *effervescent*, and yet that syllable, immediately preceding the stressed syllable, is weak. However, a medial syllable immediately before the stressed syllable is not likely to have a free vowel; note what happens to the second vowel of *invite* when that word becomes part of the bigger word *invitation*; we shall see more about such reduction in section 14.13.

halluci'nation　　　interpre'tation
w s w　S w　　　　w s　　w S w

exemplifi'cation　　Senega'lese
w s　　w w S w　　　s w w　S

When the main-stressed syllable is preceded by three or more syllables, one of the preceding syllables is strong. If the second syllable preceding has a free vowel or a consonant coda, it is naturally strong, as in the words of the first line. If that syllable is not strong by its nature, the initial syllable is strong by position, as in the second line.

In some instances it seems that the strength of a syllable is determined by analogy rather than by its nature. There is a tendency for a longer word to echo the syllables of the smaller word contained in it. Compare:

in'terpret	interpre'tation
w S w	w s w S w
'multiply	multipli'cation
S w s	s w w S w
indi'vidual	individu'ality
s w S w w	s w s wSww
'eligible	eligi'bility
Swww	sww Sww

12.7 Summary

A simple word has a stressed syllable which is strong (and there may be another strong syllable). A compound word consists of two simple words and so it has at least two strong syllables. The main stress of the compound may be in the first word of the compound (initial stress) or in the second word (final stress). Compound nouns often, but not always, have initial stress. Compound adverbs have final stress. Compound verbs which consist of a verb and a particle have greater stress on the particle, those which consist of verb and preposition have greater stress on the verb. In sequences of preposition and pronoun following a verb, the preposition and the pronoun may both be weak or either of them may be strong.

A **morphological rule** applies to nouns and verbs, and a smaller number of adjectives, which consist of a prefix and a one-syllable base. Verbs and adjectives typically are stressed on the base and nouns on the prefix, but there are numerous exceptions. As noted earlier (section 11.9), of all categories of words it is hardest to account for stress in two-syllable nouns.

Greek-type compounds consist of a limited number of first and second elements which do not occur alone but appear in a rather large number of nouns. Typically there is a connecting vowel between the two parts. If the second element of the compound is a single syllable, the word stress occurs in the first element, on the first strong syllable (or only syllable) before the connecting vowel. If the second element has more than one syllable, stress is assigned according to the usual noun rule.

The strength of syllables before the main stress of a word depends partly on the nature of syllables, partly on their number, and partly on analogy. If there is only one syllable preceding, it is heavy or light according to whether or not it has a free vowel or consonantal coda. If there are two syllables preceding, the initial syllable is strong **by position**. If there are three or more syllables preceding, either the second syllable is strong by its nature or the initial syllable is strong by position. In some instances a long, complex world has a strong syllable where the simple word from which it is derived has stress.

12A   FEEDBACK

With one example from each group:

```
'airplane 'apple tree   'fire engine   'filling station
   S    s   S  w   s     S   s   w      S w    s  w

de'partment store      'farm equipment
  w S    w    s          S   w  s   w
```

As the examples show, the stressed syllable of a compound noun is usually, but not always, in the *first* world of the compound.

12B   FEEDBACK

(a)   The verbs have greater stress on the particle, e.g. *'stand 'up* (s S). The nouns have initial stress, e.g. *'look-out* (S s).
(b)   Stress on the second word, e.g. *up 'north* (s S).
(c)   There is initial stress; e.g. *'afterthought* (S w s).
      Notice the irregularity of the noun *after'noon* (s w S).

12C   FEEDBACK

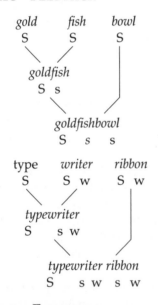

```
gold      fish     bowl
  S        S        S
   \      /          |
   goldfish          |
     S  s            |
       \             |
      goldfishbowl
        S    s    s

type     writer   ribbon
  S       S  w     S  w
   \      /          |
  typewriter         |
   S    s  w         |
        \            |
      typewriter ribbon
        S    s  w  s  w
```

12D   FEEDBACK

(a)   a 'living room   w S w s   a 'living 'wage   w s w S
      a 'brickyard   w S s   a 'brick 'house   w s S
      a 'darkroom   w S s   a 'dark 'room   w s S
      'bus-driver   S s w   'drives a 'bus   s w S

(b)   A 'Spanish-teacher (S w s w) teaches Spanish. A 'Spanish 'teacher (s w S w) is a teacher from Spain.

12E FEEDBACK

(a) Answers will vary. In general it is safe to say that the following have initial stress:

box office	dividing line
snowman	hay fever
light-year	life insurance
evening dress	X-ray
money order	cure-all
	good-for-nothing

This means that half of these items, which were chosen at random, have initial stress and half have final stress. While some specific expressions may be stressed differently by different people, it is likely that such noun expressions have this 50:50 ratio.

(b) With adjective expressions the situation is different. Again, answers will vary, but most of these expressions have final stress in the context indicated. Here are the ones most likely to have initial stress:

egg-shaped	thoroughbred
near-sighted	homesick
henpecked	trustworthy
	fireproof
	air-conditioned

12F FEEDBACK

(a) Morphological rule only: *compel, inter, permit.*
Phonological rule only: *cajole.*
Both: *console, concern, expect.*
Neither: *govern.*

(b) *Differ, offer, proffer,* and *suffer* are irregular, in terms of the morphological construction, in being stressed on the prefix rather than the base. The same is true for the verb *transfer* if it is stressed on the first syllable, as it sometimes is.

12G FEEDBACK

(a) These words follow pattern (a), verb and noun both stressed on the base:

account	collapse	rebuke	resort
advance	command	recruit	respect
appeal	control	reform	reverse
approach	decay	refrain	review
arrest	disguise	reply	revolt
assent	exchange	report	supply
attack	express	request	support
			surprise

Only three of the words clearly follow pattern (b), verb and noun stressed on the prefix: comment, interview, preview.

For the remainder, verbs and nouns are stressed differently, following pattern (c), though there is a tendency to stress some verbs on the prefix, like the corresponding nouns, perhaps because the noun is more common than the verb and influences its pronunciation. (On the other hand, the noun and verb may be semantically far apart, as is the case with *console* and *incense*). There is a verb con'tract which means 'to become or to make smaller,' and another verb 'contract, stressed like the noun, which means 'to make a contract.'

(b)   Only three of these verb–noun pairs have different stress:

con'ceive – 'concept   pro'ceed – 'process   tran'scribe – 'transcript

The others have final stress.

When *offense* means 'something which offends, a transgression,' it has final stress; as a term in sports, contrasting with *defense*, initial stress is common.

(c)   The words on the left below have initial stress and those on the right have final stress, whatever the part of speech.

aspect (N)	prospect (N, V)	inspect (V)	respect (N, V)
interlude (N)	prelude (N)	allude (V)	
district (N)		restrict (V)	
insect (N)		bisect* (V)	dissect (V)
instinct (N)		distinct (A)	
impulse (N)		repulse (N, V)	
precinct (N)		succinct (A)	

*Bisect is sometimes stressed on the initial syllable; influenced by this verb, the verb *dissect* is sometimes pronounced /'daisɛkt/ rather than /dɪ'sɛkt/.

12H   FEEDBACK

The same rule as for ordinary nouns: if the penult is heavy, stress the penult (e'lectro=, ka'leido=); if the penult is light, stress the antepenult ('cephalo=, 'biblio=).

Notes

Fudge (1984, ch. 5) gives a thorough treatment of stress in compounds. Adams (1973, chs. 5–9) treats stress in her analysis of compound formation. Bauer (1983) and Marchand (1969) are standard descriptions of English word formation, including compounding, but give little attention to stress.

13

Phonological Processes in Speech

In chapter 1 we discussed variation in language with respect to differences among users of the language and differences in their uses of it. In this chapter we study differences in pronunciation that are related to different uses of language, or different styles of speaking. We all speak faster or slower, more carefully or less, depending on what we are talking about and to whom we are speaking. Certain very common function words, mostly one-syllable words, can be strong or weak in different contexts and are pronounced differently in those different contexts. We describe these differences as the results of four different **phonological processes: vowel reduction, vowel loss, consonant loss,** and **assimilation**. These processes also affect the pronunciation of lexical words.

13.1 Full forms and reduced forms

Approximately 40 common function words vary in pronunciation according to whether they are stressed and strong or unstressed and weak. For example, consider the pronunciations of the operator, or auxiliary verb, *can* in these sentences:

1 (a) I 'can 'do it. 'Who 'says I 'can't.
  (b) 'Can I? In'deed I 'can.
2 (a) 'Who 'can?
  (b) We 'all 'can.
3 (a) 'I can 'do it.
  (b) 'What can we 'do? (or: '**What** can we 'do?)

In the sentences of group 1 *can* is accented. The word is deliberately accented for emphasis or insistence. In group 2 *can* is stressed but not accented. The emphasis is on the subject – *who, we all* – but *can* must be stressed in final position. In the sentences of group 3 *can* is typically unstressed; it occurs between stressed words.

When *can* is stressed, whether accented or not, it is pronounced /kæn/. We call this the **full form** of the word. When unstressed, it has a **reduced form** which we represent as /kən/, though the actual pronunciation may be [kən] or [kɪn] or [kn̩], depending partly on the context and partly on the speaker. In some positions *can* may be unstressed or stressed; this happens especially in utterance-initial position; for instance:

(') Can the 'doctor 'see me 'now?
(') Can you 'help me?
'What (')can you 'tell us a'bout 'this?

This function word, then, is accented when the speaker chooses to emphasize it, as in 1 (a, b), above. It must be stressed, even though not accented, in final position, as in 2 (a, b); speakers of English do not say *'Who /kən/? *We 'all /kən/. It is mostly unstressed (and reduced) when it is adjacent to a stressed word, but in initial position or in a deliberate manner of speaking it may be stressed. Other function words, examined below, are roughly similar to *can*; they occur in stressed and unstressed positions and each has a full form and one or more reduced forms.

The word *am* has a full form and two reduced forms:

'**Yes**, / I '**am**.	/æm/
'What am I sup'posed to '**do**?	/əm/
I'm '**ready**.	/m/

The last sentence illustrates a reduced form that is recognized in our written language as a contraction. Contractions are not the only reduced forms in the language.

Which are the function words that undergo reduction? There are six groups of words.

13.1a *Auxiliaries or operators like CAN*

The examples which follow are purposely kept short, and only the accented syllable is indicated – not every possible stressed syllable.

Full forms	*Reduced forms*
CAN	
Yes, I /**kæn**/.	I /kən/ **see** it.
COULD	
She /**kʊd**/ / if she **wan**ted to.	She /kəd/ **do** it / if she **wan**ted.
WILL	
Yes, we /**wɪl**/.	What /əl/ we **do**?
	He /l/ **do** it.

WOULD

He said he /wʊd/.

What /wəd/ anybody do / in that case?

He said he /d/ **do** it.

SHALL

We /ʃæl/.

What /ʃəl/ we do **now**?

SHOULD

You certainly /ʃʊd/.

I /ʃəd/ think that's **enough**.

MUST

You /mʌst/ do it, / you /mʌst/.

You /məs/ tell us a**bout** it / **later**.

IS

Yes, it /ɪz/.

Pat /s/ going.
Ann /z/ going.
Bruce /əz/ going.

ARE

Yes, they /ar/.

What /ər/ you going to **do**?
We /r/ going to **be** there.

HAVE

Yes, they /hæv/.

They must /həv/ (or /əv/) **eaten** it.
They must /həv/ (or /əv/ or /ə/) **seen** it.

HAS

Yes, he /hæz/.

Pat /s/ gone.
Ann /z/ gone.
Bruce /əz/ gone.

HAD

Yes, they /hæd/.

What /əd/ they **done**?
They /d/ already **finished**.

DO

I /duu/, / **too**.

When /də/ you **leave**?

DOES

Sue /dʌz/, / **too**.

What /dəz/ **that** mean?

DID

Yes, we /dɪd/.

When /dəd/ (or When /d/) they find **out**?

There are three other operators, *may, might,* and *ought,* which do not have reduced forms.

The reduced forms of auxiliaries *is* and *has* are the ones already discussed in chapter 8, along with the regular plural of nouns and some other suffixes. These can be written as contractions after nouns (*Pat's going, Ann's gone*), as well as pronouns (*She's going, He's gone*). Other auxiliaries which are written as contractions are those which are reduced to a single consonant phoneme, when they occur after pronouns that end with a vowel; specifically:

WILL	I'll	he'll	she'll	we'll	you'll	they'll
WOULD	I'd	he'd	she'd	we'd	you'd	they'd
AM	I'm					
ARE				we're	you're	they're
HAVE	I've			we've	you've	they've
HAD	I'd	he'd	she'd	we'd	you'd	they'd

The reduced forms of *had* and *would* are identical but of course are usually identified in context since *would* is followed by the simple form of a verb (*They'd enjoy the play if they had a chance to see it, I wish you'd be quiet*) and *had* by the past participle (*They'd wanted to see the play but hadn't been able to, I wish you'd been here earlier*).

Among the sentences above which represent the reduced forms of *have* are these two:

> They must have eaten it.
> They must have seen it.

In both of these the vowel is reduced to /ə/, and the initial /h/ is lost. The final /v/ may also disappear, a loss more likely to occur before a consonant, as in the second example, than before a vowel.

To summarize, the reduced forms of the operators are derived from the full forms by four processes or rules:

1   In all the reductions the original vowel becomes a central vowel, [ɨ] or [ə], or the sequence of vowel + /n/ becomes a syllabic [ṇ]. Using the schwa as a cover symbol for any of these results, our rule is:

   $$V \longrightarrow ə$$

2   Certain initial consonants, /h/ and /w/, are deleted.

   $$C \longrightarrow 0 \, /\# \underline{\quad\quad}$$

3(a)   If there is no initial consonant, or if the initial consonant has been deleted, the vowel may be deleted.

$$V \longrightarrow 0 \ /\# \underline{\quad\quad}$$

3(b)   In *must have, could have,* and the like the final consonant, /v/ is deleted – but this can not happen if the vowel is deleted; so 3(a) and 3(b) are mutually exclusive. The consonant is most likely to be deleted when the following word begins with a consonant.

$$C \longrightarrow 0 \ /V \underline{\quad\quad} \# \ (\# \ C \ )$$

4   When *is* and *has* have undergone the deletions or (2) and (3a), the remaining consonant adjusts to the final sound of the preceding word: *Pat*/s/ but *Ann*/z/.

$$z \longrightarrow s \ /[- \text{ voice}] \ \# \underline{\quad\quad} \#$$

The other classes of function words, examined below, undergo the same reduction rules. Before leaving operators, however, we need to note some ways in which *do-does-did* is special. First, after question words (*what, when, where, how,* etc.) the form *does* may be reduced to merely a sibilant consonant, /s/ or /z/, and is thus identical with the reduced form of *is* and *has*.

What's that sign mean?	(does)
What's that man doing?	(is)
What's the weather been like lately?	(has)
When's the bus leave?	(does)
How soon's the bus leaving?	(is)
How long's the bus been waiting?	(has)

Next, we should note that when *do, does,* or *did* follow *what,* the initial /d/ is frequently deleted in informal speech:

What do you need?	/'wʌtəjə 'niid/
What does it matter?	/'wʌtəzit 'mætər/
What did John say?	/'wʌtəd 'jɒn 'sei/

13.1b   Pronouns like HE and YOU

We have already seen that anaphoric words, including pronouns, are typically unstressed but may be accented for special emphasis.

Full forms	*Reduced forms*

HE

She didn't like it / but /hii/ did.   Did /ii/ **tell** you?

HIS

I had **mine** /and Jack had /hɪz/.   He had /ɪz/ **ten**nis racket with him.

HIM

You won't catch /hɪm/ doing that.   Did you **tell** /ɪm/?

HER

The **Browns**? / I know /ðɜr/.   Did you **tell** /ər/?

THEM

They didn't tell **me**. / I told /ðɛm/.   Did you **tell** /əm/?

YOU

This is for /juu/.   Will /jə/ **tell** them?
                     Will /ju/ **ask** them?

YOUR

Do **you** / have /jʊr/ keys?   You can leave /jər/ things **here**.

US

We didn't tell **them**. / They told /ʌs/.   They told /əs/ a**bout** it.

Pronouns SHE, WE, ME, THEY do not have reduced forms. The words I, MY, and OUR sometimes become shortened to /a/, /ma/, and /ar/, respectively, but they do not reduce to /ə/.

13A   QUESTION

For the reduced forms of *you* our illustrations were 'Will /jə/ **tell** them?' and 'Will /ju/ **ask** them?' What determines whether the reduced form is /jə/ or /ju/? (Not all speakers have this difference.)

What do you say? Some speakers consistently use /ɪm/ as the reduced form of HIM and /əm/ as the reduced form of THEM: **Tell** /ɪm/ vs. **Tell** /əm/. For other speakers both pronouns have the same reduced form: **Tell** /əm/.

13.1c   Prepositions like TO

Prepositions are usually followed by a noun, and usually the noun is stressed, the preposition unstressed. A preposition may be accented for contrastive focus, and it is often stressed, but not accented, if it is at the end of a sentence.

Full forms	*Reduced forms*
AT	
Not be**fore** noon, / /æt/ noon.	They'll be here /ət/ **noon**.
FOR	
What is it /fɔr/?	This is /fər/ **you**.
FROM	
Where are you /frʌm/? (/**frɒm**/)	I'm /frəm/ Miss**ou**ri.
OF	
Government /ʌv/ the people (/ɒv/)	a bucket /əv/ **ice**
	a cup /ə/ **coffee** (/əv/)
TO	
Talk /**tuu**/ them, not a**bout** them.	I expect him /tə/ **tell** us.
	I expect him /tu/ **ask** us.
WITH	
Who went /**wiθ**/ them? (/**wið**/)	She came /wəθ/ a **friend**.
	(/wəð/)

The prepositions BY, DOWN, IN, OFF, ON, OUT, THROUGH, UP do not have reduced forms, nor do two-syllable prepositions like ABOUT and BESIDE.

13B   QUESTIONS

(a)   When is the unstressed form of TO most likely to be /tuu/ and when is it /tə/?
(b)   When is the unstressed form of OF most likely to keep the /v/, and when is the /v/ more likely to be deleted?
(c)   Why do some children – and maybe some adults – write *would of gone, might of taken*, etc. for *would have gone, might have taken*?

13.1d   Determiners like SOME

Pronounced in isolation or with emphasis the words A, AN, THE, and SOME are, respectively, /ei/, /æn/, /ðii/, and /sʌm/. When they occur before a noun, they are usually unstressed and their respective pronunciations are:

/ə/; /ən/; /ðə/ before a consonant and /ðii/ before a vowel; /səm/. The determiner THIS, before a noun or not, is likely to be stressed and therefore unreduced ('This ma'chine is '**bro**ken), but in frequently used phrases like *this afternoon, this evening* the word is weak and reduced to /ðəs/. Other determiners such as THESE, THAT, THOSE, EACH, NO, ALL, BOTH are stressed and not reduced.

13.1e *Conjunctions like AND*

Six more function words, the conjunctions, are sometimes stressed but more often unstressed.

Full forms	*Reduced forms*
AND	
Jack /ænd/ Jill – / **both** of them.	Jack /ən/ **Jill**
OR	
Jack /ɔr/ Jill – / **ei**ther of them.	Jack /ər/ Jill
AS	
/æz/ I was **say**ing . . .	It's /əz/ sharp /əz/ a **tack**.
BUT	
Is he **clever**? / Anything /bʌt/.	He's good /bət/ not **clever**.
THAN	
What is it **worse** /ðæn/?	It's sharper /ðən/ a **tack**.
THAT	
I didn't hear **when** the accident happened/, only /ðæt/ it happened.	I'm glad /ðət/ you're **here**.

13.1f *Miscellaneous*

There are two more words which are typically, but not always, unstressed. They don't fit into any of the above categories. One is the word THERE when it functions as a sort of pronoun (not when it means 'in that place'). Stressed, /ðɛr/, unstressed /ðər/:

/ðər/'s a 'lot of 'work to be '**done**, / 'isn't '/ðɛr/?

The other word is NOT, which is different from other function words in the way that its reduced form is related to the full form. The vowel is deleted, and the initial /n/ becomes syllabic. The reduced form occurs after the auxiliaries or operators. The combinations of auxiliary + reduced form of NOT are the contractions written with *-n't*. Here is the full list:

AM	—	CAN	can't
IS	isn't	COULD	couldn't
ARE	aren't		
		WILL	won't
WAS	wasn't	WOULD	wouldn't
WERE	weren't		
		SHALL	shan't
HAS	hasn't	SHOULD	shouldn't
HAVE	haven't		
HAD	hadn't	MAY	—
		MIGHT	mightn't
DOES	doesn't		
DO	don't	MUST	mustn't
DID	didn't		
		OUGHT	oughtn't
		NEED	needn't
		DARE	daren't

The negative contraction adds /nt/ to the auxiliary, and is therefore a two-syllable word, except in the following cases:

- *Can't* is formed by dropping the final /n/ of the auxiliary and *shan't* drops a final /l/, so that the /n/ of NOT does not become syllabic.
- *Don't* and *won't* are completely irregular.
- *Aren't* and *weren't* are bisyllabic, with syllabic [n̩], in the New York City area, but elsewhere are one-syllable words.

One more negative contraction must be mentioned: AIN'T. This is in use throughout the English-speaking world though it is considered non-standard. It originated as a contraction of AM NOT but may also have been influenced by one pronunciation of AREN'T and perhaps HAVEN'T, through the form *hain't*.

Chart 13.1 summarizes the kinds of reduction that the other function words undergo. As the chart shows, the reductions are essentially four different rules which apply to the full forms, one after another:

1   The full vowel of the function word is reduced to /ə/. This applies to almost every one of the words in question.
2   An initial consonant is deleted. Obviously this does not apply to every initial consonant. It can apply to every initial /h/. It applies to the initial /w/ of WILL and WOULD, but not of WAS, WERE, or WITH. It applies to the initial /ð/ of THEM and THAN but of no other word. (Historically speaking, the reduced form *'em* /əm/ for THEM does not come from THEM but from an Old English pronoun *hem*, which otherwise does not survive in Modern English. The pronouns THEY, THEIR, THEM were brought to Britain by Scandinavian invaders.)

232 *Phonological Processes in Speech*

3(a) The vowel is deleted. This applies only to operators (not to the preposition OF, for instance) which either had no initial consonant or have deleted the initial consonant by rule 2.

3(b) A final consonant is deleted. This applies to auxiliaries which end with two consonants, MUST and AND. It also applies to HAVE and OF, which lose their final /v/.

By rules 1, 2, and 3(a) the word HAVE becomes just /v/. By rules 1, 2, and 3(b) the same word becomes just /ə/. If both 3(a) and 3(b) could apply, there would be nothing left of HAVE. However, they are mutually exclusive and that is why they are numbered 3(a) and 3(b).

4 Consonants which come together as a result of rules 1 to 3 undergo assimilation. By this rule the /z/ of HAS and IS becomes /s/ after voiceless consonants. This change is obligatory. If previous rules have deleted everything except the sibilant consonant, the sibilant consonant must be voiceless after a voiceless consonant.

	æm	ɪz	ar	wʌz	wɜr	hæv	hæz	hæd	duu	dʌz	dɪd
1	əm	əz	ər	wəz	wər	həv	həz	həd	də	dəz	dəd
2						əv	əz	əd			
3(a)	m	z	r			v	z	d			
3(b)											
4		s					s				

	kæn	kʊd	wɪl	wʊd	ʃæl	ʃʊd	mʌst
1	kən	kəd	wəl	wəd	ʃəl	ʃəd	məst
2			əl	əd			
3(a)			l	d			
3(b)							məs

	juu	jʊr	hii	hɪz	hɪm	hɜr	ɪt	ʌs	ðɛm
1	jə	jər		həz	həm	hər	ət	əs	ðəm
2			ii	ɪz	ɪm	ər			əm

	æt	fɔr	frʌm/frɒm	ʌv/ɒv	tuu	wɪθ/wɪð
1	ət	fər	frəm	əv	tə	wəθ/wəð

	ænd	ɔr	æz	bʌt	ðæt	ðæn
1	ənd	ər	əz	bət	ðət	ðən
2						ən
3(b)	ən					

	ei	æn	ðii	sʌm	ðɛr
1	ə	ən	ðə	səm	ðər

Chart 13.1

13C EXPLORATION: HOMOPHONES?

The words *to, too,* and *two* are said to be homophones, but it would be more accurate to say that they are potential homophones. They are identical in pronunciation when they are stressed, but, as we have seen, *to* has a reduced form which *too* and *two* do not have. Comment on the following sets of words.

(a)   the auxiliary verb *have* (*has, had*); the transitive verb *have*; and the catenative verb *have (to)*.

> They have bought a new **car**.
> They have a new **car**.
> They have to buy a new **car**.

Apart from stress, what pronunciation differences are there in the following?

> I have **two**.   I **have** to.
> She has **two**.   She **has** to.

(b)   The next group of sentences illustrate three words: the number *one* (different from *two, three, four,* etc.); the noun phrase substitute *one* (plural *some*); and the noun substitute *one* (plural *ones*). Which of them is unstressed and reduced?

> I have one **ticket** / – just **one**.
> I wanted to buy a **paper** / and I **bought** one.
> (I wanted to buy some **papers** / and I **bought** some).
> The committee scrapped **that** plan / and initiated a **new** one.
> (The committee scrapped **those** plans / and considered some **new** ones.

(c)   The sentences below have a word *some* in unstressed position and a word *some* in stressed – accented – position. Is it the same word? In which function does *some* seem to be the plural of the indefinite article *a, an*?

> Some people were **wait**ing. How **many**?
> **Some** people / were **wait**ing. / **Others** / had **left**.

(d)   Are the demonstrative word *that* and the conjunction or relative pronoun *that* homophones?

> Do you need that **file**?
> Did you say that you **need** it?
> Is this the file that you **need**?

13.2   More about phonological processes

In describing the variant forms of function words it was convenient to refer to full forms and reduced forms and to describe the reduced forms as derived from the full forms through the application of certain rules, which are called phonological processes. The words which undergo these processes do not lose their meanings nor change their meanings; all that changes is the pronunciation of the forms. It is important to recognize that the changes are not random or irregular. Particular vowels and consonants undergo particular changes in certain environments. That is why the changes can be stated as rules.

The same kinds of processes apply to other language forms in different styles of speech, especially the more rapid tempos and the more informal styles. We give some illustrations of all the processes already introduced: vowel reduction, vowel loss, consonant loss, and assimilation.

Vowel reduction happens frequently to checked vowels in unstressed syllables, especially, it seems, if followed by a single consonant in that syllable. The verb in each of the following sentences has a checked vowel followed by a single consonant. Each verb is unstressed and just before a word with greater stress. Vowel reduction is likely, as shown.

'You sit /sət/ 'over '**here**.
'He'll come /kəm/ 'right '**back**.
'Don't get /gət/ '**angry**.

Reduction like this does not occur with a verb that has a free vowel or a vowel followed by two consonants.

'You stand 'over '**here**.
'He'll go 'right '**back**.
'Don't stay '**angry**.

Vowel reduction, then, is a process which affects checked vowels in weak syllables, without the 'protection' of consonants. However, the word *just*, in spite of the two final consonants, is typically pronounced /jəst/ in unstressed position:

just now   just a minute

A special form of vowel reduction is that in which the high-front vowel /ii/ is changed to the glide /j/. This can happen whenever the unstressed vowel is immediately followed by another vowel. The word *alien* may be pronounced in three syllables, /'eiliən/, or in two syllables, /'eiljən/. Here is a list of common words with possible variation between /ii/ and /j/.

ammonia	champion
anemia	colonial
bacteria	furious
barrier	helium

There is a similar alternation of high-back /uu/ and the corresponding glide /w/, as in *usual*, /ˈjuuʒuəl/ or /ˈjuuʒwəl/; similarly with *casual*, *mutual* and the like.

Vowel loss is another familiar process of rapid, casual speech. A word-initial unstressed vowel may be deleted, especially after a word-final vowel, as in:

Go (a)way.   I (e)xpect so.

A schwa may be deleted in an initial unstressed syllable if the consonants on each side 'fit together'; thus

police ⟶ /pliis/
balloon ⟶ /bluun/

Especially common is the loss of a vowel in a medial posttonic syllable, as in the following:

especially /iˈspɛʃəli/ ⟶ /iˈspɛʃli/
family /ˈfæməli/ ⟶ /ˈfæmli/
history /ˈhɪstəri/ ⟶ /ˈhɪstri/
national /ˈnæʃənəl/ ⟶ /ˈnæʃnəl/

13D EXPLORATION

The following words all have a medial posttonic syllable. In some of the words the vowel of this posttonic syllable is deleted in casual speech. In the kind of speech you are most familiar with, which words are most likely to have the vowel deleted? (We may not all agree.) Can you suggest what factors are favorable to deletion?

agony	chocolate	liberal	original
aspirin	civilized	mackerel	salary
bachelor	diamond	memory	separate (adj.)
camera	factory	mystery	separate (verb)
capital	ivory	opera	temperature

This process of medial vowel loss is a kind of change going on in the English of today. It is not a new phenomenon, however. If we compare *captain* and *chimney*, for instance, with the French words *capitaine* and *cheminée*, from which the English words were derived, we see that loss of the vowel in a medial posttonic syllable is nothing new. Five centuries ago *capitain* and *chiminey* were three-syllable English words; now *captain* and *chimney* have two syllables each. We do not know the exact details of this historic change, but we can be sure about what did not happen. It was not the case that at one period everybody said *capitain* and *chiminey* and then suddenly everybody changed to *captain* and *chimney*. When change occurs, there is variation among speakers. Something like the following is a more likely kind of historic scenario:

Stage 1: All speakers of English say *capitain* (and *chiminey*) with three syllables.

Stage 2: Some speakers always say *capitain* while others vary between *capitain* and *captain*.

Stage 3: Some always say *capitain*, some vary between the two pronunciations, and others always say *captain*.

As time goes by, however many stages there may be, the number of those who have the three-syllable pronunciation decreases and the number of those who have a two-syllable pronunciation increases, until finally all speakers know only the form *captain*.

We observe a similar situation today. Some people always say *capital* and *salary*, with three syllables, /ˈkæpitəl, ˈsæləri/; others vary between these pronunciations and the two-syllable /ˈkæptəl, ˈsælri/; and others always have the two-syllable forms. The actual situation is more complex than the hypothetical one traced for *captain* because it involves a large number of words, which may be treated differently by different parts of the English-speaking population.

Consonant loss is likewise a familiar process. Like vowel loss, it is characterized by variation among different speakers and in different situations. We have already dealt (in chapter 6) with the simplification of consonant clusters as in *asks*, *risked*, *sixths*, and the like. Similar simplification, through loss of a consonant, occurs in words and phrases like these:

Ar(c)tic	san(d)wich
frien(d)ly	su(g)gest
Secon(d) Street	the firs(t) day

Since /d/ and /t/ are among the most frequently occurring consonants, it is not surprising that they are frequent in clusters and thus frequently subject to deletion. Here again we find variation among different speakers and in different situations. Consider these sets of phrases, all with a word-final /t/, which may be deleted.

(a) next time, the first day, last December
(b) last May, most people, the best night
(c) next winter, the best one, last week
(d) next afternoon, last October, the best idea
(e) the most, the best, the last

The five groups are meant to represent, roughly, a range of probability for the deletion of the consonant /t/ (which is preceded here by /s/ and perhaps another consonant). The /t/ is most likely to be dropped before a following /d/ or /t/, as in group (a); somewhat less likely before other consonants – group (b); still less likely before the glide /w/ – group (c); rather unlikely before a following vowel – group (d); and quite unlikely in final position – group (e).

Looking at the matter in a slightly different way, we may say – and again intending to make only rough descriptions – that the greatest number of people (perhaps all speakers of English) delete /t/ in phrases like those of group (a), and the smallest number consistently delete the consonant in contexts such as those of group (e). Yet it is worth noting that some people – those most likely to be considered socially deprived – have no /t/ in any of the five contexts illustrated.

The last phonological process to be considered is assimilation, a change in which a feature of one consonant, such as [+ voice], 'spreads' to a neighboring consonant. We are already familiar with some examples of assimilation. The regular plural suffix appears as /z/ in *beds* but as /s/ in *bets*. The regular past tense suffix is /d/ in *lived* but /t/ in *sniffed*. These are examples of assimilation in voicing; after a voiceless consonant /z/ is replaced by /s/ and /d/ becomes /t/. In these cases it is the second consonant which takes on the feature, [+ voice] or [– voice], of the preceding consonant. The technical term for this is **progressive assimilation**.

The opposite is **regressive assimilation**, in which one consonant 'borrows' a feature from a following consonant. We have already seen examples of this in the forms *have to*, /hæftuu/, and *has to*, /hæstuu/. Here /v/ and /z/ change to the corresponding voiceless consonants before the following /t/.

Assimilation may be a change in the articulator and/or place of articulation. In phrases like *can pay*, *can buy* the tongue-tip /n/ is likely to be replaced by a labial /m/. Similarly, before dorsal consonants /k/ and /g/, as in *can come*, *can go*, the consonant /n/ may change to /ŋ/. This assimilatory change of /n/ to /m/ or /ŋ/ occurs whether *can* is stressed or not, though it is more likely when the word is unstressed. Similar changes may occur with the /n/ of *in* and *on*: *in back*, *in part* with /m/, *in cash*, *on guard* with /ŋ/. Note that final /m/ and /ŋ/ do not become assimilated to a following consonant as final /n/ does.

Another assimilation in articulator and place of articulation is seen in the following:

is she	does she	was she	has she
/ʒʃ/	/ʒʃ/	/ʒʃ/	/ʒʃ/

The apical fricative /z/ is replaced by the frontal /ʒ/ before another frontal consonant /ʃ/. We see a similar assimilation in the compounds *horseshoe* and *spaceship*, which are more likely to be /'hɔrʃʃuu, 'speiʃʃɪp/ than /'hɔrsʃuu, 'speisʃɪp/. In this case there is complete assimilation – /s/ becomes identical with the following consonant – whereas in all the previous examples the assimilation is only partial; one segment takes on some feature or features of the neighboring segment – voicedness, labial articulation, etc. – but does not acquire all its features.

A special form of assimilation goes by the name of **palatalization**. When a tongue-tip consonant, /t d s z/ occurs at the end of a word and the next word has an initial /j/, the tongue-tip consonants may change to the corresponding tongue-front consonants, becoming, respectively, /č ǰ ʃ ʒ/. Often the /j/ is deleted when the change occurs.

won't you	/wount juu/	or	/wounčuu/
did you	/dɪd juu/	or	/dɪǰuu/
unless you . . .	/ʌnlɛs juu/	or	/ʌnlɛʃuu/
as you . . .	/æz juu/	or	/æʒuu/

Palatalization is an optional process across word-boundaries, as in the above examples. It may or may not occur. Furthermore, it does not occur, even optionally, with every word-final /t d s z/ followed by a word-initial /j/. Palatalization is usual in frequent word-groups like these:

not yet	/ . . . č . . . /
next year	/ . . . č . . . /
would you	/ . . . ǰ . . . /
this year	/ . . . ʃ . . . /
as yet	/ . . . ʒ . . . /

However, it is less usual in, for example, *that year, wide yard, this yacht,* or (he) *loves yoga.* This phonological process seems to be limited to frequently used word combinations.

13E   QUESTIONS

Casual speech forms often show the effects of several phonological processes. The forms below are transcribed two ways, one to indicate the most careful pronunciation and one to suggest the most casual; there may exist one or more in-between pronunciations. Examine each casual form and tell what process(es) account for the difference from the precise form.

pumpkin	/'pʌmpkɪn/	/'pʌŋkɪn/
probably	/'prɒbəbli/	/'prɒbli/
supposed to	/sə'pouzd tuu/	/'spoustə/
don't know	/dount 'nou/	/do'nou/

13.3 Summary

Some of the variation that exists in language is due to differences in the situations and purposes of its use and to the fact that commonly used words are likely to be pronounced differently depending on their positions within utterances. The most commonly used words in English are the so-called function words. About 40 of these, all of them monosyllabic and most of them having checked vowels, show variations that may be regarded as the result of **phonological processes**, changes which operate on the **full forms** of these words to produce **reduced forms**. The processes include **vowel reduction, vowel loss, consonant loss**, and **assimilation**.

The same processes, especially vowel reduction and consonant assimilation, apply sporadically to other language forms. In assimilation one consonant changes by taking on a feature or features of a neighboring phoneme; the most common kinds of assimilation are in voice and in place of articulation. Assimilation is said to be **progressive** when one phoneme is replaced by another under the influence of a preceding phoneme; assimilation is **regressive** when the influencing phoneme follows. Assimilation may be **mutual**: two phonemes in sequence are replaced by a single phoneme which has some features of each phoneme replaced. The most obvious example of mutual assimilation in English is **palatalization**, in which one of the tongue-tip obstruents /t d s z/ at the end of a word 'merges' with initial /j/ of the next word, resulting in a tongue-front obstruent /č ǰ ʃ ʒ/, respectively.

Phonological processes which occur in speech are **optional**.

13A FEEDBACK

The reduced form is likely to be /ju/ before a vowel and /jə/ before a consonant.

13B FEEDBACK

(a) The /tuu/ is more likely before a word which starts with a vowel, /tə/ before a word which begins with a consonant.

(b) The /v/ is more likely to be kept before a word beginning with a vowel and lost before one which begins with a consonant.

(c) OF and HAVE can have the same reduced forms, /ə/ or /əv/, and as a consequence the two words are easily confused in writing, just as other homonyms are easily confused.

13C FEEDBACK

(a) The auxiliary *have* may be reduced (contracted): *They've bought a new car.*
    The 'catenative' verb *have*, the verb that occurs before *to*, becomes partly assimilated to the /t/ of *to*. The transitive verb *have* does not become assimilated. Therefore:

I 'have '**two**. = /ai 'hæv '**tuu**/   I '**have** 'to. = /ai '**hæf**'tuu/
She 'has '**two**. = /ʃii 'hæz '**tuu**/   She '**has** 'to. = /'ʃii '**hæs**'tuu/

(b)   The number *one* and the noun phrase substitute *one* are always stressed, whether accented or not. They are pronounced /wʌn/ or /wɒn/, depending on dialect.

I 'have '/wʌn/ '**ticket**/ – 'just '/**wʌn**/.   (/wɒn/)
I 'wanted to 'buy a '**paper** / and I '**bought** '/wʌn/.   (/wɒn/)

The noun substitute *one(s)* is unstressed, /wən(z)/, if it comes right after the accented word.

The com'mittee i'nitiated a '**new** /wən/.
The com'mittee con'sidered some /səm/ '**new** /wənz/.

However, if the accented word follows, *one(s)* is stressed and pronounced /wʌn/, /wʌnz/ – or /wɒn(z), depending on dialect.

'Did you 'see the 'film at the '**Tivoli** / or the '/wʌn/ at the '**Ro**ma?
'These re'ports aren't '**rea**dy. / The '/wʌnz/ on the '**desk** 'are.

(c)   Just as *a* or *an* is used before a singular countable noun (*a pear, an apple*), the unstressed *some*, /səm/, occurs before plural countable nouns (*some pears, some apples*) and singular uncountable nouns (*some glue, some soup*) with the same general meaning, 'indefiniteness'. With stress, *some*, /sʌm/, still has the meaning of indefiniteness but the stress brings it into contrast with *all* and with *no* or *none*. The sentence, '*Some* '*people were* '*waiting*, says, in effect, 'It is not true that all people were waiting, and it is not true that no people were waiting'.
When *some* is used as an anaphoric pronoun, a substitute for an indefinite noun phrase, plural or uncountable, it is stressed.

'Would you 'like some?   '**Thanks**, / I '**have** 'some.
'These 'men are 'looking for '**jobs**.
'**Some** of them / have been 'out of 'work for '**months**.

(d)   Demonstrative *that* is stressed, /ðæt/, as are *this, these*, and *those*. The conjunction and relative pronoun *that* is unstressed, /ðət/, and it may be deleted.

Do you 'need 'that /ðæt/ '**file**?
Did you 'say (that /ðət/) you '**need** it?
Is 'this the '**file** (/ðət/) you '**need**?

13D   FEEDBACK

There seem to be three factors involved. First, the vowel is more likely to be deleted in words which form a common part of one's vocabulary than in words which are rather rare. Since some words may be common for some speakers but not so common for other speakers, there are differences in the scope of deletion. Probably *aspirin*, *chocolate*, and *memory* are common in the usage of all adults, whereas *agony*, *ivory*, and *mackerel* may not be frequently used words. Consequently, the first three are more likely to be pronounced as two-syllable words than the last three.

Second, the following syllable must be a weak syllable. The words *cantaloupe* and *civilized* have free vowels in the ult and therefore do not show deletion of the medial vowel. Similarly, there is no vowel loss in *operate* though there is in *opera*; the verb *separate* does not show vowel deletion, but the adjective *separate* does.

Third, an unstressed vowel is most likely to be dropped if the consonants on each side 'fit' well together. Notice that in most cases of vowel loss the following consonant is /l/ or /r/.

13E   FEEDBACK

Pumpkin: /'pʌmpkɪn/ to /'pʌŋkɪn/ shows deletion of /p/ between two consonants and assimilation in which /m/ becomes /ŋ/ before /k/.

Probably: /'prɒbəbli/ to /'prɒbli/ shows deletion of a medial posttonic vowel and loss of /b/ – or reduction of /bb/ to /b/.

Supposed to: /sə'pouzd tuu/ to /'spoustə/ shows vowel loss in the initial syllable; loss of /d/ before /t/; voice assimilation in which /z/ becomes /s/ before /t/; and of course the vowel reduction of /tuu/ to /tə/.

Don't know: /dount 'nou/ to /do'nou/ illustrates loss of /t/ and reduction of /nn/ to /n/.

Notes

The description of colloquial speech processes presented here is intentionally conservative. The difference between formal speech and what occurs in casual exchanges can be great. Foreign learners of English are not easily persuaded that the language has variety of this sort, and some native speakers are inclined to doubt the validity, or even the existence, of casual speech forms. Palmer and Blandford (1976), originally appearing in the 1920s, is as good a statement of these occurrences as any.

For a different description of the phonological processes treated here see Roach (1991, ch. 14).

14

Phonological Processes and the Lexicon

We have seen that some morphemes have two or more phonological forms, or allomorphs. In some instances the alternation depends on phonological factors – the difference is due to a difference of stress or to different neighboring phonemes; for example, *twelve* changes to *twelf-* before the voiceless consonant *-th*, /θ/. Such alternations are said to be **phonologically conditioned**. Other alternations cannot be explained by phonological facts; for example, *final* and *finish* have the same base with different suffixes. The base morpheme is /fain/ before *-al* and /fɪn/ before *-ish*. Alternations like this are **morphologically conditioned**. Phonologically conditioned alternations are easy to understand and describe; we can call one allomorph, like *twelve*, /twɛlv/, the basic one and show that the other allomorph is derived from it. In the case of *fin-al* and *fin-ish* there is no good reason for deriving either allomorph from the other. Instead, we establish an abstract form from which both are derived.

14.1 Words and morphemes that change

Chapter 8 dealt with processes that affect some morphemes because of phonotactic conditions: the insertion of a vowel within a morpheme-final cluster like that of *disaster* //dɪzæstr//, the deletion of a consonant from a morpheme-final cluster like that of *damn* //dæmn//, and the voice assimilation in suffixed items like *cats* //kæt#z// and *looked* //lʊk#d//. These can be called phonotactic processes.

In chapter 13 we described phonological processes which operate in the daily speech that all of us produce day by day. The phonological processes explain some of the variations that exist in different ways of speaking, how full forms like *have* /hæv/ and *for* /fɔr/ are reduced to /v/ and /fər/. For brevity we call these speech processes.

There are other morpheme alternations which cannot be attributed to phonotactic conditions nor to style of speaking; for instance:

- noun *thief* /θiif/, plural *thieve#s* /θiivz/; verb *thieve* /θiiv/; noun *thef+t* /θɛft/
- adjective *wide* /waid/, noun *wid+th* /widθ/ (or /wɪtθ/)
- noun *atom* /ætəm/, adjective *atom+ic* /ə'tɒmɪk/
- noun *circle* /'sɜrkəl/, adjective *circul+ar* /'sɜrkjulər/

As these examples show, there may be an alternation of vowels or consonants, or of stress, or the insertion (or deletion) of a vowel or consonant. More than one of these may occur in a morpheme. In fact, alternation of stress, as in *atom*, *atomic*, almost always involves vowel alternation as well.

Variations like these are due, not to phonological processes of the present time but to processes that operated in the past (though two of the processes are similar to processes operating today). We call these variations the result of **lexical processes**.

There are two kinds of alternation, **phonologically conditioned alternations** and **morphologically conditioned alternations**. An alternation is phonologically conditioned if a given phoneme (or sequence of phonemes) alternates with another phoneme (or sequence) under phonological conditions – the alternation depends on the kind of consonant or vowel which precedes or follows, or on occurrence in a stressed syllable or an unstressed one. Phonotactic processes and speech processes are phonologically conditioned, and so are some lexical processes. An alternation is morphologically conditioned if a given phoneme (or sequence) alternates with another phoneme (or sequence) under morphological conditions – the alternation depends on a specific suffix or group of suffixes which follow. In some cases the 'suffix' is really an abstract element which makes a grammatical change: it converts a singular noun to a plural, or a present tense verb to the past tense, or a noun to a verb, and the alternation is the only evidence for the abstract 'suffix.' These statements will become clear if we examine some data.

give – gif+t   twelve – twelf+th

In these two pairs the alternation of /v/ and /f/ is phonologically conditioned. The /v/ is basic and it changes to its voiceless counterpart /f/ before voiceless consonants /t/ and /θ/.

mischief – mischiev+ous   belief – believe   wife – wife'+s – wive+s

Here we see an alternation of the same two consonants, /f/ and /v/, but under quite different conditions. The /f/ of *mischief* is basic; it is replaced by /v/ before the suffix +ous, but there is no phonological reason for the change. With the next pair, *belief* and *believe*, there is no obvious reason for saying that the noun is derived from the verb or the verb from the noun. Because of other such pairs to be examined later we prefer to derive the verb from the noun; we say that *belief*, occurring in the environment ____ + {Verb}, results in, or becomes, *believe*. With regard to the last set we say that *wife* occurs as an independent word, of course, and also in the environment ____ + (Possessive) and the environment ____ + (Plural). The morphemes (Possessive) and (Plural) have the same allomorphs /s, z, ɪz/ (chapter 8), so the alternation of *wife* before the plural suffix cannot be a phonological matter. The plural and the possessive singular of *wife* would be identical if *wife* were a regular noun, but it is not. The morpheme *wife* changes to *wive-* before (Plural) but does not change before (Possessive). The choice of /z/ for (Plural) and of /s/ for (Possessive) is phonologically regular; it is the choice of *wife* or *wive-* that has no phonological basis. The lexical processes that we will examine in this chapter are partly a matter of phonological conditioning but more largely of morphological conditioning.

English has numerous sets of related words which show interchanges of vowels, alternations that reflect sound changes that occurred in the history (and pre-history) of the language. The set of vowels in *sing-sang-sung*, for instance, has come down from Proto-Indo-European, the distant ancestor of English spoken perhaps in the third millennium BC, perhaps in the area between the Black and the Caspian Seas. The vowel sets seen in *food* and *feed*, *goose* and *geese*, *man* and *men*, and other pairs reflect a number of phonetic changes that began in Proto-Germanic, a closer ancestor of Modern English, probably spoken in what is now Germany, Holland, and Denmark in the first centuries of the Christian era. The vowel sets which we are going to examine later in this chapter reflect relationships that existed, and changes that occurred, in Middle English, centering around the fourteenth and fifteenth centuries.

The English lexicon contains words of many different origins but most of the vocabulary comes from four sources. The most basic words have come down from Old English (e.g. *sun, moon, earth, mother, father, sister, brother, happy, sad, go, stay, laugh, weep*). There are numerous common words from Old French (e.g. *forest, lake, uncle, aunt, cousin, nice, pleasant, announce, enjoy*). Latin has contributed most of our more abstract terms, either directly or through French (e.g. *ambition, consequence, individual, instrument, repetitive, substance, superiority*). And most of our technical vocabulary is made up of Greek elements (e.g. *autograph, astronaut, homonym, microscope, thermometer*). All these words are now English but they have slightly different characteristics. They form different strata within the lexicon. Some of the alternations that we study in this chapter occur only in certain strata. For example, in *democrat, democrac+y; hypocrite, hypocris+y; pirate, pirac+y* we see an alternation of /t/ and /s/, which is found in various other words of Greek origin. In *electric, electric+ity; medic+al, medic+ine; italic+s, italic+ize*, words of Greek and Latin origin, there is an alternation of /k/ and /s/. There are no such alternations in words of Old English origin – no example of /t/ alternating with /s/ nor of /k/ changing to /s/. So a good account of lexical processes must include a recognition that some processes apply only to certain strata in the vocabulary. **Lexical phonology** is the name given to the theory of phonology which takes account of such lexical differences. We will have more to say about lexical phonology at the end of this chapter.

14.2 Underlying forms and lexical processes

When we describe speech processes, it seems obvious that we should begin with the isolated, careful pronunciations as the forms to which the processes apply and derive the casual, contextual pronunciations as the result of these processes. We derive the /v/ of *I've* from the full form /hæv/, *have*. The rules of derivation seem 'natural' with respect to present-day English: in this case, loss of a weak consonant and loss of a vowel (following vowel reduction). Similarly, we have recognized the naturalness of phonotactic processes, such as the insertion of a vowel between sibilants in *horses*, for instance, and the loss of /n/ in *damn*. We consider //hɔrs#z// and //dæmn// the basic, or underlying, forms from which the pronunciations, the surface forms, are derived.

When we turn to lexical processes, however, it is not so obvious which is the base form and which is the derived form or forms. Among the three allomorphs /θiif θiiv θɛf/, for instance, which one is the source from which the other two are derived? And what are the rules for derivation? The basic form should be the one from which the others can be derived by rules that seem natural. A little thought will convince us that, in this case, there are no rules which are wholly natural. To be sure, it is natural that /f/, and not /v/, occurs before a voiceless consonant (*theft*) but when we see that both /f/ and /v/ occur word-finally (*thief, thieve*), there is no reason for calling one of these basic and the other derived. Similarly, although we should expect a checked vowel like /ɛ/ rather than a free vowel like /ii/ before a consonant cluster, as in *theft*, there is nothing in the pronunciation which explains why it is these particular vowels that alternate – even though the alternation of these two vowels is fairly frequent in the vocabulary.

In short, the alternations cannot be wholly explained within the framework of present-day English phonology, and there is no basis for choosing one allomorph as basic, or underlying. The underlying form is necessarily something abstract. We can represent the morpheme this way: //θ{ii,ɛ}{f,v}//. The symbols in curly brackets, { }, indicate a choice that must be made, and the rules which apply to the underlying form tell us which choice to make in what circumstances. In this case there is choice between a free vowel and a checked vowel and between a voiceless consonant and a voiced one. We will see other instances of alternations with the {ii,ɛ} pair and alternations with the {f,v} pair and, more important, other free vowel/checked vowel pairs and other voiceless consonant/voiced consonant pairs. Recognizing kinds of alternation, like free vowel/checked vowel and voiced consonant/voiceless consonant is more important than recognizing specific alternations.

By the same token, we want to give general names to rules. The choice {ii,ɛ} is one pair affected by a rule called **vowel shift**; the choice {f,v} is one pair affected by a rule called **voicing**. Instead of the very specific notation //θ{ii,ɛ}{f,v}// we can represent the same morpheme this way:

//θiif// [V shift] [voicing].

These are equivalent notations, so long as one knows what the terms mean, of course. When we introduce alternations and rules, we will want a more specific listing. As we move on, we will prefer a more general sort of notation. The morpheme which occurs in *wide, wid-th* can be represented specifically as //w{ai,ɪ}d// and more generally as //waid// [V shift].

14.3 Checked vowel reduction

We have observed sets of words like the following in which stress occurs on different syllables of related words:

'atom   a'tomic   'continent   conti'nental   'melody   me'lodic
'origin   o'riginal   origi'nality   'tempest   tem'pestuous

We can also observe a common alternation: a checked vowel in an open stressed syllable is 'reduced' to /ə/ in an unstressed syllable, such as the first syllable of *atomic*, the second syllable of *melody*; the same reduction occurs when the vowel is followed by a single consonant or -nt or -st in word-final position, as in *atom, continent, original, tempest*. The reduced vowel may be schwa or barred I, depending on context and dialect. As before, we use schwa as a cover symbol. We show these alternations as derivations:

	//#ætɒm#//	#ætɒm+ɪk#//
Stress	S	S
V reduction	ə	ə
Surface	/'ætəm	ə'tɒmɪk/

	//#kɒntɪnɛnt#//	#kɒntɪnɛnt+æl#//
Stress	S	s S
V reduction	ə	ə
Surface	/'kɒntɪnənt	kɒntɪ'nɛntəl/

	//#mɛlɒd+i#//	#mɛlɒd+ɪk#//
Stress	S	S
V reduction	ə	ə
Surface	/'mɛlədi	mə'lɒdɪk/

	//#ɔrɪǰɪn#//	#ɔrɪǰɪn+æl#	#ɔrɪǰɪn+æl+ɪti#//
Stress	S	S	s S
V reduction	ə ə	ə ə ə	ə ə ə
Surface	/'ɔrəǰən	ə'rɪǰənəl	ərɪǰə'næləti/

	//#tɛmpɛst#	#tɛmpɛst+ju+ɒs#//	
Stress	S	s	S
V reduction	ə		ə
Surface	/'tɛmpəst	tɛm'pɛsčuəs/	

The appearance of /č/ in the surface form of *tempestuous* is the result of palatalization, a process which is examined below.

14.4 Palatalization

In chapter 13 we considered a phonological process which might apply to certain speech forms or might not, producing these variants:

won't you	/'wountjuu/	or	/'wounčuu/
did you	/'dɪdjuu/	or	/'dɪǰuu/
miss you	/'mɪsjuu/	or	/'mɪʃuu/
as you	/æzjuu/	or	/æʒuu/

The process of **palatalization** replaces a tongue-tip obstruent, //t d s z// plus //j// with the corresponding tongue-front consonant, /č ǰ ʃ ʒ/ (which are called palatal consonants by some linguists). Palatalization is optional as a speech process; that is why we can say /wountjuu/ or /wounčuu/. As a vocabulary process it is obligatory, not optional. Notice these pairs of words:

architect architecture   proceed procedure
   /t/   /č/   /d/   /ǰ/

press pressure   compose composure
  /s/   /ʃ/   /z/   /ʒ/

The suffix added is the same one which is added to *fail* to make *failure* (/feil, feiljər/), but here the /j/ of the suffix produces a change in the final consonant of the base word. The four apical consonants are replaced by the corresponding laminal consonants before /j/ and a vowel. We see the same change for /s/ and /z/ when /i/ plus a vowel follows:

face – facial   confuse – confusion

The palatalization rule is:

$$
\begin{bmatrix} t \\ d \\ s \\ z \end{bmatrix} \longrightarrow \begin{bmatrix} č \\ ǰ \\ ʃ \\ ʒ \end{bmatrix} \ / \ \underline{} \begin{Bmatrix} j \\ i \ \ [+ \text{syl}] \end{Bmatrix}
$$

(Two pairs of square brackets in a rule, with an equal number of items in each pair of brackets, is an abbreviation for that number of changes; here the rule says that *t* becomes *č*, *d* becomes *ǰ*, and so on.)

After palatalization takes place, the /j/ or /i/ which caused the palatalization is deleted if the following vowel is unstressed. We call this the I-drop rule or the J-drop rule.

$$\left\{\begin{matrix} i \\ j \end{matrix}\right\} \longrightarrow 0 \; / \; \left.\begin{matrix} \text{Palatal} \\ \text{consonant} \end{matrix}\right\} \underline{\quad} \left\{\begin{matrix} \text{Unstressed} \\ \text{vowel} \end{matrix}\right.$$

Here are two of the derivations:

	//#arkitɛkt#	#arkitɛkt+jur#//	
Stress	S s	s S	
Palatalization	—	č	
J-drop		0	
V reduction	ə	ə	ə
Surface	/'arkətɛkt	'arkətɛkčər/	

	//#feis#	#feis+i+æl#//	
Stress	S	S	
Palatalization	—	ʃ	
I-drop		0	
V reduction			ə
Surface	/feis	'feiʃəl/	

14A PRACTICE

(a) Each of the words below ends with /t/ or has /t/ before a suffix. By adding a suffix or changing the suffix you can form a related word which has /č/ instead of /t/.

   depart legislator moist sculptor spirit

(b) For each of these words which contains /d/ you can find a related word which has /ǰ/ instead.

   fraud grade grand proceed residue

(c) For each of these words with /s/ give a related word with /ʃ/.

   admissible coerce grace fallacy ferocity sacrifice

(d) For each of these words with /z/ find a related word with /ʒ/.

   compose disclose expose infuse pleasant revise

(e)   We need to look more closely at the I-drop rule. Each word below has /ʃ/, resulting from the palatalization of //s// before /i/ and another vowel. In the words on the left the /i/ which caused palatalization has been deleted. In the words on the right the /i/ has not been deleted. Why is this? (Notice that the words may be spelled with *c* or with *t*, but the spelling has nothing to do with it.)

official	officiate
partial	partiality
confidential	confidentiality

14.5   Alternation with zero

14.5a

Consider this group of base words, which end the same way:

angle   circle   fable   miracle   table   vehicle

At least one of the following suffixes can be added to each of the base words: +*ar*, +*ate*, +*ous*. Then we have, in orthographic form, *angular, circular, circulate, fabulous*, etc. The phonological forms of the first pair are /'æŋgəl/ and /'æŋgjulər/. The /ə/ of *angle* – and *circle, fable*, etc. – is the same as that of *fiddle, juggle*, etc. It is inserted by a phonotactic rule. But the /ju/ of *angular, circulate*, etc. is different. It is part of the underlying form, alternating with zero. We can represent the underlying form of *angle, angul-* this way: //æŋg{ju,0}l// or this way: //æŋg(ju)l//. Since the latter is slightly simpler, we shall use this form from now on. Material in parentheses alternates with zero; the material is present in one allomorph and absent in another. The other words listed above have these underlying forms:

//sɜrk(ju)l, f{ei,æ}b(ju)l, mɪræk(ju)l, t{ei,æ}b(ju)l, viihɪk(ju)l//

The rule which applies is:

Choose /ju/ when a non-neutral suffix follows; otherwise choose zero.

And here is a sample pair of derivations:

	//#sɜrk(ju)l#	#sɜrk(ju)l+ær#//
Stress	S	S
ju-rule	0	
V insertion	ə	
V reduction		ə
Surface	/'sɜrkəl	'sɜrkjulər/

14.5b

The adjectives *long, strong, young* end with /ŋ/. The corresponding comparative forms, *longer, stronger, younger,* and superlative forms, *longest, strongest, young-est,* have /g/ before the suffixes, /ər/ and /ɪst/. The underlying forms for the adjectives, then, are //#lɒng# #strɒng# #yung#//, and there are two rules:

an assimilation rule	n ⟶ ŋ / ___ g
a deletion rule	g ⟶ 0 / ŋ ___ #

Sample derivations would look like these:

Underlying	//#lɒng#	#lɒng+er#//
Stress	S	S
N assimilation	ŋ	ŋ
G deletion	0	
Surface	/lɒŋ	lɒŋgər/

Generative phonologists consider that there is no underlying phoneme //ŋ//. There is a surface phoneme /ŋ/, of course, but as we have seen (chapter 6), it is restricted in its occurrence. It never occurs initially, and it is rare in intervocalic position. Its principal occurrences are in final position and before /k/ and /g/. Furthermore, there is no such final cluster as /ŋg/ – at least, not in the speech of most people. Thus, from the viewpoint of generative phonology, the underlying forms of such words as *sing, sink, anger,* and *anchor* contain //n//. It is predictable that a nasal consonant in these positions must be /ŋ/, and that no /g/ will be pronounced in final position after a nasal consonant. What is predictable is stated as a rule. The underlying form gives the information about a linguistic form which is not predictable.

From this point of view the assimilation rule should be much more general:

$$[\text{+ nasal}] \longrightarrow \begin{cases} \text{m / \_\_\_ labial C} \\ \text{n / \_\_\_ apical C} \\ \text{ŋ / \_\_\_ dorsal C} \end{cases}$$

14.5c

Consider the words *normal, senatorial, intellectual.* They contain the base words *norm, senator,* and *intellect,* respectively. At first glance it might seem that they contain suffixes -*al,* -*ial,* -*ual,* respectively. But are there actually three different suffixes? In each case the suffix has the same function, making an adjective from a noun. In this respect they are alike. Is there a free choice in adding -*al,* -*ial,* or -*ual* to a particular base? Obviously not. No one can choose to say **normial* or **normual.* Nor is the choice of -*al,* -*ial,* or -*ual* dependent on some phonological feature of the base word. Thus the presence of *i* or *u* or neither of them is part of the underlying form of the base word. The underlying forms are:

$$//nɔrm// \quad //sɛnətɔr(i)// \quad //ɪntəlɛkt(ju)//$$

We call the //i// of //sɛnətɔr(i)// and the //ju// of //ɪntəlɛkt(ju)// **augments**. //sɛnətɔri// and //ɪntəlɛktju// are the augmented forms of //sɛnətɔr// and //ɪntəlɛkt//, respectively. //nɔrm// has no augmented form. If there is an augment, it is deleted when no suffix follows.

augment ⟶ 0 / ___ #

14B PROBLEM

All the words below occur with such suffixes as -*al*, -*ous*, -*ic* (//+æl//, //+ɒs//, //+ɪk//, respectively) but always in an augmented form. Give the augment for each word, using ordinary spelling – *i* for *senator(i)*, *u* for *intellect(u)*, for example.

act	aroma	contempt
habit	symptom	commerce
sense	sympath + y	event
sex	apolog + y	attitude
tempest	part	longitude
finance	manager	spasm
race	professor	drama
dogma	dictator	opera

14.6 Spirantization

Certain morphemes have an alternation of /t/ and /s/ or, as we shall put it, an underlying //{t, s}//; a rule that is called Spirantization tells when to choose each of the alternants. More simply, it tells when to choose one of these, and the other occurs under other conditions. Consider these pairs of words:

intimate, intimacy   analytic, analysis   part, partial

Let's say that the underlying forms are these:

$$//\#ɪntɪmæ\{t,s\}\#, \#ɪntɪmə\{t,s\}+i\#//$$
$$//\#ænælɪ\{t,s\}+ɪk\#, \#ænælɪ\{t,s\}+ɪs\#//$$
$$//\#par\{t,s\}(i)\# \#par\{t,s\}(i)+æl\#//$$

A tentative statement of the spirantization rule, which we will want to modify later, is this:

> In the choice {t,s} choose /s/ before the noun suffixes +i# and +is# and before the augment (i) followed by a vowel; elsewhere choose /t/.

This can also be expressed as a formula:

$$\{t,s\} \longrightarrow \begin{cases} (1) \ /s/ \\ (2) \ /t/ \end{cases} / \underline{\hspace{2em}} \begin{bmatrix} + i \, \# & \text{(a)} \\ + \text{I} \, s & \text{(b)} \\ + i + [+ \text{syl}] & \text{(c)} \end{bmatrix}$$

For *partial* the palatalization rule applies after the spirantization rule and is responsible for the /ʃ/ in that word.

Underlying	//#ɪntɪm æ{t,s}+i#//	//#ænælɪ{t,s}ɪs//
Stress	S	S
{t,s} choice	s	s
V reduction	ə ə	ə ə
Surface	/'ɪntəməsi	ə'næləsɪs/

Underlying	//#par{t,s}(i)+æl//
Stress	S
{t,s} choice	s
Palatalization	ʃ
V reduction	ə
Surface	/'parʃəl/

Rather than the notation {t,s} we can indicate morphemes affected by spirantization this way:

//ɪntɪmæt//[Spir.]   //ænælɪt//[Spir.]   //part(i)//[Spir.]

14C EXERCISES

Each of the following words has one of the suffixes mentioned in the sprirantization rule, with an /s/ immediately preceding. For each word you should be able to think of a related word which has no suffix or a different suffix and has /t/ rather than /s/. For example, the first word below, *confederacy*, should remind you of *confederate*.

confederacy	complacency	ecstasy	catharsis
delicacy	frequency	geodesy	diuresis
democracy	hesitancy	galaxy	hypnosis
diplomacy	infancy	heresy	narcosis
hypocrisy	presidency	idiocy	neurosis
literacy	vacancy	lunacy	synopsis
piracy			synthesis
prophecy			
secrecy			

14.7 Velar softening

The words *medical* and *medicine* show an alternation of /k/ and /s/. The words *analogous* and *analogy* show an alternation of /g/ and /ǰ/. Further investigation shows us that these alternations are frequent in words of Latin and Greek origin. In fact, our orthography uses the letter *c* for both /k/ and /s/ and the letter *g* for both /g/ and /ǰ/. The underlying forms of these and similar morphemes contain an alternating pair {k,s} and {g,ǰ}:

//#mɛdɪ{k,s}+æl#, #mɛdɪ{k,s}+ɪn#
#ænælɒ{g,ǰ}+ɒs#, #ænælɒ{g,ǰ}+i#.

The choice to be made in {k,s} and {g,ǰ} is slightly more complex than the choice for {t,s}. The rule will be given after you do the next exercise.

14D PRACTICE

(a) The following words all contain /k/ at or near the end. For each word think of a related word which has /s/ instead.

critical electric italic(s) reciprocal romantic

(b) The following words contain /g/ at or near the end. For each word think of a related word which has /ǰ/.

demagog fragment legal pedagog regal rigor

Rule: From the underlying pair {k,s} choose /k/ and from the pair {g,ǰ} choose /g/ before # and before the adjective suffix +ous //ɒs//, the abstract noun suffix +or //ɔr//, and the suffix +ant //ænt//; choose /s/ and /ǰ/ before this group of suffixes: +y, +ize, +ism, +ist, +ity, +ine, +ic, +id, +ent, +ile, and the augment +i+.

Examples of all of these follow:

/k/ or /g/ – electric#   pedagog#   clinic+al   reg+al   analog+ous
          rig+or
/s/ or /ǰ/ – pedagog+y   critic+ize   romantic+ism   apolog+ist
          electric+ity   medic+ine   demagog+ic   rig+id   reg+ent
          frag+ile   music+i+an   litig+i+ous   Patric+i+a

The simpler notations are, for example:

//mɛdɪk// [Vel. soft.]   //ænælɒg// [Vel. soft.]

and here are sample derivations:

	//#mɛdɪk+æl#	#mɛdɪk+ɪn#
Stress	S	S
Velar softening	—	s
V reduction	ə	
Surface	/'mɛdɪkəl	'mɛdɪsɪn/

	//#ænælɒg+ɒs#	#ænælɒg+i#//
Stress	S	S
Velar softening	—	ǰ
V reduction	ə ə ə	ə ə
Surface	/ə'næləgəs	ə'næləǰi/

14.8   The sequence of rules

The word *commerce* ends with /s/. The word *commercial* contains /ʃ/, formed by palatalization of //s// before (i) and a vowel: //kɒmɜrs(i)al//. The following words are like *commercial*. Each one is formed with an ending *iVC*, *i* followed by a vowel, followed by a consonant, added to a word that ends with /s/.

confession   gracious   malicious   palatial   spacious

Here is a pair of sample derivations:

	//#mælɪs#//	//#mælɪs(i)ɒs#//
Stress	S	S
Palatalization	—	ʃ
I-drop		0
V reduction		ə ə
	/'mælɪs	mə'lɪʃəs/

14E PROBLEM

(a) The next group of words also contains /ʃ/, and each word has an ending *iV(C)* added to a base word. However, in each of these cases the base word ends with /t/, not /s/.

> action assertion exemption inertia partial vibration
> act assert exempt inert part vibrate

Each of these base morphemes has the choice pair {t,s} and there is an augment (i). What seems to be a change from /t/ to /ʃ/ is the result of two rules. What are they?

(b) The next words also contain /ʃ/, and each word also has an ending of the form *iV(C)* added to a simpler base word. What is the final consonant of the base word? What rules account for the change of this consonant to /ʃ/?

> electrician logician mathematician magician musician
> electric logic mathematic magic music

The spirantization rule, as it was presented in section 14.6, was called a tentative statement. The rule indicated that underlying //t// becomes /s/ before the suffix +*y* as in *intimacy* (compare *intimate*); before the suffix -*is*, as in *hypnosis* (compare *hypnotic*); and before the sequence //i V// as in *partial* (compare *part*). In words like *partial* and *direction* (compared with *part* and *direct*) we see the result of both spirantization and palatalization, namely /ʃ/. But *digestion* and *exhaustion* have /č/, not /ʃ/, and so do *bestial*, *Christian* and other words in which underlying //t// is preceded by //s//. Compare these derivations for *direct*, *direction*, *digest*, and *digestion*.

	//#dɪrɛkt#	#dɪrɛkt+ion#	#dɪjɛst#	#dɪjɛst+ion#//
Stress	S	S	S	S
Spirantization	—	s	—	—
Palatalization		ʃ		č
I-drop		0		0
V reduction		ə		ə
Surface	/dɪ'rɛkt	dɪ'rɛkʃən	dɪ'jɛst	dɪ'jɛsčən/

The //t// of *direction* changes to /s/ (spirantization), and this /s/ changes to /ʃ/ (palatalization). The //t// of *digestion* does not undergo spirantization because it is preceded by //s//, so that palatalization affects the original //t//, changing it to /č/.

14.9   Change in voice

The voiceless obstruents, especially /f, θ, s/ alternate with the corresponding voiced obstruents under certain conditions. For example, we have noted these alternations which are phonologically conditioned:

give – gif+t   twelve – twelf+th

and these alternations which are morphologically conditioned:

mischief – mischiev+ous   belief – believe
wife – wife′+s – wive+s

The morphological rules for the alternation {f,v} are:

$$
\text{choose } v \; / \; \left\{
\begin{array}{l}
\underline{\hspace{1cm}} \text{+ous} \\
\underline{\hspace{1cm}} \text{\{Verb\}} \\
\underline{\hspace{1cm}} \text{\# (Plural)}
\end{array}
\right\}
$$

The underlying forms must contain the choice {f,v}. Other words like *cuff* and *hive* form the plural in the regular way: *cuffs* and *hives*, respectively.

14F   QUESTIONS

(a)   Each word below has either /f/ or /v/ in the surface form. For each word there is another form of the same word or a related word in which /f/ is replaced by /v/ or /v/ is replaced by /f/. Can you think of the word(s)? (There may be other changes, chiefly involving vowels, in some of the words.)

calf	leaf	wharf	proof	five
half	life	knife	relief	sieve
dwarf	loaf	wolf	strife	bereave
elf	scarf	shelf	grief	cleave

(b)   Which of these alternations are morphologically conditioned?
(c)   All of the following words end with voiceless /θ/. For each one there may be some related word with /ð/. Can you think of it? There are also vowel alternations in some words.

bath	cloth	north	teeth	wreath
breath	mouth	south	worth	

(d)   There is similar alternation of /s/ and /z/. For example, corresponding to the noun *glass* there is a verb *to glaze*.

(i)   What is the verb corresponding to the noun *grass*? What is the verb corresponding to the noun *advice*?

(ii)   The written words *use, abuse, excuse,* and *house* are pronounced differently depending on whether they are nouns or verbs. How do they differ?

(iii)   Are the noun *grease* and the verb *to grease* pronounced the same, or not? Does *greasy* have /s/ or /z/?

(iv)   Is the plural of *house* pronounced /ˈhawsɪz/ or /ˈhawzɪz/?

(v)   The following verbs consist of prefix and base. Examine the pronunciation of the bases.

con=serve   re=serve   per=sist   re=sist
con=sume   pre=sume   in=sert   de=sert

There is a rule which determines whether the base is pronounced with initial /s/ or /z/. What is the rule?

(vi)   In *example, executive, exert, exist, exonerate* the letter *x* represents /gz/. In *sex, taxi, execute, lexicon, taxidermy* the same letter stands for /ks/. Again, there is a rule that determines whether /gz/ or /ks/ occurs. What is the rule?

(e) The noun *absorption* is formed from the verb *absorb*. The two words should have the same underlying form, except for the ending -//tion// in the noun. Is the alternation phonologically or morphologically conditioned?

(f) The words *segment, section,* and *sector* have the same base with different suffixes. What would you propose as the underlying form of this base?

The words *fragment, fraction,* and *fracture* have the same base and different suffixes. What would you propose as the underlying form of the base?

14.10   The vowel shift rule

Prefixes and suffixes have an obvious function in the derivation of complex words from simpler words. *Befriend* and *enrich* have partly the meanings of *friend* and *rich*, respectively; *growth* and *amusement* have the meanings of *grow* and *amuse*, respectively, plus something else. Suffixes are used also for inflection, as in the plural form *horses* and the past tense form *waited*. Derivation and inflection are also accomplished by inner changes, changes in the vowels and consonants of the base words. The words *lose* and *loss* are related to each other in the same way that *grow* and *growth* are related, *full* and *fill* are related in about the same way as *deep* and *deepen* or *rich* and *enrich*. Just as the past tense of *walk* is formed by suffixation (*walked*), the past tense of *run* is made by change of vowel (*ran*). Similarly, vowel change is the mechanism for the formation of plural *feet* from singular *foot*, a function that is more frequently accomplished by suffixation. In the above examples of vowel change, the replacement of one vowel by another performs some kind of function. Sometimes, however, vowel change accompanies suffixation, as in *depth* from *deep* and *slept* from *sleep*, or change of suffix, as in *ferocious* and *ferocity*.

Consider the vowels alternating in these pairs of words:

1	wise, wisdom	4	profound, profundity
2	extreme, extremity	5	goose, gosling
3	volcano, volcanic	6	provoke, provocative

In each pair of words there is an alternation of two stressed vowels, one free and the other checked. The two vowels in each set are quite far apart in Modern English, but our school tradition refers to the two vowels in set 1 as 'long I' and 'short I'; the ones in set 2 as 'long E' and 'short E'; those in set 3 as 'long and short A,' respectively; and those of set 6 as, respectively, 'long and short O.' Our school tradition has no name for the pairs illustrated in sets 4 and 5; that is partly due to the fact that these alternations are not as common as the other four.

The vowels of each set are quite far apart in the pronunciation of our day, but in the early fourteenth century they were much closer. In each pair the two vowels were phonetically identical except that one was long (and/or tense) and the other was short (and/or lax). Then all the long vowels changed (the so-called Great Vowel Shift). Some of the short vowels changed a little, and others not at all. The consequence of these changes is that what were originally similar vowels in related words have become far apart, as the six pairs of examples above illustrate.

To explain the relationships that exist in Modern English we use underlying forms which contain a choice pair of vowels, one free and one checked. The underlying forms for the six sets of words above are:

1	//#w{ai,ɪ}z (+dəm)#//	4	//#prɒf{au,ʌ}nd (+iti)#//
2	//#ɛkstr{ii,ɛ}m (+iti)#//	5	//#g{uu,ɒ}s(+ling)#//
3	//#vɒlk{ei,æ}n(o/+ik)#//	6	//#prɒv{ou,ɒ}k (+æt+iv)#//

To simplify and generalize, we list such morphemes with the free vowel indicated and the following notation, '[V shift]':

//waiz//[V shift]	//prɒfaund//[V shift]
//ɛkstriim//[V shift]	//guus//[V shift]
//vɒlkein-//[V shift]	//prɒvouk//[V shift]

Thus the morpheme which appears in *wise* and *wisdom* has the underlying form //w{ai,ɪ}z//. In the surface forms the free vowel appears in the unsuffixed word (*wise*) and the checked vowel in the suffixed word (*wisdom*). The other five pairs of words also have a single morpheme with alternating free and checked vowels. In these pairs also the free vowel occurs, generally, in the word without a suffix and the checked vowel in a suffixed word. However, the conditions for choice of the free or the checked vowel are somewhat more complicated than this.

The checked vowel is the one which is chosen when two or more consonants follow (unless the two consonants are *nd*, *ld*, or *st*); when two or more syllables follow in the same word; and when certain suffixes follow – namely, *-ic* as in *volcanic*, *-id* as in *valid*, and *-ish* as in *demolish*. Only the first of these is important here.

We can re-state the preceding paragraph in a formula:

$$\text{Vowel} \longrightarrow \text{checked} / \underline{\hspace{1cm}} \left\{ \begin{matrix} C_2 \\ C\,V\,C\,v \ldots \# \\ +\text{ɪk, ɪd, ɪʃ}\# \end{matrix} \right\}$$

This rule affects the second word in each of the six sets above.

	//#w{ai,ɪ}z#	w{ai,ɪz+dəm)#//
Stress	S	S
V shift	ai	ɪ
	/waiz	'wɪzdəm/

	//#ɛkstr{ii,ɛ}m#	#ɛkstr{ii,ɛ}m+iti#//
Stress	s S	s S
V shift	ii	ɛ
V reduction		ə
Surface	/ɛk'striim	ɛk'strɛməti/

	//#vɒlk{ei,æ}no#	#vɒlk{ei,æ}n+ɪk#//
Stress	s S	s S
V shift	ei	æ
Surface	/vɒl'keino	vɒl'kænɪk/

	//#prɒf{au,ʌ}nd#	#prɒf{au,ʌ}nd+iti#//
Stress	S	S
V shift	au	ʌ
V reduction	ə	ə ə
Surface	/prə'faund	prə'fʌndəti/

	//#g{uu,ɒ}s#	#g{uu,ɒ}s+lɪng#//
Stress	S	S
V shift	uu	ɒ
Voice assimilation		z
NG rule		ŋ
Surface	/guus	'gɒzlɪŋ/

	//#prɒv{ou,ɒ}k#	#prɒv{ou,ɒ}k(æt)+ɪv#//
Stress	S	S
V shift	ou	ɒ
V reduction	ə	ə ə
Surface	/prə'vouk	prə'vɒkətɪv/

(The augment (æt) seen in *provocative* is discussed in section 14.12, 'More about augments.')

14G   PRACTICE

Here are more words with checked vowels in six sets. Each word has a suffix. Remove the suffix and identify the word with the corresponding free vowel.

(i)   width fifty typical derivative divinity Biblical wilderness
precision Palestinian Cypriot   (For this last word add a new ending
-*us*.)

(ii)   kept obscenity supremacy competitive adrenalin intervention
shepherd

(iii)   sanity chastity explanatory urbanity profanity Spanish
inflammatory

(iv)   abundant southern pronunciation

(v)   fodder lost

(vi)   phonic composite jocular nostril diagnostic microscopic

---

14.11   Free and checked vowels

The use of underlying forms helps us to see the systematic relationships which exist between the allomorphs of certain morphemes, as in *compose* and *composite*, *volcano* and *volcanic*. But the facts that we have observed do more than tell us about specific morphemes; they point to some general facts about the language. Free and checked vowels are in contrast in some environments, for example, before a single final consonant, as in *pane* and *pan*. But in certain other environments only free vowels occur or only checked vowels; there is no contrast.

We have seen that a checked vowel occurs in a syllable that is closed by a consonant.

candy   rapture
detective   November
malignant   relinquish
doctrine   option
indulgent   reluctant

Usually when the antepenult of a word is stressed, its vowel is a checked vowel, but this does not apply to *u*.

anecdote calendar
democrat ebony
curriculum minimum
document monitor
but: funeral ludicrous

A vowel is typically checked if it occurs before the suffixes +*ic*, +*id*, and the verbal suffix +*ish* (as in *vanish*; not the adjective suffix, as in *Danish*). But note that the vowel *u* is not checked before the first two of these suffixes.

mechanic	vocalic	placid	valid	banish	establish
epidemic	prophetic	fetid	intrepid	blemish	replenish
terrific	critic	frigid	insipid	diminish	finish
economic	logic	solid	stolid	astonish	demolish
				publish	punish

but: cubic music   lucid putrid

On the other hand, a free vowel occurs in an open syllable.

chaos laity
neon peony
lion science
poet boa
cruel fluid

In the environment,

_____ C¹ (r) i V . . .

$$\_\_\_\_ \; C^1 \; (r) \; i \; V \ldots$$

that is, before one consonant (plus, possibly, /r/), then /i/ and another vowel only the free vowels /ei ii ou/ occur, and not the corresponding checked vowels /æ ɛ ɒ/.

radium patriot audacious nation
amnesia completion devious medium
atrocious jovial podium notion

But in this position checked /ɪ/ occurs and not free /ai/.

ambition civilian nutritious Virginia

(Note that palatalization may occur if the consonant is /s/.)
  The rule for free vowel choice can be stated in this formula:

$$\text{Vowel} \longrightarrow \text{Free} \; / \; \left\{ \begin{array}{l} \left[\underline{} \text{ vowel} \right] \\[4pt] \left[\begin{array}{c} \underline{} \\ \text{non-low} \end{array} \right] \# \\[6pt] \left[\begin{array}{c} \underline{} \\ \text{non-high} \end{array} \right] C^1 \; (r) \; i \; \text{Vowel} \end{array} \right\}$$

This rule applies after the stress rules; this means that stress rules apply as if the final vowel of *macaroni, continue, volcano,* etc. is a checked vowel.

14H   PRACTICE

A large number of (originally) related words follow, showing the opposition of free vowel and checked vowel. You should have no trouble in accounting for the environment of the checked vowel. (There is no feedback. In the unlikely case that you can't explain why a particular word has a checked vowel, review the preceding section.)

/ei, æ/
depraved, depravity
fable, fabulous
grain, granary
inane, inanity
Kate, Katherine
labor, elaborate
opaque, opacity
page, paginate
sacred, sacrament

/ai ɪ/
Bible, Biblical
crime, criminal
file, filament
imbibe, bibulous
mine, mineral
rabbi, rabbinical
reside, residual
sine, sinuous
title, titular
tyrant, tyranny

/ii ɛ/
bereave, bereft
clean, cleanse
heal, health
redeem, redemption

/ii, ɛ/
creed, credulous
female, feminine
femur, femoral
gene, generate
helix, helical
hero, heroine
legal, legislate
repeat, repetitive
species, specimen

/ou ɒ/
code, codify
globe, globular
local, locative
mediocre, mediocrity
mode, modify
omen, ominous
onus, onerous
opus, opera
provoke, provocative
sole, solitude

/ai ɪ/
defile, filth
drive, drift
scribe, script
thrive, thrift

/ei æ/
grave, gravid
pale, pallid
prevail, valid
rabies, rabid

/ai ɪ/
arthritis, arthritic
cycle, cyclic
lyre, lyric
parasite, parasitic
satire, satiric
bile, bilious
collide, collision
expedite, expeditious
Palestine, Palestinian
reconcile, reconciliation
reptile, reptilian
suffice, sufficient

/ii ɛ/
athlete, athletic
exegesis, exegetic
kinesis, kinetic
meter, metric

/ou ɒ/
colon, colic
embryo, embryonic
episode, episodic
neurosis, neurotic

There exist a number of pairs of words with the same vowel contrasts which cannot be explained within the rules given. Examples:

cave, cavern
face, facet
glaze, glass
Jane, Janet
shade, shadow
vale, valley
dine, dinner
final, finish
dike, ditch
pike, pickerel
whine, whinny

feet, fetters
heath, heather
mead, meadow
please, pleasant
sheep, shepherd
zeal, zealous
close, closet
coal, collier
hole, hollow
know, knowledge
throat, throttle

The relationships seen in these word-pairs are the result of the same historic processes as those previously considered, but the original conditioning factors have been lost: *shadow* and *southern* once had an extra syllable at the end; *valley, dinner, closet* were originally stressed on the ult, for which reason the vowel of the initial syllable was lax; *ditch* and *shepherd* have lax vowels because the vowels were once followed by two consonants. It is interesting to note that some of these pairs are still semantically related but others, like *feet* and *fetters*, *mead* and *meadow*, now have no common meaning. Other historically related pairs with no present semantic kinship can be cited. No speaker of Modern English would see what *bonfires* have to do with *bones*, or *shackles* with *shaking*, or *spaniels* with *Spain*.

14.12 More about augments

Consider these sets of words:

admire – admiration	imagine – imaginative
define – definition	describe – descriptive
convene – convention	exclaim – exclamatory
inscribe – inscription	expose – expository

Here there is a problem of deciding how much belongs to the base and how much is a suffix. The right-hand words of the pairs are apparently formed by adding suffixes *-tion*, *-tive*, *-tory* to the verbs on the left-hand side, but there seems to be something else in between.

It is simplest to recognize special augments which are added to many Latin-derived verbs when any of the suffixes +*ion*, +*ive*, +*ory* (or +*or* as in *compositor*) follow. The augment is (æt), (ɪt), or just (t) depending on the base, and in all of them the *t* is subject to spirantization (t → s) and *s* is subject to palatalization (s → ʃ) before *-ion*. The augment is part of the underlying form. It is not predictable and thus cannot be stated as a rule. It is part of the knowledge of any person who uses such words as *invite, invitation; expose, expository; describe, descriptive*, and the like. The augmented underlying forms of the bases in the words above are:

//ædm{ai,ɪ}r(æt)//	//ɪmæǰɪn(æt)//
//-f{ai,ɪ}n(ɪt)//	//-kl{ei,æ}m(æt)//
//-v{ii,ɛ}n(t)//	//-p{ou,ɒ}z(ɪt)//
//-skr{ai,ɪ}b(t)//	

Many augmented forms are irregular. Some examples:

resolve, resolution	//-sɒlv(ᴀᴜɢ)// = /solut/
inquire, inquisitive	//-kwair(ᴀᴜɢ)// = /kwɪzɪt/
introduce, introductory	//-d(j)uus(ᴀᴜɢ)// = /dʌkt/
retain, retentive	//-tein(ᴀᴜɢ)// = /tɛnt/

A number of bases which end in //t// or //d// have an augmented form in which that final consonant is replaced by /s/. Some examples:

include, inclusive	//-kluud(ᴀᴜɢ)// = /kluus/
divide, division	//-v{ai,ɪ}d(ᴀᴜɢ)// = /vɪs/
respond, responsive	//-spɒnd(ᴀᴜɢ)// = /spɒns/
permit, permission	//-mɪt(ᴀᴜɢ)// = /mɪs/

14I   EXERCISE

Here is an opportunity for you to prove that you know the augmented underlying forms for certain words which are similar to the ones discussed above.
You probably have not thought about these words in terms of underlying
forms and augments, but these terms simply refer to concepts which are our
way of accounting for the knowledge that speakers of English have.

If you add *+ion* to *propel*, the result is *propulsion*. Let's state it simply, this
way:

  propel +ion = propulsion

What are the results of these additions?

intrude +ion	=		submit +ive	=
revolve +ion	=		compel +ory	=
offend +ive	=		inform +ion	=
evoke +ive	=		suspend +ion	=
define +ive	=		comprehend +ive	=
inflame +ory	=		preserve +ion	=

14.13   Applications

Consider the following pairs of words:

1	*2*
Canada	Canadian
comedy	comedian
felony	felonious
melody	melodious
remedy	remedial

Each pair of words must have the same underlying form, except for the ending. The same set of rules should apply to all the words in column 1, and
another set of rules should apply to all the words in column 2.

All words in column 1 have the canonical form CVCəCV; all words in column
2 have the canonical form CəCV:CiVC. The first vowel in all the underlying
forms must be a checked vowel; it remains a checked vowel when stressed,
as in column 1, and it becomes schwa when unstressed, as in column 2. The
second vowel must also be a lax vowel in the underlying form; otherwise the
stress would not be on the antepenult in the words of column 1. How then do
we account for the free vowel in the surface forms of the words in column 2?
We observe that there is an environment for free vowel choice, ____ C i V. So
the derivation for the first pair of words is like this:

Underlying	//#kænædæ#	#kænæd+i+æn#//	
Stress	S	S	
V shift	æ	ei	
V reduction	ə ə	ə	ə
Surface	/'kænədə	kə'neidiən/	

Write out the derivations for the other four pairs of words.

Study the derivations for the words *rite* /rait/ and *ritual* /'rɪčuəl/.

Underlying	//#rait(ju)#	#rait(ju)+æl#//	
Augment choice	0	ju	
Stress	S	S	
V choice	ai	ɪ	
Palatalization		č	
J-drop		0	
V reduction		ə	
Surface	/'rait	'rɪčuəl/	

14J PRACTICE

Using the above as models, determine what should be the derivations for the following:

vice /vais/   vicious /'vɪʃəs/
habit /'hæbɪt/   habitual /hə'bɪčuəl/

14.14 Summary

Just as phonemes, the units of sound, have variant pronunciations called allophones, so many of the meaningful units of the language, the morphemes, have variant forms called **allomorphs**. In this chapter we have taken the point of view that each variable morpheme has a single abstract form, the **underlying representation** or **underlying form**, and the allomorphs are different **surface forms** which are derived from the underlying form by application of certain **rules**, or **processes**.

A few rules are quite special, but we have not investigated any of them in this chapter. The classic example of a special rule in English is the formation of the past tense of the verb *go*: go + Past = went. No other verb – in fact, nothing else in English – is like this. We come to a better understanding of the language by considering the most common rules that govern alternations.

Some alternations are **phonologically conditioned**. In this chapter we have dealt with three of these, all of which resemble processes discussed in previous chapters. Obstruents are affected by **voice assimilation**, so that they agree in voice with a following obstruent. Checked vowels in unstressed open syllables or final syllables undergo **vowel reduction**. And the tongue-tip consonants /t d s z/ are affected by **palatalization** when they are followed by /j/ plus a vowel or, in the case of the fricatives, by /i/ and a vowel.

If the allomorphs of a morpheme are **morphologically conditioned**, the choice of one or another depends on the morphemes that occur next, including **abstract morphemes** such as **past tense** or **verb**. An alternation, such as that between /f/ and /v/ may be phonologically conditioned in some environments and morphologically conditioned in others.

When allomorphs are at least partly morphologically conditioned, we have followed the procedure of showing the alternating phonemes as a **choice pair** in the underlying form, with symbols in curly brackets, thus: {f,v}, {ii,ɛ}, and others. The rules which affect specific choice pairs are called by traditional names. **Spirantization** is the rule which applies to the pair {t,s}. The rule of **velar softening** applies to two pairs, {k,s} and {g,j}. The **voicing** rule affects {f,v}, {θ,ð}, and {s,z}. The **vowel shift** rule operates on six pairs of free and checked vowels, {ii,ɛ}, {ei,æ}, {ai,ɪ}, {ou,ɒ}, {uu,ʌ}, and {au,ʌ}, of which the first four are frequent in alternation, the last two uncommon.

The vowel shift rule and vowel reduction rule should help us to understand an important characteristic of English orthography. Our spelling patterns are often a kind of underlying form. Consider such sets of words as these:

define, definitive, definition
compete, competitive, competition
provoke, provocative, provocation

The spelling *defin-* does not represent one single pronunciation, but three of them, and the same is true of *compet-* and *provok-/provoc-*. The variation, however, is not irregular. Those who speak, read, and write English have become accustomed to the fact that one vowel letter has different values in different places. In a way they have acquired the rules which are described in this chapter.

Another kind of allomorphic variation is alternation of a phoneme with zero. Certain of these phonemes are called **augments**. Before the adjective suffixes +al, +an, +ous the augments (i) and (u) – /ju/ – are common. Verbs of Latin origin often have (a{t,s}), (i{t,s}), ({t,s}), or an irregular augment before suffixes +ion, +or, +ory, +ive.

Describing the phonology of a language in terms of rules which apply to an abstract, underlying form leads to another observation: some rules apply to part of the vocabulary but not to all words. The vocabulary of English is made up of words of different origins, most notably Old English, Old French, Latin, and Greek, and these have somewhat different phonological characteristics. The Velar Softening rule applies to words that have come from Latin and

Greek – for example, *electric* with /k/, *electricity* with /s/, *analogous* with /g/, *analogy* with /ǰ/ – but we do not find such alterations in words of Old English origin. On the other hand, we see the effects of the Vowel Shift rule and Voice Assimilation rule in *drive, drift*, of Old English origin, and in *scribe, script*, which came from Latin. Lexical Phonology is a recently developed approach to phonological description which takes into account the different components of the lexicon and the different processes which apply to these components. See the Notes below for references.

14A FEEDBACK

(a) departure legislature moisture sculpture spiritual
(b) fraudulent gradual grandeur procedure residual
(c) admission coercion gracious fallacious ferocious sacrificial
      (Notice the vowel alternation in *ferocious* and *ferocity* and the vowel alternation in *sacrifice* and *sacrificial*.)
(d) composure disclosure exposure infusion pleasure revision
(e) The rule says that /i/ is deleted before a checked vowel in a weak syllable; this applies to *official, partial, confidential*. On the other hand, in *officiate, partiality*, and *confidentiality* /i/ is right before a vowel in a strong syllable and is not deleted.

14B FEEDBACK

act(u)	aroma(t)	contempt(u)
habit(u)	symptom(at)	commerc(i)
sens(u)	sympath(et)	event(u)
sex(u)	apolog(et)	attitud(in)
tempest(u)	part(i)	longitud(in)
financ(i)	manager(i)	spasm(od)
rac(i)	professor(i)	drama(t)
dogma(t)	dictator(i)	opera(t)

14C FEEDBACK

confederate	complacent	ecstatic	cathartic
delicate	frequent	geodetic	diuretic
democrat(ic)	hesitant	galactic	hypnotic
diplomat(ic)	infant	heretic	narcotic
hypocrite	president	idiot(ic)	neurotic
literate	vacant	lunatic	synoptic
pirate			synthetic
prophet(ic)			
secret			

As these examples show, from the underlying //{t,s}// we choose /t/ in final position and before the suffix +*ic*.

Note the alternation of vowels in *diure/ii/sis, diure/ɛ/tic* and in *hypno/ou/sis, hypno/ɒ/tic; narco/ou/sis, narco/ɒ/tic*. These alternations are treated in the vowel shift rule, section 14.10.

14D FEEDBACK

(a) criticize criticism electricity italicize reciprocity romanticism
(b) demagogic fragile legislate legitimate pedagogy regent rigid

14E FEEDBACK

(a) First, //t// → /s/ through spirantization; then /s/ → /ʃ/ through palatalization. Here is a sample derivation:

	//#æk{t,s}#	#æk{t,s}+ion#//	
Stress	S	S	
Spirantization	t	s	
Palatalization		ʃ	
I-drop		0	
V reduction			ə
Surface	/ækt	'ækʃən/	

(b) The final consonant is /k/: *electric, logic, mathematic, magic, music.* Velar softening yields /s/ from the underlying {k,s}, and then /s/ becomes /ʃ/ through palatalization. A pair of sample derivations:

	//#ɛlɛktr+ɪ{k,s}#		#ɛlɛktr+ɪ{k,s}+i+an#//	
Stress	S		S	
Velar softening	—	k	—	s
Palatalization			ʃ	
I-drop			0	
V reduction	ə		ə	ə
Surface	/ə'lɛktrik		əlɛk'trɪʃən/	

14F FEEDBACK

(a)

calf: pl. calves, verb calve   leaf: pl. leaves
half: pl. halves, verb halve   life: pl. lives, verb live,
dwarf: pl. dwarves (also dwarfs)   loaf: pl. loaves
elf: pl. elves   scarf: pl. scarves (also scarfs)
wharf: pl. wharves (also wharfs)   proof: verb prove

knife: pl. knives   relief: verb relieve
wolf: pl. wolves   strife: verb strive
shelf: verb shelve   grief: verb grieve

five: fifth, fifteen, fifty
sieve: sift
bereave: bereft
cleave: cleft

(b) The last group (*five, sieve, bereave, cleave*) are the only ones in which the alternation of /v/ and /f/ is phonologically conditioned. The vowel alternations are also phonologically conditioned, except for *sieve* and *sift*, as we shall see.

(c)

bath: verb bathe
breath: verb breathe
cloth: verb clothe
mouth /-θ/:   verb mouth /-ð/
north: northern
south: southern
teeth: verb teethe
worth: worthy
wreath: verb wreathe

All these alternations are morphologically conditioned.

(d) (i)   graze; advise
     (ii)   The nouns *use, abuse, excuse,* and *house* all end with /s/. The corresponding verbs end with /z/.
     (iii)   That depends on dialect. Generally in Britain and in the South and South Midland of the United States the noun and verb are different, the noun having /s/ and the verb /z/. In Scotland and the greater part of the US and Canada noun and verb are identical, /griis/. In Britain and in the South and South Midland of the US the adjective is /'griizi/. In the rest of North America the word is /'griisi/.
     (iv)   For most speakers of English the plural of *house* is /'hauzɪz/. In some areas the form is /'hausɪz/.
     (v)   In words of this type there is an initial /s/ in the base if the prefix ends with a consonant. If the prefix ends with a vowel, the base has initial /z/.
     (vi)   Compare *e'xecutive* and *'execute.* /gz/ occurs before a stressed vowel, /ks/ after a stressed vowel.
              Incidentally, the words *exile* and *exit* are pronouned with either /gz/ or /ks/. Several centuries ago the verbs *exile* and *exit* were pronounced with /gz/, the corresponding nouns with /ks/.

(e) A phonological change

(f)   To judge from these words alone, we might with equal reason choose either
of two approaches. (1) We might say the underlying forms are //seg//
and //frag// and there is a rule which changes //g// to /k/ before a
following voiceless consonant (as in +*tion*, +*tor*, +*ture*). Or (2) we might
say that the underlying forms are //sek// and //frak// and there is a
rule which changes //k// to /g/ before a following voiced consonant
(such as +*ment*). If we look beyond these examples, we find that voiceless
consonants do occur before /m/ (as in *appointment*) and other voiced
consonants, but voiced consonants do not ordinarily occur before voiceless ones. These considerations make the first of our two approaches
seem preferable to the other.

14G   FEEDBACK

(i)   wide   five   type   derive   divine   divine   Bible   wild   precise
Palestine   Cyprus
(ii)   keep   obscene   supreme   compete   adrenal   intervene   sheep
(iii) sane   chaste   explain   urbane   profane   Spain   inflame
(iv)   abound   south   pronounce
(v)   food   lose
(vi)   phone   compose   joke   nose   diagnose   microscope

   Notice the words *wild, chaste, abound, pronounce*. Before final consonant
clusters /ld, st, nd, ns/ a free vowel may occur, but not before other consonant
clusters.

14I   FEEDBACK

intrusion	submissive
revolution	compulsory
offensive	information
evocative	suspension
definitive	comprehensive
inflammatory	preservation

14J   FEEDBACK

Underlying	//#vais(i)#	#vais(i)+ɒs#//
Augment choice	0	i
Stress	S	S
V choice	ai	ɪ
Palatalizatiom		ʃ
I-drop		0
V reduction		ə
Surface	/vais	'vɪʃəs/

Underlying	//#hæbɪt(ju)#	#hæbɪt(ju)+æl//	
Augment choice		0	ju
Stress	S		S
Palatalization			č
J-drop			0
V reduction		ə	ə
Surface	/ˈhæbɪt	həˈbɪčuəl/	

Notes

The rules presented are derived from Chomsky and Halle (1968). The examples of vowel alternation in section 14.11 are largely drawn from Lightner (1972). On the relationship between spelling and pronunciation see Dickerson (1978), Venezky (1970), Wijk (1966).

The terms *palatalization* and *velar softening* are intended to be merely labels. To call the consonants /t d s z/ 'dentals' and /č ǰ ʃ ʒ/ 'palatals' is traditional but not realistic since both series are articulated at the alveolar ridge, the former with the tongue-tip, the latter with the tongue-front. The term 'velar softening' derives from the custom of referring to /s/ and /ǰ/ as the 'soft' values of the letters C and G, respectively, and /k/ and /g/ as the respective 'hard' values.

For introductions to lexical phonology see Kaisse and Shaw (1985), Jensen (1993), Booij (1994), Spencer (1996).

Appendix: A List of Word-endings and their Effects on Stress

1 Neutral suffixes

A neutral suffix has no effect on stress. It is added to a word which has independent status, and the stress in the suffixed word is on the same syllable as in the word to which the suffix is added, e.g. *pro'pose, pro'posal*. However, there are sometimes changes in the vowels or consonants of the base word, as shown below.

#al₁ (makes abstract nouns from verbs) (dis)approval, arrival, burial, denial, dismissal, proposal, rehearsal . . .

#dom (rare: makes abstract nouns from adjectives and nouns) freedom, martyrdom, officialdom . . . Note the vowel change in *wisdom*.

#ed (forms participles of verbs, many of which are used as adjectives; forms adjectives from nouns; frequent in compound adjectives) bearded, candied, interested, (un)prejudiced, privileged, salaried, absent-minded, three-legged . . .

#en₁ (forms verbs from nouns and adjectives) broaden, cheapen, heighten, lengthen, sharpen, strengthen, threaten

#en₂ (forms adjectives from nouns of material) earthen, golden, wooden, woolen

#en₃ (makes participles from certain verbs, used as adjectives) drunken, forsaken, mistaken, swollen, (un)written . . .

#er (nouns of agent or instrument from certain verbs; nouns meaning 'inhabitant' from some nouns and adjectives; frequent in noun compounds) announcer, carrier, divider, islander, laborer, Londoner, southerner, busdriver, dish-washer, two-wheeler . . .

#ess (forms feminine nouns from other nouns) actress, laundress, sorceress, waitress . . .

#ful₁ (makes nouns of measurement from other nouns; the suffix is a heavy syllable with /ʊ/)   'armful, 'handful, 'houseful, 'mouthful . . .

#ful₂ (makes adjectives from nouns and verbs; a light suffix with /ə/)   cheerful, graceful, joyful, mournful, resentful, tactful . . .

#hood (makes abstract nouns from nouns and adjectives)   childhood, falsehood, likelihood, motherhood, neighborhood . . .

#ing (a versatile and frequent suffix, forms adjectives and nouns, including compounds, from various sources)   absorbing, (un)compromising, gathering, intoxicating, opening . . .

#ish₁ (forms adjectives from various sources)   devilish, feverish, ticklish, yellowish, old-maidish, five-o'clockish . . .

#less (makes adjectives, mostly from nouns)   bottomless, humorless, penniless, regardless, relentless . . .

#ling (rare; makes nouns from nouns and verbs)   changeling, fledgeling, hireling, underling

#ly₁ (makes adjectives, mostly from nouns)   cowardly, friendly, neighborly, slovenly, westerly . . .

#ly₂ (makes adverbs from adjectives)   completely, joyfully, similarly, thoroughly, tremendously . . .

Note that *daily, weekly, monthly, yearly* are both adjective and adverb.

#ness (makes abstract nouns from adjectives)   consciousness, exactness, heartiness, preparedness, thoroughness . . .

#ship (makes abstract nouns from adjectives and nouns)   censorship, partnership, scholarship . . .

#some (makes adjectives from various sources)   burdensome, cumbersome, quarrelsome, venturesome . . .

#wise (makes adverbs from various sources)   (counter)clockwise, crosswise, lengthwise . . .

#th₁ (rare; makes abstract nouns from adjectives and one verb; note vowel change in most words)   breadth, depth, growth, length, width, strength

#th₂ or eth (forms ordinal numbers)   seventh, tenth, twentieth
Note vowel and consonant change in *fifth*.

#y₁ (makes adjectives, mostly from nouns)   feathery, hungry, silky, (un)wieldy . . .

Note vowel deletion in *angry, hungry*.

#y₂ (rare; forms nouns, mostly from other nouns)   ministry, smithy

#y₃ (alternating in spelling with -ie, forms diminutives)   cookie, dolly, kitty, mommy . . .

Note that when -*ly* is added to adjectives of more than one syllable which end in /l/, such as *careful, partial*, only one /l/ is pronounced. There may be two /l/s pronounced in such words as *coolly, fully, solely, wholly*.

The words *able, gentle, humble, noble, simple* have two syllables each. When the adverbial suffix #*ly₂* is added to one of them, it still has two syllables and one /l/.

When #*ly*₂ or #*ness* is added to words which end in #*ed*, such as *alleged, confused, marked*, there is a vowel insertion before /d/:   /əˈlɛjɪdli, kənˈfjuuzɪdli ˈmarkɪdnəs/.

2   Tonic endings

A tonic ending is always stressed (chapter 11). As was also indicated in that chapter, there has been a tendency in the history of the English language for stress to move forward, mostly from the ult to the antepenult. Numerous words which originally had tonic endings are now stressed on the antepenult. We find the same tendency at work today, so that some of the words listed below may be stressed – sometimes and by some people – on the antepenult instead of the ult.

+*aire*   (in nouns and adjectives)   debonaire, doctrinaire, concessionaire, millionaire, questionnaire
+*ee*   (pronounced /ii/; productive now in formation of new nouns)   absentee, endorsee, internee, licensee, nominee, refugee
-*e(e)*, -*et*   (pronounced /ei/; in various words)   ballet, bouquet, cafe, crochet, matinee, negligee, valet
   [In British English these have stress on the initial syllable.]
+*eer*, +*ier*   (nouns which indicate persons)   auctioneer, conventioneer, engineer, mountaineer; bombardier, grenadier
+*esce*   (in a small group of verbs)   acquiesce, coalesce, convalesce, effervesce, rejuvenesce
   [Perhaps the verb *reminisce* might be included here.]
+*ese*   (nouns and adjectives of nationality)   Burmese, Congolese, Japanese, Senegalese, Sudanese, Vietnamese
+*esque*   (in certain adjectives)   grotesque, picturesque, Romanesque
+*ette*   (in nouns, originally with a meaning of diminutive)   brunette, kitchenette, marionette
-*eur*, -*euse*   (in nouns denoting people)   chauffeur, connoisseur, masseuse, raconteur
-*ique*   (in a few nouns and adjectives)   antique, critique, oblique, physique, technique, unique
-*oon*   (in nouns)   baboon, balloon, cartoon, cocoon, harpoon, lagoon

3   Heavy endings

What we call a heavy ending here is a single syllable with a free vowel. Some of the endings listed here might qualify as suffixes, at least in some of the words in which they occur, in which case they might be so designated with a + preceding, but they are all marked here with a hyphen. If a word with a heavy ending has three or more syllables, main stress is on the antepenult. Two-syllable verbs and adjectives have stress on the ult, while two-syllable nouns have stress on the penult.

Here are nine typical heavy endings, with examples in this order: (a) words of 3 or more syllables; (b) 2-syllable verbs and adjectives; (c) 2-syllable nouns.

-ane   (a) cellophane, hurricane; (b) germane, inane, mundane; (c) membrane, methane, propane.

-ene   (a) acetylene, ethylene, kerosene; (b) obscene, serene; (c) benzene, hygiene, phosgene.

-ide   (a) cyanide, sulfanilamide; (b) — ; (c) bromide, chloride, oxide.

-ine   (a) alkaline, aquiline, asinine, concubine, porcupine; (b) divine; (c) carbine, quinine, strychnine, turbine.

   The adjective *alpine* is exceptionally stressed on the initial syllable; such words as *bovine, canine, equine, feline*, which function as nouns and adjectives, are stressed like nouns.

-ite   (a) anthracite, appetite, dynamite, erudite, extradite, parasite, satellite; (b) contrite, ignite, polite, unite; (c) calcite, graphite, lignite, quartzite, termite.

   Exceptions: The nouns *stalactite* and *stalagmite* may be stressed on the penult or on the antepenult; the same is true for the adjective *recondite*.

   Note the adjective *'finite*. In three-syllable adjectives like *definite, infinite* the ult is not heavy.

-oid   (a) adenoid, alkaloid, asteroid, anthropoid, trapezoid; (b) — ; (c) deltoid, mastoid, rhomboid, typhoid, spheroid.

-ose   (a) bellicose, comatose, grandiose, diagnose, varicose; (b) jocose, morose; (c) dextrose, glucose, lactose, sucrose.

-ule   (a) minuscule, molecule, ridicule, vestibule; (b) — ; (c) capsule, globule, module, ovule, schedule.

-ute   (a) constitute, destitute, dissolute, institute, persecute; (b) acute, astute, dilute, pollute, salute; (c) statute, tribute.

   Exceptions: The verbs *at'tribute* and *con'tribute* are stressed on the penult. The adjectives *absolute* and *resolute* vary; stress may be on the antepenult or on the ult.

In addition to these nine endings there are other, less well-defined words with a tense vowel in the ult. Here are some random examples:

(a)   anecdote, exercise, formaldehyde, hypotenuse
(b)   amuse, anoint, cajole, extreme, obey, supreme, sublime
(c)   alcove, athlete

4   Light endings

In almost all cases these 'endings' can be called suffixes. Each is a single syllable with a checked vowel and occurs in nouns and adjectives. Stress is on the penult if the penult is heavy or the first syllable of the word, and otherwise on the antepenult. Ten of these suffixes are listed below (we call *+ant* and *+ent* one suffix and *+ance* and *+ence* one suffix).

+a   (in numerous nouns)   delta, lava, mimosa, placenta; opera, taffeta.

+al₂   (in adjectives)   fatal, tribal, anecdotal, eternal, oriental, universal; criminal, general, radical.

+ar   (a variant of *+al* occurring after bases which have an /l/)   lunar, polar, stellar; perpendicular, similar, triangular.

+ant/+ent   (adjectives and some nouns)   dormant, prudent, silent, vacant, adherent, defiant, resistant; evident, permanent, vigilant.

+ance/+ence   (nouns, many of them corresponding to adjectives with *+ant/ +ent*)   balance, hindrance, prudence, sentence, contrivance, interference; extravagance, reverence.

+is   (in abstract nouns of Greek origin)   crisis, thesis, catharsis, hypnosis, synopsis; emphasis, genesis, metropolis.

+on   (in certain nouns of Greek origin or made up by modern scientists from Greek and other elements)   This is actually two different suffixes, one pronounced /ən/, the other /ɒn/, with variation among speakers as to the pronunciation in specific words. In general, these are pronounced with /ən/:

colon, mammon, cotyledon, horizon, rhododendron; phenomenon, skeleton.

The following are pronounced with /ɒn/:

neutron, nylon, proton, electron; automaton, cyclotron, silicon.

+ous   (an adjective suffix)   callous, pompous, desirous, disastrous, stupendous; onerous, magnanimous, preposterous.

In *hazardous* the suffix is neutral, added to a free word *hazard*.

+um   (in nouns of Latin origin)   album, fulcrum, quorum, decorum, memorandum; curriculum, platinum.

+us   (in nouns of Latin origin, or where a Latin ending has replaced an original Greek ending)   circus, focus, alumnus, papyrus; abacus, phosphorus.

In addition, there are endings which cannot properly be called suffixes. Three groups can be recognized:

-an, -en, -ine pronounced /ɪn/ or /ɨn/
-ace, -ice -ise pronounced /ɪs/ or /ɨs/
-it, -ite pronounced /ɪt/ or /ɨt/

Examples with initial syllable or heavy penult preceding:

menace, premise, promise; affidavit, intestine

Examples with light penult preceding:

cardigan, citizen, deficit, gelatin, javelin, nitrogen, oxygen, pelican, precipice, puritan, specimen, veteran

The penult is heavy if it ends in a consonant, as in *agenda, alumnus, amalgam*, or has a free vowel. Of course the spelling of the word indicates that there are two consonants, and so we know by looking that the penult is heavy and is stressed. On the other hand, our spelling does not indicate whether the penult vowel is free, and therefore stressed, or checked, and therefore not stressed. Compare these two groups of words:

(a)   angina, arena, aroma, diploma, emphysema, empyema, glaucoma, idea, Korea, mimosa, sonata
(b)   camera, cholera, cinema, cupola, formula, malaria, nebula, opera, spatula, tempera, uvula

It would be good if our orthography indicated when a vowel letter stands for a 'long' vowel and when it stands for a 'short' vowel. As we saw in chapter 14, there are some clues derived from redundancy; only free vowels occur in certain positions and only checked vowels in certain other positions. However, in an open penult either a free or a checked vowel may occur, as in the examples above, and our spelling does not indicate the difference. Note that the letter *e* is especially ambiguous, as the following two sets of words show:

idea, panacea	cornea, nausea
museum	cameo, stereo, nucleus
emphysema, empyema	cinema, enema
European	Caesarean

It may be helpful to look at some more words which have a light penult. Note that the vowel letter is *e, i, o,* or *u* but seldom *a*.

-e-   'cerebral, 'competent, 'covetous, 'federal, 'integral, i'tinerant, 'liberal, pe'ripheral, phe'nomenal, 'tolerant
-i-   ab'dominal, 'abstinence, 'decimal, 'dominant, 'eminent, ex'orbitant, in'heritance, in'telligent, 'lubricant, 'madrigal, 'medical, 'militant, 'negligent, par'ticipant, 'pestilence, 'principal, py'ramidal, 'radical
-o-   di'agonal, 'eloquence, 'ignorant, 'resonance
-u-   'ambulance, 'casual, cen'trifugal, con'stituent, ha'bitual, 'opulent, 'petulant, 'rapturous, 'stimulant, 'turbulence, 'virtuous

5 Posttonic suffixes

It is helpful to recognize certain suffixes, few in number but frequent in occurrence, which always follow the stressed syllable of the word in which they occur. Three of them are one syllable long: +*ic*, +*id*, +*ish*₂; others are two syllables long with a light penult: +*ify*, +*itude*, +*ity*; and one of them, +*ion*, may be considered two syllables in the underlying form with loss of the first vowel through palatalization.

+*ic*   (forming adjectives, some of which are also nouns)   academic, automatic, barbaric, dynamic, economic, periodic . . .
   Exceptions: '*Arabic*, '*catholic*, '*lunatic*, '*politic*; also compare the nouns *a'rith-metic*, '*heretic*, '*rhetoric* with the adjectives *arith'metic*, *he'retic(al)*, *rhe'toric(al)*.
+*ics*   (in nouns which designate fields of study)   acoustics, ballistics, calisthenics, economics, semantics . . .
   Exception: '*politics*
+*id*   (in certain adjectives, some of which are also nouns)   acid, arid, candid, insipid, intrepid, lucid, timid, vivid . . .
   Note: Compare the noun '*invalid* and the adjective *in'valid*.
+*ify*/+*efy*   (in a large group of verbs)   amplify, diversify, exemplify, identify, liquefy, personify . . .
+*ion*   (in thousands of abstract nouns)   adoption, communion, intention, opinion, solution, simplification, volition . . .
+*ish*₂   (in a small number of verbs)   abolish, astonish, demolish, diminish, extinguish, relinquish, replenish, vanish . . .
   Exception: *im'poverish*
+*itude*   (in certain abstract nouns)   altitude, exactitude, fortitude, longitude, solicitude, vicissitude . . .
+*ity*/+*ety*   (in a large number of abstract nouns)   absurdity, complexity, continuity, humidity, notoriety, society . . .

(There is often more than one way of classifying and labeling. Instead of calling +*fy*/ +*efy* and +*itude* posttonic suffixes, we could just as well say that +*fy* and +*tude* are heavy endings. The effect would be the same.)

6 Some special suffixes

There are some suffixes of high frequency which cannot be categorized in any simple way. They are treated in this section.

#*able*, +*able*   This adjective suffix is neutral in many words: acceptable, break-able, (in)excusable, foreseeable, impressionable, regrettable.
   In all formations like these #*able* is added to an existing independent word. When not added to an independent word, it is like a light suffix. Stress is on the preceding syllable if that syllable is heavy or initial:

delectable;   affable   capable   durable   liable

If the preceding syllable is light and not initial, stress is on the next syllable to the left:

abominable   amiable   charitable   (in)habitable   memorable
navigable   reputable   (in)separable   venerable

The next group of words vary. They may be stressed on the first syllable or the second syllable of the base word . .

(in)applicable   despicable   (in)hospitable

In some other words the suffix may act as a neutral suffix or as a light suffix:

(in)com'par#able   (in)'compar+able
pre'fer#able   'prefer+able
re'pair#able   (ir)'repar+able
(ir)re'voke#able   (ir)'revoc+able

Notice that the word *admirable* is not what it would seem. It is not *ad'mir-#able* but instead it has a light suffix: *'admir+able*.

+*ible*   is best considered a light syllable. In a few cases it is added to an independent word (for example, *convertible, repressible*), but mostly it appears in words where the base is not an independent word. Then stress is on the preceding syllable if that syllable is heavy or word-initial:

edible   (in)defensible

If the preceding syllable is light and not initial, stress is one syllable to the left:

(in)eligible   negligible

#*age, +age*   Although spelling does not differentiate, there are two different noun endings. One is a neutral suffix pronounced /ɪ̆ǰ/:

acreage   bondage mileage, percentage . . .

The other ending, pronounced /-aʒ/ or /aǰ/, is a tonic ending in two-syllable nouns:

barrage   corsage   massage . . .

and a heavy ending in words of three syllables:

camouflage   fuselage   sabotage

The word *espionage* shows a regular, though uncommon, phenomenon: if the antepenultimate vowel is itself followed immediately by a vowel, stress is on the preantepenult.

+ate,   a frequent suffix in verbs, where it is pronounced /eit/, in adjectives, where it is pronounced /ət/, and in nouns, where the pronunciation is usually /ət/.

In *create* and *equate* the stress is on the ult. In other two-syllable verbs, like those below, stress may be on the first or the second syllable.

collate   cremate   dictate   migrate   narrate   vibrate . . .

Verbs of more than two syllables which have this ending (there are more than 1,000 of them) are stressed on the antepenult:

'designate   'elevate   'hibernate   in'terrogate   per'petuate . . .

There are a handful of exceptions.

Stress on the preantepenult:
de'teriorate   'oxygenate   'peregrinate
Stress on the penult or antepenult:
eructate   impregnate   infiltrate   remonstrate

Nouns and adjectives of more than two syllables are likewise stressed on the antepenult. The following are exceptionally stressed on the penult:

ap'pellate   a'postate   in'carnate   in'sensate   in'testate

+ive   This frequent adjective suffix appears in words with four different stress patterns. Except for the word *conducive* it is always preceded by *t* or *s*. These are the five patterns:

(1)   'x + ive

(2)   x 'x + ive   (3)   (x) 'x $\begin{Bmatrix} a \\ e \\ i \\ u \end{Bmatrix}$ t + ive

(4)   . . . 'x x-at- + ive

The first pattern is, of course, what occurs when the suffix is preceded by a single syllable:

'active   'captive   'cursive   'massive   'missive . . .

Pattern (2) is usual when the suffix is preceded by a prefix and a one-syllable base:

    col'lective   de'cisive   ex'pansive   of'fensive   per'missive . . .

Pattern (3) occurs when *at, et, it,* or *ut* follows a single syllable:

    'additive   'expletive   'lucrative   'negative   'relative   'positive
    'sedative   'talkative   'tentative . . .

It is also the pattern when there is a prefix and a one-syllable base before *at, it,* or *ut*:

    ac'cusative   con'servative   con'secutive   di'minutive
    e'vocative   in'formative   pro'hibitive . . .

    Pattern (4) is found when *at* follows a base of more than one syllable. There are two sub-patterns. In one of them the syllable with *a* is light and the ult is heavy:

    'generative   'nominative   'operative

In the other sub-pattern the syllable with *a* is heavy and the ult is light.

    'imitative   'legislative   'meditative

A number of words vary between the two sub-patterns:

    ad'ministrative   com'municative   'decorative   i'maginative
    re'munerative

Finally, note the variation between pattern (3) *con'templative* and pattern (4) *'contemplative.*

+or   This is actually three different endings. One, which is spelled *-our* in British English, occurs in a number of abstract nouns, always with stress on the preceding syllable:

    ardor   behavior   candor   color   demeanor   favor   fervor . . .

A second ending, more properly identified as *-ior,* is found in words derived from Latin comparative adjectives. Stress is on the syllable preceding the suffix:

    anterior   exterior   inferior   interior   junior   senior   superior

The third *or* ending is always preceded by *t* or *s.* Nouns with this ending designate actors or instruments. There are several stress patterns.

'*x-or*   when a single syllable precedes:
actor   censor   doctor
x '*x-or*   when there is a prefix and a one-syllable base:
aggressor   collector   conductor   detector   inventor   incisor ...
(x) '*x it-or, (x)* '*x ut-or*:   when the *-or* is preceded by *it* or *ut*:
auditor   contributor   editor   exhibitor   executor   monitor   solicitor ...

Notice that in a number of these nouns *or* is like a neutral suffix added to an existing verb (contribute, edit, exhibit). When a noun ends in *-ator*, the *or* is almost always like a neutral suffix added to a verb that ends in *+ate*. Therefore the penult is heavy and the stress is on the preantepenult of the word:

'agitator   'elevator   'illustrator   'percolator ...

Note, in contrast, the noun *con'spirator* from the verb *con'spire*.
   As noted above, two-syllable verbs like *dictate, narrate, spectate, translate* are commonly stressed on the second syllable in British English but the first syllable in American English. This means that the corresponding nouns, *dictator, narrator, spectator, translator,* and so on are stressed on the second syllable in British but the first syllable in American English.

+*ure*   This ending also occurs after *t* or *s*. There are several patterns, very similar to the patterns for +*ive* and +*or*.

'*x-ure*   This is the pattern for words of two syllables:

capture   censure   lecture   pressure   sculpture ...

x '*x-ure*   The pattern of prefix plus one-syllable base:

composure   departure   erasure   exposure   indenture ...

'*x-at-ure,* '*x-it-ure*   The first syllable is not a prefix:

armature   curvature   furniture   ligature   signature ...

x '*x-it-ure*   The first syllable is a prefix:

expenditure   investiture ...

'*x x ature*   Only six words; in four of them the penult is light:

caricature   literature   miniature   temperature;

and in two the penult is heavy:

legislature   nomenclature.

Glossary of Technical Terms

accent   In ordinary usage this term refers to a particular way of speaking (e.g. a Scottish accent, a foreign accent) or to one of several marks used in some languages to indicate pronunciations (e.g. é, è, ê). In this book accent means the heaviest stress on one syllable in a phrase or sentence, giving the word in which the syllable occurs greatest emphasis.

adjective   A word that expresses some attribute of a noun and is modified by *very*, *more*, and other qualifiers: *a very nice day*.

adverb   A term used in the grammatical classification of words to refer to a heterogeneous group of items; the most frequent function is to modify the verb; can be classified by relating to such question words as *where*, *when*, *how*, *why*.

affix   A meaningful element which does not occur alone but is always atached to a **base**. English, like many languages, has two kinds of affixes, **prefixes**, which occur before the base (e.g. *co-author*, *repay*, *unable*), and **suffixes**, which follow the base (e.g. *sharpen*, *happiness*, *employment*). Also see **base**.

affricate   A complex consonant made by stopping the flow of air in the mouth, then releasing the air stream just enough to cause friction – in other words, it consists of a stop and a fricative articulated with the same articulator in the same place. English has two affricates, made with the front of the tongue, /č/ as in *church* and /ǰ/ as in *judge*.

air stream   The breath as it goes from lungs to mouth or nose, or vice versa.

allomorph   One of two or more different forms which have the same meaning or function and are therefore members of the same **morpheme**. For example, *long* and *leng*(th) are allomorphs of one morpheme. See section 14.1 for further discussion. Also see **morpheme**.

allophone   One of two or more similar speech sounds which together compose a **phoneme**. Allophones are not in contrast; they may vary freely (e.g.

one can pronounce the word *cup* with an aspirated /p/ or an unaspirated /p/ and it will be recognized as the same word) or they may occur in different environments (e.g. English /p/ is aspirated when it occurs at the beginning of a strong syllable (e.g. *pair, repair*) but is unaspirated when it occurs after /s/ and when it is ambisyllabic (e.g. *spare, open*). See chapter 7 for extended discussion. Also see **phoneme**.

alternation   Variation of a linguistic unit – a phoneme, a morpheme, a phoneme occurring in a specific morpheme or morphemes (thus, allophone, allomorph).

alveolar   A term used in classifying consonants on the basis of their place of articulation – specifically, at or near the alveolar ridge.

ambisyllabic   Said of a consonant that occurs between two vowels (intervocalic), therefore on the boundary of two syllables, and belongs to both syllables; e.g. the /l/ of '*melody*. The consonant is ambisyllabic only if the second syllable is weak; compare *me'lodious*, where the second syllable is strong and /l/ is in that syllable.

amplitude   The greatest distance a particle of air travels in a sound wave. See section 2.10.

antepenult   The third syllable from the end of a word; e.g. *animal, humility, individual*.

anterior   A term used by Chomsky and Halle (1968) in their phonological theory to make a distinction in place of articulation; anterior sounds are made at the alveolar ridge or more forward.

apex   The tip of the tongue. A speech sound articulated with the apex is **apical**. More specifically, it is **apicodental** if the apex is near or touching the upper teeth, **apicoalveolar** if the apex is near or touching the alveolar ridge.

articulation   (1) The act of producing a speech sound. (2) The speech sound produced.

articulator   The mobile body part which articulates a consonant; it can be the lower lip, the tip, front, or back of the tongue.

articulatory feature   See **feature**.

aspiration   The audible breath which may accompany the articulation of a sound, as when English /p t k/ are released in word-initial position or before a stressed vowel.

assimilation   The influence of one sound segment on another so that they become more alike, by spreading of one or more features. See sections 7.1 to 7.4.

augment   When a morpheme has a short form and a longer form, the difference between them is an augment. In *sympathy* and *sympathetic* the base is *sympath-*, +*y* and +*ic* are suffixes and -*et*- is an augment added to *sympath-*; *sympathet-* is the **augmented form**.

autonomous phoneme   A term in phonology used to characterize the notion of a phoneme when no reference is made to its relationships with grammatical structure.

autosegmental phonology   An approach to phonology which sees phonology as made up of several tiers, each made up of a linear sequence of segments linked to one another by association lines.

auxiliary verb   A verb used with a lexical verb to make grammatical modifications, as in <u>*are working, have seen, will go.*</u>

back vowel   A vowel produced with the back of the tongue in the back of the mouth; phoneticians have traditionally described vowel sounds as front, central, or back; for English (and some other languages) it is enough to make a two-way distinction, either [– back] and [+ back] or, as in this book, [+ front] and [– front].

base   The linguistic form to which affixes are added – or, from the opposite point of view, what is left of a word when all affixes are removed. A base may be free, like the word *friend* of *friendly, friendliness, friendship, unfriendly,* or bound, like *ident-* in *identical, identify, identity.*

bilabial   Produced with both lips.

binary feature   A characteristic of a speech sound or phoneme in a system that classifies in terms of two mutually exclusive possibilities, designated as + or – in square brackets; for example, any speech sound is made either with the vocal cords vibrating or not – it is either [+ voice] or [– voice], with air moving out of the mouth or not – [+ continuant] or [– continuant].

blade   The part of the tongue's upper surface from the center to the tip; it consists of the tip (apex) and front.

borrowed words   Words that have spread from one language to another; English 'borrowed' *chance* from French in the twelfth century and *soprano* from Italian in the sixteenth century, but these are now like native words. In the twentieth century some speakers of English began to use the Yiddish word *shlep* and the Japanese word *tsunami*; these borrowings have consonant clusters which are not usual in English words.

bound morpheme   A meaningful element that does not occur as an independent word; affixes like *un-* and *-ness* are bound morphemes and so is a base like *ident-*. See **base**.

canonical form   A way of showing how classes of phonemes are arranged in certain syllables, morphemes, and words; for example, the words *top, big, fan,* and *sum* consist of a consonant, a vowel, and another consonant; these four, and many other English words, have the canonical form CVC. If we use more precise class names, we see that *top* and *big* consist of a stop, a vowel, and a stop (SVS) while *fan* and *sum* have a fricative, a vowel, and a nasal (FVN). Canonical forms help us state what arrangements are possible in a language and, by extension, what cannot occur in that language. See **constraint**.

checked vowel   An English vowel that never occurs as the coda of a stressed syllable: the vowels of *bit, bet, bat, put, cut, pot.*

clause   A construction of words that could be an independent sentence but forms part of a sentence rather than being a sentence in itself: *She told us* <u>*she will wait.*</u>

cluster   A sequence of consonants which can occur initially or finally in a syllable; e.g. pr- (*prize*), sk- (*school*), -kst (*next*).

coda   The final consonant or consonant cluster of a syllable; if there is no final consonant or cluster, we say there is a zero coda.

complex word   See **word**.

compound   A word made of two or more independent words: bedroom, dining room, near-sighted. As these examples show, the parts may be written together, with a space, or with a hyphen between them. See also **compound verb** and **Greek-type compound**.

compound verb   (As used here) a combination of verb + particle or verb + preposition, which acts as a single semantic unit: *stand up, listen to*.

conjunction   One of a class of words whose chief function is to connect words or phrases; it is usual to distinguish between subordinating conjunctions such as *if, when, as, because, unless*, which typically introduce clauses, and coordinating conjunctions (*and, or, but*) which link two or more nouns, adjectives, phrases, clauses, etc.

consonant   One of several speech sounds produced with some kind of obstruction of the air stream in the vocal tract. There may be complete obstruction (a stop or plosive); complete obstruction in the mouth but with air escaping through the nose (a nasal); partial obstruction that produces turbulence in the air stream (a fricative); or obstruction along the center line of the tongue with air escaping at the sides (a lateral). The English phonemes /r w j/ are not consonants in a phonetic sense but occur in the positions of consonants, adjacent to vowels.

constraint   A statement of what cannot occur in a given language or perhaps in any language; a speech sound cannot be voiceless and voiced at the same time (a universal constraint); an English word can begin with one, two, or three consonants (C-, CC-, CCC-) but not with four consonants (*CCCC-); in Finnish a word can begin with one consonant (C-) but not more (*CC-) – these are language-specific constraints.

context   The linguistic environment of a form in a sentence; the social, spatial, temporal situation in which a form is produced. The place that a unit (a sound, a word) occupies in terms of what precedes and/or what follows.

continuant   Term describing a feature of a speech sound based on whether the air stream is (+) or is not (–) moving out of the mouth during its articulation; vowels, glides, and fricatives are [+ continuant], stops and nasals are [– continuant].

coronal   Describing the feature of a speech sound determined by whether the blade of the tongue is (+) or is not (–) raised from its neutral position; apical and frontal consonants are [+ coronal], labial and dorsal consonants are [– coronal].

deep structure   The underlying, or abstract, form of a word, phrase, or sentence from which the surface form (the actual pronunciation) is derived by general rules.

deletion   The omission of some language element.

derivation   (1) A process in which one word is formed from another: *writer* from *write*. (2) A process in which the pronunciation of a word – the surface form – is derived from an abstract form – the underlying form, or the underlying representation.

determiners   A class of words that occur before nouns and express quantity, specificity, or relative position; e.g. *the, a, an, some, any, all, no, this, that, several.*

dialect   A variety of a language associated with a particular geographic area or a group of speakers who are distinct from other groups in terms of social class.

diphthong   A speech sound produced with the tongue moving from one position to another in the mouth, often with a change in the position of the lips also; examples are *bite, loud, noise.*

discourse   A continuous stretch of spoken or written language, consisting of at least one sentence and usually more than one.

distinctive feature   See **feature**.

distribution   The total set of linguistic contexts in which a phoneme can occur.

dorsum   The back of the tongue; sounds produced with the dorsum are called **dorsal**: the final consonants of *lock, log, long*. A distinction can be made between **dorsopalatal**, referring to articulation of the dorsum with the hard palate and **dorsovelar**, to articulation of the dorsum with the soft palate or velum.

ellipsis   The omission of part of a sentence, where the missing part is understood from context: *'Where are you going?' 'Out.'*

ending   A term used in this book to include the following: *-acy, -ancy/-ency, -ary, -ory, -y*; these forms occur in word-final position and they are important for the statement of stress rules, but they cannot be called suffixes because none of them has a specific meaning or group of meanings.

environment   The parts of an utterance that are adjacent to a word; in *The dog is barking* the environment of *bark* is *The dog is ___ing*.

feature   Any position or action in the vocal tract which is part of the articulation of a speech sound; the initial consonants of *mat, bat,* and *pat* share the feature [labial]. As explained in chapter 2, some features of a phoneme are distinctive and others are non-distinctive.

final   Occurring at the end (of a syllable, word, phrase).

focus   Special attention to one element in a sentence: *Henry* in *Henry is the one I told what you said.* In speech focus is often accomplished through accent: *I told Hénry what you said.*

foot   A unit of rhythm consisting of one strong syllable and perhaps one or more weak syllables; *stop, agree, soda, animal* consist of one foot each; *understand, elevator, ammunition* consist of two feet each.

frequency   The number of cycles in a period of time that a particle of air vibrates; frequencies are usually stated in cycles per second.

functional load   The comparative importance of the contrast between two phonemes; there are few pairs of words like *thigh* and *thy*, *teeth* and *teethe*, minimal pairs differentiated by /θ/ and /ð/, so the contrast of /θ/ and /ð/ has a low functional load; on the contrary, the contrast of /t/ and /d/ has a high functional load: *tie/die, try/dry, coat/code, tent/tend*, etc.

glide   The term used here for a speech sound or phoneme which is vowel-like but does not occur as the peak of a syllable, specifically, the phonemes /j w h/ as in *yet, wet, head*; /j/ and /w/ are called semivowels or semi-consonants by some linguists.

glottis   The area between the vocal cords.

grammar   The rules by which a language operates, and therefore the implicit knowledge that speakers of that language have which makes them competent to use the language. Also, an account of the rules.

grammatical suffixes   Suffixes that express grammatical meanings, such as past tense, plural number, or possessive (*walked*, *books*, *David's*), as distinct from suffixes that create new words (*teacher*, *useful*, *happiness*).

Great Vowel Shift   A term used for an event in the history of the English language, occurring in the fourteenth and fifteenth centuries. Middle English had sets of long and short vowels which can be illustrated in these words:

iː wise i wisdom	uː house u husband, Monday
eː sheep e shepherd, health	oː moon o nostril
ɛː heal	ɔː nose
aː sane	a sanity

The long vowels 'shifted', iː and uː becoming diphthongs, /ai/ and /au/, respectively; other long vowels moved up: eː and ɛː ⟶ /ii/, aː ⟶ /ei/, oː ⟶ /uu/, ɔː ⟶ /ou/. Short vowels changed little except that u became lowered to /ʌ/. The result is that Modern English has related words such as *wise* and *wisdom* with vowels that were once quite similar but are now quite different.

Greek-type compound   A term for words like *astronaut, microphone, phono-graph*, which consist of two recognizable morphemes that occur in various combinations but are not ordinarily independent words. Many of these morphemes, but not all, are of Greek origin. See section 12.6.

homonyms   Words with the same pronunciation but different meanings: *club* 'a heavy stick' and *club* 'a social organization.'

homorganic   A term describing phonemes which have the same articulator and the same place of articulation: e.g. /m/ and /p/ in *limp*, /n/ and /t/ in *lint*, /ŋ/ and /k/ in *link*.

initial   Occurring at the beginning of a syllable, word, or phrase.

initiation   Expulsion of air from the lungs, providing the force or energy for the production of speech.

intervocalic consonant   A consonant occurring between two vowels: /k/ in *bacon*.

intonation   The distinctive patterns of melodies that are part of speech communication; notice that we cannot say that an intonation pattern has a specific meaning, but different intonation patterns with the same sequence of words have different meanings.

intrusive R   The pronunciation of /r/ at the end of a word which originally did not have this phoneme when a word with initial vowel follows closely: *the idea-r of it.*

larynx   The structure of muscle and cartilage at the top of the trachea, containing the vocal cords.

lexicon   All the meaningful elements of a language – morphemes, words, and idiomatic phrases like *kick the bucket* (meaning 'to die'), together with information about the pronunciation, use, and meaning of each item. No speaker of a language knows the entire lexicon but each speaker has a personal lexicon.

linking R   A term used in describing the fact that many speakers of English pronounce /r/ when a vowel follows closely, as in *Where is it?* but not when a consonant follows, as in *Where can it be?*

liquid   A term for speech sounds that are produced with some obstruction of the air stream but with regular patterns of vibration; in other words, sounds that are [+ consonantal] and [+ sonorant]; English /l/ and /r/.

medial   Referring to anything which is in the middle of a syllable, word, or phrase.

minimal pair   Two words (or other linguistic forms) which differ by one phoneme in what is otherwise the same sequence of phonemes; thus *pat* and *bat* are a minimal pair, *pat* and *pet* are another minimal pair, and *pat* and *pack* are another.

morpheme   The smallest contrastive unit of meaning: a single word like *cat* or an affix such as *un-* and *-ness* in *unhappiness.*

morphologically conditioned alternations   Two (or more) different forms of a morpheme which occur in different environments, not phonological in nature. See section 8.2 for an example.

morphology   The part of language description that studies the formation of words.

nasal cavity   The area above the mouth, connected to the pharynx in back and the nostrils in front.

neutralization   The lack of contrast between two phonemes in a certain position or in a certain dialect; /ii/ and /ɪ/ are in contrast in many pairs of words (*beat, bit,* etc.) but in final position (e.g. *happy*) the vowel could be more like /ii/ or more like /ɪ/ – there is no contrast. In Scottish English there is no contrast of /uu/ and /ʊ/, which other dialects have – for instance, *pool* and *pull* are homonyms. In such cases we say that a contrast has been **neutralized**.

non-verbal   Said of communication without words; this includes gestures used by a speaker and sometimes the appearance of the speaker. See also **paralanguage**.

noun   A class of words with a naming function. In English nouns are either proper (*George, London*) or common (*man, city*) and either countable (*man, apple*) or uncountable (*rice, information*); countable nouns distinguish singular and plural.

onset   The part of a syllable that comes before the vowel (the **peak** of the syllable); see section 5.2.

orthography   The writing system used for a language.

palate   The structure of bones that forms the roof of the mouth in front, separating the mouth from the nasal cavity; sometimes called the 'hard palate'; see also **velar**.

paradigmatic   The relation of items that can substitute for one another at the same place in a language form; the following are 27 short sentences:

$$
\left. \begin{matrix} I \\ You \\ They \end{matrix} \right\} \left\{ \begin{matrix} can \\ should \\ will \end{matrix} \right\} \left\{ \begin{matrix} wait. \\ hurry. \\ go. \end{matrix} \right.
$$

I, you, they form one paradigmatic set, *can, should, will* are another paradigmatic set, and *wait, hurry, go* are a third set. In this display 'paradigmatic' is a vertical relationship. The horizontal relationship – the relation of *can* to *I* and *wait*, for example – is **syntagmatic**.

paralanguage   Characteristics of the voice, apart from the words spoken, which can communicate something about the speaker's attitude – extra loudness, exaggerated intonation, rapid or slow speech.

particles   Words that combine with verbs to make compound verbs: *in, out, on, off, up, down, over, away, through*; see section 12.3.

peak   The center of a syllable, which is always a vowel or a syllabic consonant.

penult   The next to last syllable of a word, e.g. <u>co</u>mic, co<u>me</u>dy, come<u>di</u>an; the vowel of the penult is called the **penultimate vowel**.

person   A grammatical category of reference, in English expressed with pronouns, referring to the speaker and perhaps others (1st person: *I, we*), the addressee(s) (2nd person: *you*), or others (3rd person: *he, she, it, they*).

pharynx   The cavity composed of muscle and membrane located above the larynx and connecting with the mouth and the nasal cavity.

phonation   The production of vibration by the vocal cords.

phoneme   A unit in the sound system of a language, which combines with other such units to form syllables and words; English *cash* and *shack* have the same three phonemes differently arranged.

phonetics   The scientific study of speech sounds used in human languages, with three divisions: **acoustic phonetics**   the branch of phonetics which studies the physical properties of speech sounds, as transmitted from mouth to ear, using instrumental techniques of investigation; **articulatory phonetics** the branch of phonetics which studies the ways in which speech sounds are produced by the vocal organs; and **auditory phonetics**   the branch of phonetics which studies how the ears, auditory nerves, and brain process speech.

phonology   The branch of linguistics which studies the sound systems of languages or of a particular language.

phonotactics   The study and description of how the phonemes of a language go together to form syllables and words.

phrase   A group of words smaller than a clause, forming a grammatical unit.

pitch   The auditory effect of a sound that correlates with frequency of vibration; the greater the vibration of any material the higher the pitch that results.

plosive   Another name for a **stop** consonant.

prefix   See **affix**.

preposition   One of a class of function words that tie a following noun phrase to the rest of the sentence: *at, for, with*. See section 12.3.

prosody   A term used to refer to variations in pitch, stress, and tempo, the elements that occur simultaneously with a stream of speech sounds.

quality   The nature of a sonorant speech sound due to the pattern of vibrations in the air stream during the articulation of the sound. The pattern of vibrations depends on the size and shape of the vocal tract, so that vowels, especially, differ in quality because of the different positions of the tongue and the shape of the lips.

Received Pronunciation (RP)   A name for the pronunciation of English which is typical of the upper middle class in southern England and which is widely taught in foreign language classes in Europe and in the Commonwealth.

redundant   (1) Said of any item that is more than necessary in a message for conveying the meaning; in the phrase *three houses* the plural ending is redundant because the number *three* expresses the notion of plurality more precisely. (2) Said of a feature which is predictable, not distinctive; comparing English /n/, a voiced apical nasal, with /d/, a voiced apical stop, and /m/, a voiced labial nasal, we see that 'nasal' distinguishes /n/ from /d/, and 'apical' distinguishes /n/ from /m/ but the feature 'voiced' is redundant for /n/ because it does not distinguish that phoneme from anything else.

reference   The relation between a language form and something outside of language. For example, *this window* and *that idea* can be associated with a large number of different things, but in a particular place and time a speaker uses either expression in association with a particular window or idea, and other speakers of English who are present generally know what the speaker intends to communicate.

regional dialects   See **dialect**.

release   A term used to describe the movement or non-movement of an articulator after a consonantal sound; e.g. after the tongue-tip touches the alveolar ridge in pronouncing *bat*, the tongue may remain in place with nothing following (no release) or may be released with aspiration (aspirated release), or without aspiration (unaspirated release); in, *batting, battle, button* the tongue is released into the next speech sound.

resonance chamber   Any kind of container with air where a vibration is modified because the air in the container responds to the vibration but with different frequencies, which depend on the size and shape of the resonance chamber. See section 2.4.

rhotic dialect   A dialect in which /r/ is pronounced as a sonorant consonant in any position of occurrence.

rhyme   The part of a syllable which follows the onset and which includes the peak and coda.

rising   A term used to describe an intonation in which the vocal cords increase their frequency of vibration to the end of the tone unit.

round   A feature of a speech sound articulated with the lips rounded.

rule   A statement that describes some characteristic of how a language operates: e.g. in English statements the subject typically precedes the verb and the object follows it; English verbs distinguish present and past tense; the peak of a stressed syllable is a vowel. In the generative treatment followed in this book an underlying (abstract) form is converted into the surface (pronounced) form through the application of rules. These are the rules covered in this book.

schwa   The name for a neutral vowel, represented as /ə/, which occurs, for instance, at the beginning and end of the word *aroma*; it occurs frequently in unstressed syllables of English words.

segment   A name for a speech sound considered as one element in a stream of speech.

semantics   The study of how meaning is expressed in language.

sentence   A grammatical construction that is complete in itself.

sibilant   A fricative or affricate produced with a groove along the center line of the tongue blade; English /s z ʃ ʒ č ǰ/.

simple word   See **word**.

sonorant   A term which describes speech sounds that are not obstruents; in the articulation of a sonorant air flows freely and the vocal cords are in a position to vibrate freely – thus sonorants are typically voiced. Sonorants in English include all vowels, glides, liquids, and nasals.

sonority scale   A ranking of speech sounds according to their relative loudness or 'carrying power'; low vowels are more sonorous than higher vowels, all vowels are more sonorous than sonorant consonants, which are more sonorous than fricatives, and fricatives are more sonorous than stops; among fricatives the sibilant sounds like [s] are more sonorous than non-sibilant ones like [θ].

stop   A speech sound which is produced with complete closure in some part of the vocal tract; also called **plosive**.

stress   The degree of force with which a syllable is pronounced; in English stressed syllables are louder and longer than unstressed syllables.

stress timing   The kind of rhythm found in English and some other languages in which stressed syllables are longer than unstressed syllables; cf. **syllable timing**.

suffix   See **affix**.

surface forms   The actual pronunciation of a word after all the relevant rules have been applied to the underlying form.

syllabic   A term describing the feature of a phoneme which can be the peak of a syllable.

syllabic consonant   A consonant that is the peak of a syllable; in English /l r m n ŋ/ can be syllabic but only in unstressed syllables. See section 5.8.

syllable   A unit of speech which has one peak – usually a vowel – and may have an onset and a coda.

syllable timing   The kind of rhythm found in French and some other languages in which each syllable has equal weight and equal length.

syntagmatic   Describing the relation of words to one another when they form a construction; see **paradigmatic**.

syntax   The study of the rules governing the arrangement of words in sentences; cf. **morphology**.

tag   A phrase or clause that occurs attached to the end of an utterance; it may be a question (*She's lovely, isn't she?*), a name used in address (*It's nice to see you again, Mrs. Smith*), or a brief statement (*You won't like this, I'm afraid*).

tone   The distinctive pitch level of a syllable.

tone unit   A term for a unit of intonation; a word or a sequence of words, even a whole sentence, constitutes a tone unit if it has a sequence of pitches centering on one syllable, the accented syllable.

triphthong   A vowel unit which consists of three simple vowels in quick sequence; in non-rhotic dialects, for example, *tire* is /taiᵊ/ and *tower* is /tauᵊ/.

ult   The last syllable of a word.

underlying form   An abstract representation of a linguistic form – sentence, phrase, or word – from which the actual pronunciation (the surface form) is derived by rules. The underlying form (or underlying representation) contains only the information that is relevant for identification.

utterance   Any stretch of speech produced by one speaker without a notable pause.

velar   Pertaining to any speech sound produced at or near the **velum**, the soft palate.

vocal cords/bands   Two muscular folds which run from the thyroid cartilage at the front of the larynx to the arytenoid cartilages in back; if they vibrate during the production of speech, the sounds articulated are voiced.

vocal tract   The air passage above the larynx, the shape of which determines the quality of any speech sound; it consists of three interconnected parts, the pharynx, the nasal cavity, and the oral cavity.

voice   A term used in classifying speech sounds according to whether the vocal cords vibrate or not in the articulation.

vowel   Phonetically, a speech sound produced without any closure or friction, so that the quality of the vowel depends entirely on the shape of the oral cavity (with possible contribution from the shape of the pharynx and the movement of air through the nasal cavity).

word   A unit of expression in a language which native speakers recognize as a unit intuitively but which is difficult to define scientifically. It is common to distinguish between a **simple word**, which contains just one morpheme (e.g. *cat, good, swim*), and a **complex word**, consisting of a base and one or more affixes.

Bibliography

Adams, Valerie. 1973. *An Introduction to Modern English Word-Formation*. London: Longman.

Allerton, D. J. 1978. The notion of 'givenness' and its relation to presupposition and to theme. *Lingua*, 34: 1–29.

Anderson, Stephen R. 1974. *The Organization of Phonology*. New York: Seminar Press.

Anderson, R. 1995. *Phonology in the Twentieth Century: Theories of Rules and Theories of Representations*. Chicago, IL: University of Chicago Press.

Arnold, G. F. 1957. Stress in English words. *Lingua*, 6: 221–67.

Bailey, Charles-James N. 1968. Dialectal differences in the syllabication of non-nasal sonorants in American English. *General Linguistics*, 8: 79–91.

—— 1973. *Variation and Linguistic Theory*. Arlington, VA: Center for Applied Linguistics.

—— 1980. Evidence for variable syllable boundaries in English. In Waugh, L. R., and Schooneveld, C. H. (eds.). *The Melody of Language*. Baltimore, MD: University Park Press, 25–39.

Bailey, Richard W., and Görlach, Manfred (eds.). 1982. *English as a World Language*. Ann Arbor, MI: University of Michigan Press.

Bailey, Richard W., and Robinson, Jay L. (eds.). 1973. *Varieties of Present-Day English*. New York: Macmillan.

Bauer, Laurie. 1983. *English Word Formation*. Cambridge: Cambridge University Press.

Bell, Alan, and Hooper, Joan Bybee (eds.). 1978a. *Syllables and Segments*. Amsterdam: North Holland.

—— 1978b. Issues and evidence in syllabic phonology. In: Bell and Hooper 1978a: 3–22.

Berger, Marshall D. 1968. Accent, pattern, and dialect in North American English. *Word*, 24: 55–61.

Berko, Jean. 1958. The child's learning of English morphology. *Word*, 14: 150–77.

Bickerton, Derek. 1990. *Language and Species*. Chicago, IL: University of Chicago Press.

Bing, Janet M. 1980. *Aspects of English Prosody*. Bloomington, IN: Indiana University Linguistics Club.

—— 1983. Contrastive stress, contrastive intonation and contrastive meaning. *Journal of Semantics*, 2: 141–56.

Bloomfield, Leonard. 1935. The stressed vowels of American English. *Language*, 11: 97–116.

Bolinger, Dwight L. 1958. A theory of word accent in English. *Word*, 14: 109–48.

—— 1961a. Contrastive accent and contrastive stress. *Language*, 37: 83–96.

—— 1961b. *Generality, Gradience and the All-or-none*. The Hague: Mouton.

—— 1983. Where does intonation begin? *Journal of Semantics*, 2: 101–20.

—— 1986. *Intonation and its Parts: Melody in Spoken English*. Stanford, CA: Stanford University Press.

Booij, Geert. 1994. Lexical phonology: a review. *Lingua e Stile*, 29: 525–55 (also in Kreidler 2000: 5.460–90).

Brazil, David, Coulthard, Malcolm, and Johns, Catherine. 1980. *Discourse, Intonation and Language Teaching*. London: Longman.

Bronstein, A. J. 1960. *The Pronunciation of American English*. Englewood Cliffs, NJ: Prentice-Hall.

Brown, Gillian, Currie, Karen L., and Kenworthy, Joanne. 1980. *Questions of Intonation*. Baltimore, MD: University Park Press.

Burzio, Luigi. 1994. *Principles of English Stress*. Cambridge: Cambridge University Press.

Chafe, Wallace L. 1976. Givenness, contrastiveness, definiteness, subjects, topics and points of view. In Li, Charles N. (ed.). *Subject and Topic*. New York: Academic Press, 25–55.

Chomsky, Noam. 1971. Deep structure, surface structure, and semantic interpretation. In Steinberg, D. D., and Jakobovits, L. A. (eds.). *Semantics*. Cambridge: Cambridge University Press, 183–216.

Chomsky, Noam, and Halle, Morris. 1968. *The Sound Pattern of English*. New York: Harper and Row.

Clark, Herbert H., and Clark, Eve V. 1977. *Psychology and Language: An Introduction to Psycholinguistics*. New York: Harcourt Brace Jovanovich.

Clark, John, and Yallop, Colin. 1995. *An Introduction to Phonetics and Phonology*. Oxford: Blackwell.

Clements, George N., and Keyser, Samuel Jay. 1983. *CV Phonology: A Generative Theory of the Syllable*. Cambridge, MA: MIT Press.

Clements, George N. 1985. The geometry of phonological features. *Phonology Yearbook*, 2: 225–52 (also in Goldsmith 1999: 201–23 and Kreidler 2000: 2.143–71).

Coulthard, Malcolm. 1977. *An Introduction to Discourse Analysis*. London: Longman.

Couper-Kuhlen, Elizabeth. 1986. *An Introduction to English Prosody*. London: Edward Arnold.

Cruttenden, Alan. 1986. *Intonation*. Cambridge: Cambridge University Press.

Crystal, David. 1969. *Prosodic Systems and Intonation in English*. Cambridge: Cambridge University Press.

—— 1991. *A Dictionary of Linguistics and Phonetics*, 3rd edn. Oxford: Blackwell.

Crystal, David, and Quirk, Randolph. 1964. *Systems of Prosodic and Paralinguistic Features in English*. The Hague: Mouton.

Currie, Karen L. 1980. An initial 'search for tonics.' *Language and Speech*, 23: 329–46.

—— 1981. Further experiments in the 'search for tonics'. *Language and Speech*, 24: 1–28.

Dale, P. S. 1976. *Language Development*, 2nd edn. New York: Holt, Rinehart, and Winston.

Daneš, Frantisek. 1960. Sentence intonation from a functional point of view. *Word*, 16: 34–54.

Delattre, Pierre. 1963. Comparing the prosodic features of English, German, Spanish, and French. *International Review of Applied Linguistics*, 1: 193–210.

Denes, Peter, and Pinson, E. N. 1968. *The Speech Chain*. New York: Harper and Row.

Dickerson, Wayne. 1975. Predicting word stress: generative rules in an ESL context. *TESL Studies*, 1: 38–52.

—— 1978. English orthography: a guide to word stress and vowel quality. *International Review of Applied Linguistics* 16: 127–47.

Fallows, Deborah. 1981. Experimental evidence for English syllabification and syllable structure. *Journal of Linguistics*, 17: 309–317.

Fasold, Ralph W. 1984. *The Sociolinguistics of Society*. Oxford: Blackwell.

Francis, W. Nelson. 1958. *The Structure of American English*. New York: Ronald Press.

Friederich, Wolf. 1967. *Englische Aussprachelehre*. Munich: Max Hieber Verlag.

Fries, Charles C. 1964. On the intonation of 'yes–no' questions in English. In Abercrombie, D. D. et al. (eds.). *In Honour of Daniel Jones*. London: Longman, 242–54.

Fromkin, Victoria A. (ed.). 1978. *Tone: A Linguistic Survey*. New York: Academic Press.

Fudge, Erik. 1984. *English Word Stress*. London: Edward Arnold.

Gandour, Jackson T. 1978. The perception of tone In: Fromkin 1978: 41–76.

Giegerich, Heinz J. 1992. *English Phonology: An Introduction*. Cambridge: Cambridge University Press.

Gimson, A. C. 1994. *An Introduction to the Pronunciation of English*, 5th edn. London: Edward Arnold/New York: St. Martin's Press.

Glenn, Marilyn. 1976. *Pragmatic Functions of Intonation*. PhD dissertation, Georgetown University, Washington, DC.

Goldsmith, John A. 1990. *Autosegmental and Metrical Phonology*. Oxford: Blackwell.

—— (ed.). 1995. *The Handbook of Phonological Theory*. Oxford: Blackwell.

—— (ed.). 1999. *Phonological Theory: The Essential Readings*. Oxford: Blackwell.

Goyvaerts, D. L., and Pullum, G. K. (eds.). 1975. *Essays on the Sound Pattern of English*. Ghent: Story-Scientia.

Guierre, Lionel. 1970. *Drills in English Stress Patterns*. London: Longman.

—— 1984. *Drills in English Stress Patterns*. Paris: Colin, Librairie Armand.

Gunter, Richard. 1974. *Sentences in Dialog*. Charleston, SC: Hornbeam Press.

Halle, Morris. 1973. Stress rules in English: a new version. *Linguistic Inquiry*, 4: 451–64.

Halle, Morris, and Clements, George N. 1982. *Problem Book in Phonology: A Workbook for Introductory Courses in Linguistics and in Modern Phonology*. Cambridge, MA: MIT Press.

Halle, Morris, and Keyser, Samuel Jay. 1971. *English Stress: Its Form, its Growth, and its Role in Verse*. New York: Harper and Row.

Halle, Morris, and Mohanan, K. P. 1985. Segmental phonology of modern English. *Linguistic Inquiry*, 16: 57–116.

Halle, Morris, and Vergnaud, Roger. 1987. *An Essay on Stress*. Cambridge, MA: MIT Press.

Halliday, M. A. K. 1967. *Intonation and Grammar in British English*. The Hague: Mouton.

—— 1970. *A Course in Spoken English: Intonation*. London: Oxford University Press.

Halliday, M. A. K., and Hasan, Ruqaiya. 1976. *Cohesion in English*. London: Longman.

Halliday, M. A. K., McIntosh, Angus, and Strevens, Peter. 1964. *The Linguistic Sciences and Language Teaching*. London: Longman.

Harris, John. 1994. *The English Sound Structure*. Oxford: Blackwell.

Hayes, Bruce. 1995. *Metrical Stress Theory: Principles and Case Studies*. Chicago, IL: University of Chicago Press.

Hoard, J. E. 1971. Aspiration, tenseness, and syllabification in English. *Language*, 47: 133–40.

Hockett, Charles F. 1955. *Manual of Phonology* (*International Journal of American Linguistics*, Memoir 11).

————— 1958. *A Course in Modern Linguistics*. New York: Macmillan.

Hogg, Richard, and McCully, C. B. 1987. *Metrical Phonology: A Coursebook*. Cambridge: Cambridge University Press.

Hooper, Joan. 1972. The syllable in phonological theory. *Language*, 48: 525–40.

Hubbell, Allen F. 1950. *The Pronunciation of English in New York City: Consonants and Vowels*. New York: King's Crown Press.

Hughes, Arthur, and Trudgill, Peter. 1987. *English Accents and Dialects*, 2nd edn. London: Edward Arnold.

Hyman, Larry. 1975. *Phonology: Theory and Analysis*. New York: Holt, Rinehart, and Winston.

Jakobson, Roman. 1941. *Kindersprache, Aphasie und allgemeine Lautgesetze*. Uppsala: Universitetsarskrift 9. (Tr. Allan R. Keiler, *Child Language, Aphasia, and Phonological Universals*. The Hague: Mouton, 1968.)

Jensen, John T. 1993. *English Phonology*. Amsterdam and Philadelphia: John Benjamins.

Jespersen, Jens Otto Harry. 1909–49. *A Modern English Grammar on Historical Principles*. Copenhagen: Ejnar Munksgaard.

Johnson, Samuel. 1755. *Dictionary of the English Language*. London: W. Strahan (Reprinted, New York: Arons Press, 1979).

Jones, Daniel. 1967. *Everyman's Pronouncing Dictionary, Containing over 58,000 Words in International Phonetic Transcription*, 13th edn., ed. A. C. Gimson. London: Dent.

————— 1976. *An Outline of English Phonetics*, 9th edn. Cambridge: Cambridge University Press.

Kachru, Braj B. (ed.). 1982. *The Other Tongue: English across Cultures*. Champaign/Urbana, IL: University of Illinois Press.

Kahn, Daniel. 1976. *Syllable-based Generalizations in English Phonology*. Bloomington, IN: Indiana University Linguistics Club.

Kaisse, Ellen M., and Shaw, Patricia A. 1985. On the theory of lexical phonology. *Phonology Yearbook*, 2: 1–30 (also in Kreidler 2000: 5.378–410).

Katamba, Francis. 1989. *An Introduction to Phonology*. London: Longman.

Kenstowicz, M., and Kisseberth, C. 1979. *Generative Phonology: Description and Theory*. New York: Academic Press.

Kenyon, John S. 1958. *American Pronunciation*, 10th edn. Ann Arbor, MI: George Wahr.

Kenyon, John S., and Knott, Thomas A. 1953. *A Pronouncing Dictionary of American English*. Springfield, MA: Merriam.

Keyser, Samuel Jay, and Stevens, Kenneth N. 1994. Feature geometry and the vocal tract. *Phonology*, 11: 207–36 (also in Kreidler 2000: 2.172–202).

Kingdon, Roger. 1958a. *The Groundwork of English Stress*. London: Longman.

————— 1958b. *The Groundwork of English Intonation*. London: Longman.

Knapp, Mark L. 1972. *Nonverbal Communication in Human Interaction*. New York: Holt, Rinehart, and Winston.

Kreidler, Charles W. 1972a. English orthography: a generative approach. In Alatis, James E. (ed.), *Studies in Honor of Albert H. Marckwardt*. Washington, DC: Teachers of English to Speakers of Other Languages, 81–91.

————— 1972b. Teaching English spelling and pronunciation. *TESOL Quarterly*, 5: 3–12.

————— 1984. The uses of accent in English sentences. *SECOL Review*, 8: 9–27.

————— 1990. Toward a pan-dialect phonology of English. *Word*, 41: 69–80.

————— (ed.). 2000. *Phonology: Critical Concepts*, 6 vols. London: Routledge.

Kurath, Hans. 1967. *A Phonology and Prosody of Modern English*. Ann Arbor, MI: University of Michigan Press.

Kurath, Hans, and McDavid, Raven I., Jr. 1961. *The Pronunciation of English in the Atlantic States*. Ann Arbor, MI: University of Michigan Press.

Labov, William. 1966. *The Social Stratification of English in New York City*. Washington, DC: Center for Applied Linguistics.

Ladd, D. Robert. 1980. *The Structure of Intonational Meaning*. Bloomington, IN: Indiana University Press.

Ladefoged, Peter. 1962. *Elements of Acoustic Phonetics*. Chicago, IL: University of Chicago Press.

—— 1993. *A Course in Phonetics*, 3rd edn. Fort Worth, TX: Harcourt, Brace, Jovanovich.

Lane, Harlan L. 1965. The motor theory of speech perception: a critical review. *Psychological Review*, 72: 275–309.

Lass, Roger. 1984. *Phonology: An Introduction to Basic Concepts*. Cambridge: Cambridge University Press.

Leben, William R. 1976. The tones in English intonation. *Linguistic Analysis*, 2: 69–107.

Lehiste, Ilse. 1970. *Suprasegmentals*. Cambridge, MA: MIT Press.

Lenneberg, E. 1967. *Biological Foundations of Language*. New York: Wiley.

Li, Charles N., and Thompson, Sandra A. 1978. The acquisition of tone. In: Fromkin 1978: 271–84.

Liberman, Mark, and Prince, Alan. 1977. On stress and linguistic rhythm. *Linguistic Inquiry*, 8: 249–336.

Lieberman, Philip. 1977. *Speech Physiology and Acoustic Phonetics*. New York: Macmillan.

Lightner, T. M. 1972. *Problems in the Theory of Phonology*, vol. 1. Edmonton: Linguistic Research.

Lowth, Robert. 1762. *A Short Introduction to English Grammar*. London: A. Miller and R. and J. Dodsby. Facsimile reprint, Menston: Scolar Press, 1967.

Lyons, John. 1968. *Introduction to Theoretical Linguistics*. Cambridge: Cambridge University Press.

Makkai, Valerie Becker (ed.). 1972. *Phonological Theory: Evolution and Current Practice*. New York: Holt, Rinehart, and Winston.

Malécot, André. 1960. Vowel nasality as a distinctive feature in American English. *Language*, 36: 222–9.

Malmberg, Bertil. 1955. The phonetic basis for syllable division. In Lehiste, Ilse (ed.). *Readings in Acoustic Phonetics*. Cambridge, MA: MIT Press.

Marchand, Hans. 1969. *The Categories and Types of Present-Day English Word Formation*, 2nd edn. Munich: C. H. Beck.

Newman, Stanley S. 1946. On the stress system of English. *Word*, 2: 171–87.

O'Connor, J. D. 1973. *Phonetics*. Harmondsworth: Penguin.

O'Conner, J. D., and Arnold, G. F. 1973. *Intonation of Colloquial English: A Practical Handbook*, 2nd edn. London: Longman.

O'Conner, J. D., and Trim, J. L. M. 1953. Vowel, consonant, and syllable: a phonological definition. *Word*, 9: 103–22.

Osherson, Daniel N., and Lasnik, Howard. 1990. *Language* (vol. 1 of *An Invitation to Cognitive Science*). Cambridge, MA: MIT Press.

Palmer, Harold, and Blanford, F. G. 1976. *A Grammar of Spoken English*, 3rd edn., revised and rewritten by Roger Kingdon. Cambridge: Cambridge University Press.

Pierrehumbert, Janet Breckenridge. 1987. *The Phonology and Phonetics of English Intonation*. Bloomington, IN: Indiana University Linguistics Club.

Pike, Kenneth L. 1943. *Phonetics: A Critical Analysis of Phonetic Theory and a Technique for Transcribing*. Ann Arbor, MI: University of Michigan Press.

—— 1945. *The Intonation of American English*. Ann Arbor, MI: University of Michigan Press.

Poldauf, Ivan. 1984. *English Word Stress: A Theory of Word Stress in English*. Oxford: Pergamon.

Pulgram, Ernst. 1970. *Syllable, Word, Nexus, Cursus*. The Hague: Mouton.

Pyles, Thomas. 1971. *The Origins and Development of the English Language*, 2nd edn. New York: Harcourt Brace Jovanovich.

Quirk, Randolph, Greenbaum, Sidney, Leech, Geoffrey, and Svartvik, Ian. 1984. *A Comprehensive Grammar of English*. London: Longman.

Roach, Peter. 1991. *English Phonetics and Phonology: A Practical Course*, 2nd edn. Cambridge: Cambridge University Press.

Ross, John Robert. 1972. A reanalysis of English word stress. In Brame, M. K. (ed.), *Contributions to Generative Phonology*. Austin, TX: University of Texas Press.

Rudes, Blair A. 1977. *Another Look at Syllable Structure*. Bloomington, IN: Indiana University Linguistics Club.

Sag, Ivan A., and Liberman, Mark. 1975. The intonational disambiguation of indirect speech acts. *Chicago Linguistic Society*, 11: 487–97.

Schane, Sanford A. 1975. Noncyclic English word stress. In: Goyvaerts and Pullum 1975: 249–59.

—— 1979. The rhythmic nature of English word accentuation. *Language*, 55: 559–602.

Sherman, Donald. 1975. Noun–verb stress alternation: an example of the lexical diffusion of sound change in English. *Linguistics*, 159: 43–71.

Sloat, Clarence, and Taylor, Sharon. 1983. *The Structure of English Words*, 3rd edn. Eugene, OR: Pacific Language Associates.

Sommerstein, Alan. 1977. *Modern Phonology*. London: Edward Arnold.

Spencer, Andrew. 1996. *Phonology: Theory and Description*. Oxford: Blackwell.

Stampe, David. 1969. The acquisition of phonetic representation. *Chicago Linguistic Society*, 5: 443–54.

—— 1972. A dissertation on natural phonology. PhD dissertation, University of Chicago.

Stockwell, Robert, and Minkova, Donka. 2001. *English Words: History and Structure*. Cambridge: Cambridge University Press.

Tench, Paul. 1990. *The Roles of Intonation in English Discourse*. Frankfurt am Main: Peter Lang.

Thompson, Henry S. 1981. *Stress and Salience in English: Theory and Practice*. Palo Alto, CA: Xerox.

Trager, George L. 1949. *The Field of Linguistics*. Baltimore, MD: Battenburg Press.

Trager, George L., and Smith, Henry Lee, Jr. 1951. *Outline of English Structure* (*Studies in Linguistics*, Occasional Papers 3).

Traugott, Elizabeth Closs. 1972. *A History of English Syntax*. New York: Holt, Rinehart, and Winston.

Trnka, Bohumil. 1966. *A Phonological Analysis of Present-day Standard English*. Tokyo: Hokeiou. Re-issued by University of Alabama Press, 1968. Originally published 1935.

Troubetzkoy, N. S. 1935. Phonologie et géographie linguistique. *Travaux du Cercle Linguistique de Prague*, 4: 228–34.

—— 1939. *Grundzüge der Phonologie* (Travaux du Cercle Linguistique de Prague VII), tr. J. Cantineau, *Principes de Phonologie*. Paris: C. Klincksieck. 1949; tr. Christiane A. M. Baltaxe, *Principles of Phonology*. Berkeley/Los Angeles, CA: University of California Press, 1982.

Trudgill, Peter. 1974. *Sociolinguistics: An Introduction to Language and Society*. Harmondsworth: Penguin.

——— 1990. *The Dialects of England*. Oxford: Blackwell.

Trudgill, Peter, and Hannah, Jean. 1991. *International English: A Guide to Varieties of Standard English*, 3rd edn. London: Edward Arnold.

Vanderslice, Ralph, and Ladefoged, Peter. 1972. Binary suprasegmental features and transformational word-accentuation rules. *Language*, 48: 819–38.

Venezky, Richard L. 1970. *The Structure of English Orthography*. The Hague: Mouton.

Vennemann, Theo. 1972. On the theory of syllabic phonology. *Linguistische Berichte*, 18: 1–18.

Walker, John. 1791. *A Critical Pronouncing Dictionary*. London: Robinson. (Facsimile reprint, Menston: Scolar Press. 1968).

Wardhaugh, Ronald. 1993. *Investigating Language: Central Problems in Linguistics*. Oxford: Blackwell.

Wells, J. C. 1982. *Accents of English*, 3 vols. Cambridge: Cambridge University Press.

Wijk, Axel. 1966. *Rules of Pronunciation for the English Language*. London: Oxford University Press.

Willems, Nico. 1982. *English Intonation from a Dutch Point of View*. Dordrecht: Foris Publications.

Wolfram, Walt, and Johnson, Robert. 1982. *Phonological Analysis: Focus on American English*. Washington, DC: Center for Applied Linguistics.

Zwicky, Arnold. 1970. Auxiliary reduction in English. *Linguistic Inquiry*, 1: 323–36.

Index

The index lists all technical terms and names mentioned in the book, with the number of the chapter(s) and section(s) in which the term or name is introduced and discussed. A number in **boldface** indicates that the term is (part of) the title of the chapter or section. Since some terms – e.g. *vowel*, *syllable*, *stress* – appear on almost every page, it would not be productive to cite every occurrence, but the index does contain a citation for the discussion of every term.